D1498456

A Latin Epic
Reader

BC LATIN Readers

Series Editor:

Ronnie Ancona, Hunter College and CUNY Graduate Center

These readers provide well annotated Latin selections written by experts in the field, to be used as authoritative introductions to Latin authors, genres, topics, or themes for intermediate or advanced college Latin study. Their relatively small size (approximately 600 lines) makes them ideal to use in combination. Each volume includes a comprehensive introduction, bibliography for further reading, Latin text with notes at the back, and complete vocabulary. Nineteen volumes are currently scheduled for publication; others are under consideration. Check our website for updates: www.BOLCHAZY.com.

A Latin Epic Reader
Selections from Ten Epics

Alison Keith

Bolchazy-Carducci Publishers, Inc.
Mundelein, Illinois USA

Series Editor: Ronnie Ancona
Volume Editor: Laurie Haight Keenan
Cover Design & Typography: Adam Phillip Velez
Maps: Mapping Specialists, Ltd.

A Latin Epic Reader
Selections from Ten Epics

Alison Keith

Bolchazy-Carducci Publishers, Inc.
1570 Baskin Road
Mundelein, Illinois 60060
www.bolchazy.com

Printed in the United States of America
2012
by United Graphics

ISBN 978-0-86516-686-8

Library of Congress Cataloging-in-Publication Data

Keith, Alison.
 A Latin epic reader : selections from ten epics / Alison Keith.
   pages. cm. -- (BC Latin readers)
 Includes bibliographical references and index.
 ISBN 978-0-86516-686-8 (pbk. : alk. paper) 1. Epic poetry, Latin--History and criticism.
2. Epic poetry, Latin. I. Title. II. Series: BC Latin readers.
 PA6054.K445 2012
 873'.0108--dc23

                                                          2012036753

Contents

List of Illustrations

Preface

Vergil's *Aeneid* and Ovid's *Metamorphoses* first inspired my love of Latin epic, but the wealth and diversity of Roman contributions to the genre from Ennius to Claudian remain a source of delight and interest to me. This is poetry that tackles subjects of the highest importance—the nature of the universe and the dictates of history, politics, and society—and explores Rome's foundational responses not only to her own history and political culture, but also to the art, history, and (especially) literature of ancient Greece. It is my hope that students exposed to the ten epics here anthologized will be moved to further immersion in this stimulating poetry, whether in the Augustan masterpieces of Vergil and Ovid or beyond, in the republican philosophical epic of Lucretius and the historical and mythological epics of the imperial writers Lucan, Valerius Flaccus, Statius, and Silius Italicus.

I am very grateful to Ronnie Ancona for offering me the opportunity to assemble a reader in Latin Epic for Bolchazy-Carducci Publishers. She and Laurie Haight Keenan at the Press have been unstinting in their guidance and help at every stage of the process. My colleague Jarrett Welsh generously read drafts of the commentaries and improved every page of the volume. I also had the benefit of feedback on an initial draft of the text and notes from my Dalhousie colleague Peter O'Brien and his students in an intermediate Latin class, and I am grateful to them for the care with which they read the materials. Finally, a team of graduate and undergraduate students in the Department of Classics at the University of Toronto rendered material assistance in a variety of ways: commenting on drafts, proofreading texts and commentaries, and compiling the

Latin Vocabulary for the volume as a whole. My thanks to John MacCormick, Sarah McCallum, Nicholas Arrigo, Susan Dunning, Spencer Gough, Jen Oliver, and Melanie Racette-Campbell for their indefatigable assistance on the project. I am delighted to dedicate this *opusculum* to them.

ALISON KEITH
Toronto, Canada

Introduction

Epic stood at the pinnacle of the classical hierarchy of genres. Its subject matter—the establishment and maintenance of divine and human order—was felt to be the most important material for commemoration in verse, and therein lay its prestige. The genre's literary and national significance in ancient Rome can be felt from the very inception of Latin literature, in the adaptation of Homer's *Odyssey* into Latin Saturnians by L. Livius Andronicus (*fl.* 240–207 BCE) and, a generation later, in the *Carmen belli poenici* of his younger contemporary Cn. Naevius (*fl.* 235–204 BCE), which celebrated Rome's defeat of Carthage in the First Punic War (264–241 BCE) and consequent acquisition of an overseas empire. The adaptation of the Greek dactylic hexameter into Latin by Q. **Ennius** (239–169 BCE) in his magisterial epic of Rome's rise to Mediterranean dominance, *Annales*, ensured the primacy of epic in Latin literary culture as a narrative vehicle for the celebration of Roman *imperium*. Ennius' metrical experiment inspired the further refinement of the dactylic hexameter in the Latin verse of T. **Lucretius** Carus (ca. 95–55 BCE) and C. Valerius **Catullus** (ca. 84–54 BCE), and the form flourished in the early Principate in the hands of P. **Vergil**ius Maro (70–19 BCE) and his successors—P. **Ovid**ius Naso (43 BCE–17 CE), M. **Manilius** (*fl.* first quarter of the first century CE), M. Annaeus **Lucan**us (39–65 CE), C. **Valerius** Flaccus Setinus Balbus (dead by 95 CE), P. Papinius **Statius** (ca. 50–96 CE), and Ti. Catius Asconius **Silius** Italicus (ca. 26–102 CE). This rich corpus of Roman epic poetry ensured the continuing preeminence of the genre in late antique Latin (Claudian, Ausonius, Prudentius), medieval romance (Dante, the poet of the Cid), and early modern European literature (Tasso, Ariosto, Milton), and is still reflected in our application of the adjective "epic" to the novel in high culture (e.g., James Joyce's *Ulysses*) and to Hollywood movies in popular culture (e.g., "Gladiator," "Titanic").

∾ *Mid-republican epic: Ennius*

Ennius, the earliest Latin author included in this volume, records that he was Messapian by birth (*Ann.* 524) and came from Rudiae (*Ann.* 525), an Oscan-speaking town in southern Italy, in the heart of *Magna Graecia*. There he received an impressive education in Greek literature, but he served in Rome's army, reportedly in Sardinia, where he met the elder Cato and returned with him to Rome in 204 BCE. At Rome he earned a living by teaching the sons of the upper classes (Suet. *Gramm.* 1), and in this way he came to enjoy the patronage of some of the leading politicians and generals of the mid-republic, including M. Fulvius Nobilior, who took him on campaign in Aetolia in 189 BCE and for whom he wrote a drama, *Ambracia*, commemorating the general's achievements in war. His epic poem *Annales*, "yearly records," seems to be a late work, perhaps begun after his return from Aetolia in 187 BCE. Originally conceived and apparently published in fifteen books, the poem celebrated Rome's rise to Mediterranean dominion from the mythological pre-history of the city's foundation down to the poet's own day. Ennius updated the work at least once, adding another three books to the original fifteen in order to take his chronicle down to 171 BCE and include the Istrian and Macedonian Wars. Tradition put Ennius' death in the year 169 BCE, presumably soon after he finished the three additional books of the *Annales*.

Ennius broke with his predecessors Livius Andronicus and Naevius, who had written their Latin epic poems in Saturnian verse, by adopting the meter of Homeric epic, dactylic hexameter, for the composition of his *Annales*. This was an extraordinary choice and its impact cannot be overstated for the subsequent tradition of Latin epic at Rome. By writing in a Greek meter, Ennius acknowledged the importance of Greek culture in contemporary Rome and paraded the sophistication of his Hellenism while implicitly deriding his

uncouth predecessors for their reliance on an old-fashioned, paro-
chial Italian form. His metrical innovation was complemented by his
narrative innovation in making the history of Rome into a universal
history of the Mediterranean. For where his Latin predecessors had
focused their efforts on a Homeric theme (Livius' *Odussia*) or a Roman war (Naevius' *Carmen belli poenici*), Ennius took all of Roman
myth, legend, and history as his subject and integrated it into the
Greek epic traditions of cosmogonic, historical, and mythological
epic. Moreover, the title *Annales* resonates against the annual cal-
endar of religious holidays and the inscribed records of consuls and
censors that adorned the porticoes of the temple of Hercules and the
Muses, which Fulvius Nobilior constructed in Rome after his return
from Ambracia.

Although the *Annales* is no longer extant in its entirety, substantial fragments survive, preserved in quotations by Cicero, who was
clearly a great admirer of Ennius' poetry, and Vergil's commentators,
who were interested in the Augustan poet's use in the *Aeneid* of his
great republican predecessor's poem. Thus in his treatise *On Divination*, Cicero quotes the first two excerpts in this *Reader*, Ilia's dream
(*Div.* 1.40–41) and Romulus' taking of the auspices (*Div.* 1.107–8),
while Macrobius quotes the third, on felling trees for funeral pyres
(*Sat.* 6.2.27), in his *Saturnalia*, an early fifth-century CE work of con-
vivial literature, which focuses in part on Vergil's achievement in the
Aeneid by measuring him against his Greek and Latin models.

◌ *Late republican epic: Lucretius and Catullus*

We know very little about Lucretius: his full name appears only in
the manuscripts of his poem "On the Nature of the Universe" (*De
rerum natura*), and we know nothing whatsoever about his family
background or social standing. The only contemporary reference to
the poet appears in a letter that Cicero wrote to his brother Quintus
in February 54 BCE, praising Lucretius' poetry as possessing both
ingenium, "genius," and *ars*, "artistry" (*QFr.* 2.10[9].3), and it is likely
that the *De rerum natura* was in circulation by this time. The poem
itself was composed in six books of dactylic hexameter, and Lucretius

makes clear his admiration for Ennius' foundational achievement in the meter early in the work (Lucr. 1.117–19): "as our **Ennius** sang, who first brought down from lovely Helicon a garland of per**enni**al foliage, which brought him great fame through the Italian races of men." Lucretius' encomium of Ennius' "eternal verses" stands in striking contrast to his disdain for Ennius' mytho-historical subject-matter. Lucretius' own theme is cosmogonic and philosophical—the Epicurean nature of the universe—and he treats his subject in the didactic mode, all three features (cosmogony, philosophy, and didacticism) characteristic of grand epic. Drawing on the cosmogonic and ethical writings of the Athenian philosopher Epicurus (341–270 BCE), Lucretius offers an atomist account of the natural world and explains the goal of a happy life as pleasure, defined ascetically as *ataraxia*, "freedom from disturbance."

The addressee of the *De rerum natura* (1.25–43) is a certain Memmius, whom scholars have long agreed must be the Roman politician C. Memmius, active in the 50s BCE. Memmius had literary interests in oratory and poetry and was obviously an important literary patron in this period for, in addition to receiving Lucretius' dedication, he was on familiar terms with the "neoteric" poets Catullus and Cinna (tribune in 44 BCE), whom he included in his gubernatorial entourage in Bithynia in 57 BCE (Cat. 28 and 10). Catullus, Cinna, and their friend Calvus, were Italian aristocrats who pursued political careers at Rome in the mid-50s BCE and the most prominent exponents of the "new poetry"—short, personal, intensely emotional, and artistically mannered verse in a variety of lyric meters. Each of them, however, also tried his hand at hexameter composition in brief compass. Calvus composed an *epyllion* or "short epic" entitled *Io*, about Juno's unfortunate priestess who was raped by Jupiter, transformed into a cow, and pursued round the Mediterranean by a gadfly, while Cinna wrote an epyllion about a mythological heroine, *Zmyrna* (i.e., Myrrha), whose incestuous love for her father Cinyras resulted in her transformation into a myrrh tree, and the ensuing birth from the tree of her son Adonis. Neither poem survives, though both heroines receive extensive notice in Ovid's *Metamorphoses*. Catullus' poem 64, however, about the wedding of Peleus and Thetis, which features an inset panel describing Theseus' desertion of Ariadne (from which the excerpt in this volume has been drawn), furnishes a magnificent extant example of neoteric hexameter artistry. At four hundred and eight lines, Catullus 64 is by far the shortest "epic" composition in Latin literature. Its influence on Vergil and Ovid, however, was profound, and through them the formal techniques of neoteric poetry were naturalized in imperial Latin epic.

∾ Augustan epic: Vergil and Ovid

Already in his own lifetime, Vergil was hailed as the greatest poet Rome had produced. His book of pastoral poems (*Bucolics* or *Eclogues*), published ca. 37 BCE, made him famous and his publication in late 29 of a four-book poem on farming, *Georgics*, consolidated his status as the greatest living Latin poet. Individual eclogues were performed as mimes and pantomimes on stage to the accompaniment of music and drew huge crowds, while he himself personally recited the four books of *Georgics* to Augustus on the princeps' return to Italy from Egypt after the civil wars. So famous was Vergil's poetry that contemporary schoolteachers included it in their lessons during his lifetime. From 29 BCE until his untimely death in 19, Vergil labored at his masterpiece, the *Aeneid*, a mythological epic about the Trojan hero Aeneas' journey to Italy, where he is destined to found the Roman race through a dynastic marriage to the daughter of a Latin king. On arrival in Italy, however, Aeneas must contend for his Latin bride against local suitors, especially Turnus, who leads the Italian forces ranged against the Trojans. En route to Italy, moreover, Aeneas diverges from his mission to dally with the Carthaginian queen Dido in the "wrong" dynastic marriage. In the disastrous coupling (and subsequent rupture) of Aeneas and Dido, Vergil locates the origin of the Punic wars, a century of conflict between the empires of Rome and Carthage for control of the western Mediterranean (264–146 BCE).

Vergil died unexpectedly in September of 19 BCE, reportedly asking on his deathbed that the manuscript of the *Aeneid* be consigned to the flames. The emperor Augustus, however, in whose entourage the poet died, refused to countenance the destruction of the poem, and entrusted it instead to Vergil's friends and literary executors, Varius and Tucca. The result of their efforts was put into circulation some time later and became an instant classic. Vergil's epic project was common knowledge in literary circles at Rome long before his death and stimulated great excitement. Suetonius quotes letters from Augustus to Vergil asking to see "either the first draft of the poem or whatever section you like," while the elegiac poet Propertius, Vergil's contemporary, hails the poem already in the mid-20s BCE as "something greater than the *Iliad*" (Prop. 2.34.66). A century later the first professor of rhetoric at Rome, Quintilian (ca. 35–95 CE), acclaims Vergil as the supreme exponent of Latin epic (*Inst. Or.* 10.1.85–86).

Ovid, by far the youngest of the Augustan poets, relates in his poetic autobiography (*Tristia* 4.10) that he only "saw" Vergil but never really knew him, although he venerated the famous poets of the early Augustan period. His own earliest verse, for Corinna "so-called under a false name," Ovid says he first performed publicly when his beard had been cut once or twice, perhaps around the age of eighteen in 25 BCE. These poems, later collected into several books of *Amores*, made him famous (or infamous) at an early age, and Ovid claims that younger poets revered him as he had his elders. He himself seems to have regarded his fifteen-book hexameter poem *Metamorphoses*, which treats over 200 myths of transformation, as his masterpiece. His decision to compose the poem in dactylic hexameters has often been explained as arising from a desire to emulate Vergil's model in the *Aeneid*, and the influence of Vergil is everywhere apparent in the poem, from the renovation of Vergilian diction and metrical techniques to the appropriation of Vergilian themes and subjects, including the fall of Troy and Aeneas' wanderings in the Mediterranean in a mini-"Aeneid" (*Met.* 13.623–14.608). Yet while Vergil may have been the most immediate spur to Ovid's epic production, the whole of the classical epic tradition informs his essay in hexameter poetry, and the selections in this volume bear witness to his interest in Ennius, Lucretius, and Catullus as well as Homer and Vergil, whose epics Ovid mined for myths of metamorphosis.

∾ Imperial epic: Manilius, Lucan, Valerius Flaccus, Statius, Silius Italicus

Like Ovid, the Latin poets of the first century CE responded with enthusiasm to the challenge of the *Aeneid*, producing a substantial body of epic poetry on didactic, historical, and mythological themes. The shadowy figure of Manilius is the earliest exponent of imperial epic with his *Astronomica*, a work whose composition spanned the reigns of Augustus and Tiberius and which avowedly supports the institution of the Principate. The poem furnishes a Stoic counterpart to Lucretius' Epicurean masterpiece in its focus on celestial harmony in relation to earthly order and human government. Like Epicurus, the Stoics offered a materialist account of the nature of the universe, but they differed from the Epicureans in holding that fire was the basic material from which the cosmos emerged, and they identified virtue rather than pleasure as the highest ethical good and chief goal of human happiness. Although Manilius' didactic subject aligns the *Astronomica* with Lucretius' *De Rerum Natura* (and Vergil's didactic poem on farming, *Georgics*), the passage included in this volume—Perseus' rescue of Andromeda from a sea-monster— reworks an Ovidian episode (also included in this volume) and illustrates Manilius' considerable debt to Ovid's *Metamorphoses* as well as to Vergil's *Aeneid*.

Like Manilius, the poet Lucan was a Stoic, but he wrote historical epic in the *Bellum Ciuile*, which took as its subject the clash between Caesar and Pompey for authority over Rome and her empire in 49– 48 BCE, and he offers a compelling antithesis to Manilius in the oppositional stance he adopts towards the Caesars. The nephew of the philosopher Seneca, Lucan reveals his immersion in Stoic philosophy in almost every line of his civil war epic (including the proem to *BC* 2, included in this volume). Lucan was admitted to Nero's inner circle as a youth and early in the emperor's reign enjoyed his favor, holding the offices of quaestor and augur before the legal age. He was a literary prodigy, earning acclaim during his rhetorical studies and later a prize for his poem on Nero at the first celebration of the *Neronia* in 60 CE. He had published the first three books of the

Bellum Ciuile by 63 CE, but increasing hostility between poet and emperor led Nero to forbid Lucan to speak in the lawcourts or recite his poetry in public. Many scholars have assumed that this ban precipitated Lucan's participation in the Pisonian conspiracy of 65 CE, the discovery of which led to his condemnation by Nero and his suicide in 65 CE at the age of 25.

Rounding out the volume are selections from the epics of three poets who wrote at the end of the first century CE, under the emperors of the so-called Flavian dynasty, T. Flavius Vespasianus (Vespasian) and his sons Titus and Domitian: the *Argonautica* of Valerius Flaccus, the *Thebaid* of Statius, and the *Punica* of Silius Italicus. Quintilian mentions neither Statius nor Silius in his survey of Latin epic in the *Education of the Orator*, but refers to the recent death of Valerius, whose poetic talent he praises by implication (*Inst. Or.* 10.1.90). Of Valerius we know nothing beyond Quintilian's notice of his recent death and his apparent support for the Flavian dynasty, on display in the proem of the *Argonautica*, which alludes to all three Flavian emperors. His epic rehearses the theme—already put into epic form by the Hellenistic Greek poet Apollonius of Rhodes and emulated by an Augustan Latin poet, P. Terentius Varro Atacinus, whose version is no longer extant—of the voyage of Jason and the Argonauts to Colchis on the Black Sea, in order to retrieve the Golden Fleece from Medea's father, King Aeetes. Valerius' epic breaks off abruptly in the eighth book, as Medea beseeches Jason (with whom she has fallen in love), not to hand her over to her brother Absyrtus, who has been sent by their father to recover her from the Argonauts.

Like Valerius, Quintilian's contemporary Statius composed mythological epic but it is clear that he attained far greater fame than the Argonautic poet with his epic *Thebaid*, which narrates the war of the Seven against Thebes. The satirist Juvenal records the rapturous response of the Roman rabble to Statius' recital of his epic (*Sat.* 7.82–87):

> They rush to hear his pleasant voice reciting the poem
> of his sweetheart *Thebais*, when Statius has made
> the city happy and promised a day: with such great
> sweetness does he capture and ensnare their souls,

and with such great pleasure the audience listens. But
though the benches break [under the crowds] at his
verse, he goes hungry unless he sells the pantomime
actor Paris a virgin "Agave."

Statius himself reports that the *Thebaid* entered the school curriculum
in his own lifetime (*Theb.* 12.815) and the existence of a late antique
commentary on the epic bears witness to its enduring appeal.

Of Silius Italicus we know considerably more than we do about
either Valerius or Statius, thanks to Martial, who mentions him in
his *Epigrams* (6.64, 7.63, 8.66, 9.86, 11.48–49), and to the younger
Pliny, who supplies a death notice (*Epist.* 3.7). The latter reports that
Silius rose to prominence under Nero with accusations of treason
against leading politicians and that he held the consulship in 68
CE, the year of Nero's overthrow and death. In this capacity, he was
closely involved in negotiating the transfer of power to Vespasian in
69, and his senatorial career flourished under the new dynasty, cul-
minating a decade later (ca. 77 CE) with the governorship of Asia, the
peak of senatorial success. His literary aspirations were as lofty as his
political ambitions: he revered Cicero, one of whose villas he owned,
and Vergil, whose tomb he owned and whose *Aeneid* supplied the
subject of his seventeen-book epic *Punica*. Silius' epic treats the Second Punic War (218–201 BCE) and locates the origin of the enmity
between Carthage and Rome in Dido's curse (*Aeneid* 4.622–9).

Statius himself offers an epic poet's guide to the masters of the
genre at Rome at *Silvae* 2.7.75–80, in a poem commemorating Lucan's birthday. Statius' catalogue of Roman epic poets and their poems in *Silvae* 2.7 furnishes the core of the texts assembled in this
Reader, which brings together some of the most important passages
in the history of the genre of Latin epic at Rome. The volume focuses
especially on the intertextual literary relations of authors and epics for, from Ennius on, the Latin epic poets echo and re-echo their
Greek and Roman predecessors' hexameter poems and thereby establish a self-consciously Roman tradition of epic poetry. The bulk
of the passages in this volume are drawn from republican and Augustan epic, to complement H. MacL. Currie's Bolchazy-Carducci/

Bristol Classical Press reader in *Silver Latin Epic* (1985) and Susanna Braund's *Lucan Reader*, the inaugural volume in this series (2009). But representative passages from imperial Latin epic are included to illustrate the continuation of republican and Augustan themes in the later authors.

∾ *Latin epic style and meter*

The introductory lines of all classical verse (and prose for that matter), and especially of epic poetry, offer the audience important information—thematic, philosophical, poetic, political—about the stance of the author and the aims and contents of his work. A number of such passages, called "proems," are included in this *Reader* to illustrate the variety of possible approaches to opening a long narrative poem. Other scenes conventional to classical epic poetry include the ecphrasis, in which the poet describes an object, often a work of art, or a place (the description of which is also called *topographia*); the duel, often between rival heroes (e.g., Aeneas and Turnus in *Aeneid* 12, included in this volume) but also between hero and beast (e.g., Theseus and the Minotaur); the hero's abandonment of a princess who has fallen in love with him (e.g., Theseus' abandonment of Ariadne in Cat. 64, included in this volume); the pitched battle and the felling of trees for the pyres of war-dead (several examples of which are included in this volume); the storm; and the shipwreck. In addition to conventional scenes, epic typically employs a wide range of figures of speech, both figures of syntax and figures of rhetoric, many of which are illustrated in the passages in this volume (see the Glossary).

Ennius made dactylic hexameter the standard meter of Latin epic, as it had been of Greek epic from Homer onwards, and his successors refined the verse over the course of the two and a half centuries of classical Latin epic composition. The word meter is used to mean a system of poetic versification and, in the case of the dactylic hexameter, the system of versification takes its name from the number (six, whence "hexameter") of feet (or basic metrical units) that prevail in it (whence "dactylic" from dactyl). The dactyl (D), which takes its name from the human "finger" with its three bones articulated by two joints, is composed of one long syllable (*longum*) followed by two short syllables (plural *breuia*, from singular *breue*): $-\cup\cup$. In each of the first five feet of the dactylic hexameter, a dactyl can be replaced by a spondee (S), a foot that takes the form of two long syllables (plural *longa*): $--$. The sixth and final foot of the dactylic hexameter is never a dactyl, but always either a spondee ($--$) or a trochee ($-\cup$). A short syllable at line-end is sometimes called *breuis in longo* (with the final short syllable treated as long because of the following pause) or "final *anceps*," and the variable quantity of the final syllable is marked as "doubtful" with an $\times$ ($-\times$). The full range of possibilities for the dactylic hexameter line are represented thus:

$$-\underline{\cup\cup}|-\underline{\cup\cup}|-\underline{\cup\cup}|-\underline{\cup\cup}|-\underline{\cup\cup}|-\times$$

The division of a line of verse according to feet is called scansion. When dividing the dactylic hexameter according to feet, there are three basic rules: the first four feet may take the form either of dactyls ($-\cup\cup$) or spondees ($--$); the fifth foot is almost always a dactyl (although Catullus favors an unusual fifth-foot spondee; see my note on Cat. 64.67); and the sixth foot is always either a spondee or trochee ($-\times$). The ending of a foot and word together is called a "DI-AERESIS," while the place within a foot where a word ends is called a "CAESURA" (strong after a long syllable, weak after a short syllable); the CAESURA is commonly indicated by the symbol //. By far the most common CAESURA in the classical Latin dactylic hexameter is the strong third-foot CAESURA. The opening verse of Vergil's *Aeneid* offers a good example, and is scanned as follows:

$$-\quad\cup\ \cup|-\quad\cup\ \cup|-//\ -\ |-\ -\ |\ -\ \cup\ \cup\ |-\ \times$$
arma uirumque cano Tro(j)a qui primus ab oris

If a word ending in a vowel (or vowel + *m*) is directly followed by a word that begins with a vowel (or *h* + vowel), the first vowel is elided (suppressed). For example, in the third line of Vergil's *Aeneid*, the second word (*multum*) elides with the third (*ille*) and the third (*ille*) with the fourth (*et*). The line is thus scanned:

$$–\cup\cup| \quad – \quad – | \quad –//– |– \quad –|– \cup \cup|– \times$$
litora, mult(um) ill(e) et terris (j)actatus et alto

The Roman poets experimented continuously with the dactylic hexameter from Ennius' introduction of the measure into Latin verse all the way to the imperial epic poets and beyond. A verse in which the end of every foot coincides with the end of a word (as almost happens in, e.g., Enn. *Ann.* 41) sounded harsh to the classical Latin poets and so they avoided such lines. Similarly, the suppression of final -*s*, normal in Ennius' day (see my note on Enn. *Ann.* 37), sounded old-fashioned to the classical Latin poets, who shun it altogether. Catullus is especially innovative in his approach to the dactylic hexameter, experimenting with the sound effects of different rhythms (e.g., with a spondaic fifth-foot) and number of words in a line (e.g., with a four-word hexameter; see my note on Cat. 64.77). Vergil is generally agreed to have brought the meter to perfection in Latin by developing a complex pattern of sound and sense over several lines through variation (1) of syntax and sense pauses from line to line, and (2) of word emphasis (accent) against the metrical beat (i.e., the initial position of the foot, normally a long syllable) within the line. After Vergil, the Latin epic poets follow or diverge from his metrical principles according to their poetic ends. Thus, for example, Ovid "lightens" the Latin dactylic hexameter with his preference for dactyls over spondees in the first four feet of the line in order to keep the pace of his narrative swift, while Lucan dispenses with Vergil's variety of tone and tempo in order to communicate the relentless pressure of Caesar's assault on the institutions of republican government at Rome.

∾ *Suggested reading*

Ahl, F. M. *Lucan, An Introduction*. Ithaca and London: Cornell University Press, 1976.

Anderson, W. S., ed. *Ovid's* METAMORPHOSES *Books 6–10*. Norman OK: University of Oklahoma Press, 1972.

Armstrong, R. *Cretan Women*. Oxford: Oxford University Press, 2006.

Augoustakis, A., ed. *Brill's Companion to Silius Italicus*. Leiden: Brill, 2010.

Bailey, C., ed. *Titi Lucreti Cari, De Rerum Natura Libri Sex*. 3 vols. Oxford: Clarendon Press, 1947.

Boyd, B. W., ed. *Brill's Companion to Ovid*. Leiden: Brill, 2002.

Boyle, A. J., ed. *The Imperial Muse. Ramus Essays on Roman Literature of the Empire: Flavian Epicist to Claudian*. Victoria, Australia: Aureal Publications, 1990.

———. *Roman Epic*. New York and London: Routledge, 1993.

Braund, S. *A Lucan Reader: Selections from Civil War*. Mundelein: Bolchazy-Carducci Publishers, 2009.

Conte, G. B. *The Rhetoric of Imitation*. Translated by C. Segal. Ithaca and London: Cornell University Press, 1986.

Currie, H. MacL. *Silver Latin Epic: A Selection from Lucan, Valerius Flaccus, Silius Italicus & Statius with Introduction, Commentary & an Appendix of Comparative Passages*. Bristol and Chicago: Bristol Classical Press and Bolchazy-Carducci Publishers, 1985.

Ehlers, W., ed. *Valerius Flaccus*. Stuttgart: Teubner, 1980.

Gale, M. R. *Myth and Poetry in Lucretius*. Cambridge: Cambridge University Press, 1994.

———. *Lucretius and the Didactic Epic*. London: Bristol Classical Press, 2001.

———, ed. *Lucretius*. Oxford: Oxford University Press, 2007.

Gillespie, S., and P. Hardie, eds. *The Cambridge Companion to Lucretius*. Cambridge: Cambridge University Press, 2007.

Gratwick, A. S. "Ennius' *Annales*." In *The Cambridge History of Classical Literature*, Vol. 2, 60–76. Cambridge, Cambridge University Press, 1982.

Hardie. P. *Virgil's Aeneid: Cosmos and Imperium*. Oxford: Clarendon Press, 1986.

————. *The Epic Successors of Virgil*. Cambridge: Cambridge University Press, 1993.

————, ed. *The Cambridge Companion to Ovid*. Cambridge: Cambridge University Press, 2002.

Hardie, P., A. Barchiesi, and S. Hinds, eds. *Ovidian Transformations: Essays on the METAMORPHOSES and its Reception*. Cambridge: Cambridge Philological Society, 1999.

Hinds, S. *Intertext and Allusion*. Cambridge: Cambridge University Press, 1998.

Hollis, A. S., ed. *Ovid, METAMORPHOSES BOOK VIII*. Oxford: Clarendon Press, 1970.

Keith, A. M. *Engendering Rome: Women in Latin Epic*. Cambridge: Cambridge University Press, 2000.

Lee, A. G., ed. *Ovid, METAMORPHOSES I*. Cambridge: Cambridge University Press, 1953; repr. Bristol and Chicago: Bristol Classical Press and Bolchazy-Carducci Publishers, 1984.

Leigh, M. *Lucan: Spectacle and Engagement*. New York: Clarendon Press, 1997.

Martindale, C., ed. *The Cambridge Companion to Virgil*. Cambridge: Cambridge University Press, 1997.

Masters, J. *Poetry and Civil War in Lucan's BELLUM CIVILE*. Cambridge: Cambridge University Press, 1992.

Morgan, Llewelyn. *MUSA PEDESTRIS: Metre and Meaning in Roman Verse*. Oxford, 2010.

O'Hara, J. J. *True Names: Vergil and the Alexandrian Tradition of Etymological Wordplay*. Ann Arbor: University of Michigan Press, 1996.

————. *Inconsistency in Roman Epic*. Cambridge: Cambridge University Press, 2007.

Paschalis, M., ed. *Roman and Greek Imperial Epic. Rethymnon Classical Studies 2*. Rethymmon: Crete University Press, 2005.

Pöschl, V. *The Art of Vergil: Image and Symbol in the AENEID*. Translated by G. Seligson. Ann Arbor: University of Michigan Press, 1962.

Quint, D. *Epic and Empire.* Princeton: Princeton University Press, 1993.

Rosati, G. *Ovidio, Metamorphosi,* vol. 2. Edited by A. Barchiesi. Rome: Fondazione Lorenzo Valla, 2007.

Sedley, D. *Lucretius and the Transformation of Greek Wisdom.* New York: Cambridge University Press, 1998.

Sklenár, R. *The Taste for Nothingness: A Study of Virtus and Related Themes in Lucan's Bellum Civile.* Ann Arbor: University of Michigan Press, 2003.

Volk, K. *Manilius and his Intellectual Background.* Oxford: Oxford University Press, 2009.

Warmington, E. H., ed. *Remains of Old Latin.* 4 vols. Cambridge MA: Harvard University Press, 1967.

Wills, J. *Repetition in Latin Poetry: Figures of Allusion.* Oxford: Clarendon Press, 1996.

Latin Text

Skutsch, O., ed. *The Annals of Q. Ennius.* Oxford: Clarendon Press, 1985.

Bailey, C., ed. *Titi Lucreti Cari.* Oxford: Clarendon Press, 1947.

Mynors, R. A. B., ed. *C. Valeri Catulli Carmina.* Oxford: Clarendon Press, 1958.

Mynors, R. A. B., ed. *P. Vergili Maronis, Opera.* Oxford: Clarendon Press, 1969.

Tarrant, R. J., ed. *P. Ovidi Nasonis, METAMORPHOSES.* Oxford: Oxford University Press, 2004.

Housman, A. E., ed. *M. Manilii ASTRONOMICA.* Cambridge: Cambridge University Press, 1932.

Housman, A. E., ed. *M. Annaei Lucani, BELLI CIVILIS libri decem.* Oxford: Blackwell, 1958.

Poortvliet, H. M., ed. *C. Valerius Flaccus, ARGONAUTICA Book II: A Commentary.* Amsterdam: VU University Press, 1991.

Hill, D. E., ed. *P. Papini Stati THEBAIDOS Libri XII.* Leiden: E. J. Brill, 1983.

Delz, J., ed. *Sili Italici PUNICA.* Stuttgart: Teubner, 1987.

NB: I have regularized all texts to consistently lower case presentation (except for proper nouns and adjectives, which are capitalized) and consonantal *u* (even though students find the latter challenging compared to the alternative, *v*).

Specific divergences from the texts are listed below:

Enn. *Ann.* 34	period removed after **lumen**
Enn. *Ann.* 74	**Murco** printed instead of †*monte*
Verg. *Aen.* 4.167	**Aether** capitalized
V. Fl. *Arg.* 2.518	daggers removed from **illa simul**
Stat. *Theb.* 6.88	**Tempe** capitalized
Stat. *Theb.* 6.88–89	square brackets removed

∾ *Ennius, ANNALES 34–50*
Ilia's dream

    et cita cum tremulis anus attulit artubus lumen

35 talia tum memorat lacrimans, exterrita somno:

    'Eurydica prognata, pater quam noster amauit,

    uires uitaque corpus meum nunc deserit omne.

    nam me uisus homo pulcer per amoena salicta

    et ripas raptare locosque nouos. ita sola

40 postilla, germana soror, errare uidebar

    tardaque uestigare et quaerere te neque posse

    corde capessere: semita nulla pedem stabilibat.

    exim compellare pater me uoce uidetur

    his uerbis: "o gnata, tibi sunt ante gerendae

45 aerumnae, post ex fluuio fortuna resistet."

    haec ecfatus pater, germana, repente recessit

    nec sese dedit in conspectum corde cupitus,

    quamquam multa manus ad caeli caerula templa

    tendebam lacrumans et blanda uoce uocabam.

50 uix aegro cum corde meo me somnus reliquit.'

∾ *Ennius,* ANNALES *72–91*
Romulus and Remus take the auspices

curantes magna cum cura tum cupientes

regni dant operam simul auspicio augurioque.

in Murco Remus auspicio sedet atque secundam

75 solus auem seruat. at Romulus pulcer in alto

quaerit Auentino, seruat genus altiuolantum.

certabant urbem Romam Remoramne uocarent.

omnibus cura uiris uter esset induperator.

expectant ueluti consul quom mittere signum

80 uolt, omnes auidi spectant ad carceris oras

quam mox emittat pictos e faucibus currus:

sic expectabat populus atque ore timebat

rebus utri magni uictoria sit data regni.

interea sol albus recessit in infera noctis.

85 exin candida se radiis dedit icta foras lux

et simul ex alto longe pulcerrima praepes

laeua uolauit auis. simul aureus exoritur sol

cedunt de caelo ter quattuor corpora sancta

auium, praepetibus sese pulcrisque locis dant.

90 conspicit inde sibi data Romulus esse propritim

auspicio regni stabilita scamna solumque.

∾ *Ennius, Annales 175–79*
Felling of trees

175   incedunt arbusta per alta, securibus caedunt,

      percellunt magnas quercus, exciditur ilex,

      fraxinus frangitur atque abies consternitur alta,

      pinus proceras peruortunt: omne sonabat

      arbustum fremitu siluai frondosai.

∾ *Lucretius, De rerum natura 1.1–43*
Invocation of Venus

      Aeneadum genetrix, hominum diuumque uoluptas

      alma Venus, caeli subter labentia signa

      quae mare nauigerum, quae terras frugiferentis

      concelebras, per te quoniam genus omne animantum

5   concipitur uisitque exortum lumina solis:

      te, dea, te fugiunt uenti, te nubila caeli

      aduentumque tuum, tibi suauis daedala tellus

      summittit flores, tibi rident aequora ponti

      placatumque nitet diffuso lumine caelum.

10   nam simul ac species patefactast uerna diei

      et reserata uiget genitabilis aura fauoni,

      aeriae primum uolucris te, diua, tuumque

      significant initum perculsae corda tua ui.

      inde ferae pecudes persultant pabula laeta

15   et rapidos tranant amnis: ita capta lepore

      te sequitur cupide quo quamque inducere pergis.

      denique per maria ac montis fluuiosque rapacis

frondiferasque domos auium camposque uirentis
omnibus incutiens blandum per pectora amorem
20   efficis ut cupide generatim saecla propagent.
quae quoniam rerum naturam sola gubernas
nec sine te quicquam dias in luminis oras
exoritur neque fit laetum neque amabile quicquam,
te sociam studeo scribendis uersibus esse
25   quos ego de rerum natura pangere conor
Memmiadae nostro, quem tu, dea, tempore in omni
omnibus ornatum uoluisti excellere rebus.
quo magis aeternum da dictis, diua, leporem.
effice ut interea fera moenera militiai
30   per maria ac terras omnis sopita quiescant.
nam tu sola potes tranquilla pace iuuare
mortalis, quoniam belli fera moenera Mauors
armipotens regit, in gremium qui saepe tuum se
reicit aeterno deuictus uulnere amoris,
35   atque ita suspiciens tereti ceruice reposta
pascit amore auidos inhians in te, dea, uisus,
eque tuo pendet resupini spiritus ore.
hunc tu, diua, tuo recubantem corpore sancto
circumfusa super, suauis ex ore loquellas
40   funde petens placidam Romanis, incluta, pacem.
nam neque nos agere hoc patriai tempore iniquo
possumus aequo animo nec Memmi clara propago
talibus in rebus communi desse saluti.

∾ *Lucretius, DE RERUM NATURA 1.936–50*
The honey round the cup

    sed ueluti pueris absinthia taetra medentes

    cum dare conantur, prius oras pocula circum

    contingunt mellis dulci flauoque liquore,

    ut puerorum aetas improuida ludificetur

940 labrorum tenus, interea perpotet amarum

    absinthi laticem deceptaque non capiatur,

    sed potius tali pacto recreata ualescat,

    sic ego nunc, quoniam haec ratio plerumque uidetur

    tristior esse quibus non est tractata, retroque

945 uulgus abhorret ab hac, uolui tibi suauiloquenti

    carmine Pierio rationem exponere nostram

    et quasi musaeo dulci contingere melle,

    si tibi forte animum tali ratione tenere

    uersibus in nostris possem, dum perspicis omnem

950 naturam rerum qua constet compta figura.

∾ *Catullus, CARMEN 64.50–93*
Ariadne in love

50 haec uestis priscis hominum uariata figuris

    heroum mira uirtutes indicat arte.

    namque fluentisono prospectans litore Diae,

    Thesea cedentem celeri cum classe tuetur

    indomitos in corde gerens Ariadna furores,

55 necdum etiam sese quae uisit uisere credit,

    utpote fallaci quae tum primum excita somno

desertam in sola miseram se cernat harena.

immemor at iuuenis fugiens pellit uada remis,

irrita uentosae linquens promissa procellae.

60 quem procul ex alga maestis Minois ocellis,

saxea ut effigies bacchantis, prospicit, eheu,

prospicit et magnis curarum fluctuat undis,

non flauo retinens subtilem uertice mitram,

non contecta leui uelatum pectus amictu,

65 non tereti strophio lactentis uincta papillas,

omnia quae toto delapsa e corpore passim

ipsius ante pedes fluctus salis alludebant.

sed neque tum mitrae neque tum fluitantis amictus

illa uicem curans toto ex te pectore, Theseu,

70 toto animo, tota pendebat perdita mente.

a misera, assiduis quam luctibus externauit

spinosas Erycina serens in pectore curas,

illa tempestate, ferox quo ex tempore Theseus

egressus curuis e litoribus Piraei

75 attigit iniusti regis Gortynia templa.

nam perhibent olim crudeli peste coactam

Androgeoneae poenas exsoluere caedis

electos iuuenes simul et decus innuptarum

Cecropiam solitam esse dapem dare Minotauro.

80 quis angusta malis cum moenia uexarentur,

ipse suum Theseus pro caris corpus Athenis

proicere optauit potius quam talia Cretam

funera Cecropiae nec funera portarentur.

atque ita naue leui nitens ac lenibus auris

85 magnanimum ad Minoa uenit sedesque superbas.
hunc simul ac cupido conspexit lumine uirgo
regia, quam suauis exspirans castus odores
lectulus in molli complexu matris alebat,
quales Eurotae praecingunt flumina myrtus
90 auraue distinctos educit uerna colores,
non prius ex illo flagrantia declinauit
lumina, quam cuncto concepit corpore flammam
funditus atque imis exarsit tota medullis.

∾ *Vergil, Aeneid 1.1–11*
Proem

arma uirumque cano, Troiae qui primus ab oris
Italiam fato profugus Lauiniaque uenit
litora, multum ille et terris iactatus et alto
ui superum, saeuae memorem Iunonis ob iram,
5 multa quoque et bello passus, dum conderet urbem
inferretque deos Latio; genus unde Latinum
Albanique patres atque altae moenia Romae.
Musa, mihi causas memora, quo numine laeso
quidue dolens regina deum tot uoluere casus
10 insignem pietate uirum, tot adire labores
impulerit. tantaene animis caelestibus irae?

❧ *Vergil,* Aeneid *1.148–56*
First simile, Neptune calms the sea

ac ueluti magno in populo cum saepe coorta est

seditio saeuitque animis ignobile uulgus

150 iamque faces et saxa uolant, furor arma ministrat;

tum, pietate grauem ac meritis si forte uirum quem

conspexere, silent arrectisque auribus astant;

ille regit dictis animos et pectora mulcet:

sic cunctus pelagi cecidit fragor, aequora postquam

155 prospiciens genitor caeloque inuectus aperto

flectit equos curruque uolans dat lora secundo.

❧ *Vergil,* Aeneid *1.338–68*
Dido's family background

Punica regna uides, Tyrios et Agenoris urbem;

sed fines Libyci, genus intractabile bello.

340 imperium Dido Tyria regit urbe profecta,

germanum fugiens. longa est iniuria, longae

ambages; sed summa sequar fastigia rerum.

huic coniunx Sychaeus erat, ditissimus auri

Phoenicum, et magno miserae dilectus amore,

345 cui pater intactam dederat primisque iugarat

ominibus. sed regna Tyri germanus habebat

Pygmalion, scelere ante alios immanior omnis.

quos inter medius uenit furor. ille Sychaeum

impius ante aras atque auri caecus amore

350 clam ferro incautum superat, securus amorum

germanae; factumque diu celauit et aegram

multa malus simulans uana spe lusit amantem.

ipsa sed in somnis inhumati uenit imago

coniugis ora modis attollens pallida miris;

355   crudelis aras traiectaque pectora ferro

nudauit, caecumque domus scelus omne retexit.

tum celerare fugam patriaque excedere suadet

auxiliumque uiae ueteres tellure recludit

thesauros, ignotum argenti pondus et auri.

360   his commota fugam Dido sociosque parabat.

conueniunt quibus aut odium crudele tyranni

aut metus acer erat; nauis, quae forte paratae,

corripiunt onerantque auro. portantur auari

Pygmalionis opes pelago; dux femina facti.

365   deuenere locos ubi nunc ingentia cernes

moenia surgentemque nouae Karthaginis arcem,

mercatique solum, facti de nomine Byrsam,

taurino quantum possent circumdare tergo.

∾ Vergil, Aeneid 4.1–30
Dido in love

at regina graui iamdudum saucia cura

uulnus alit uenis et caeco carpitur igni.

multa uiri uirtus animo multusque recursat

gentis honos; haerent infixi pectore uultus

5   uerbaque nec placidam membris dat cura quietem.

postera Phoebea lustrabat lampade terras
umentemque Aurora polo dimouerat umbram,
cum sic unanimam adloquitur male sana sororem:
'Anna soror, quae me suspensam insomnia terrent!
10 quis nouus hic nostris successit sedibus hospes,
quem sese ore ferens, quam forti pectore et armis!
credo equidem, nec uana fides, genus esse deorum.
degeneres animos timor arguit. heu, quibus ille
iactatus fatis! quae bella exhausta canebat!
15 si mihi non animo fixum immotumque sederet
ne cui me uinclo uellem sociare iugali,
postquam primus amor deceptam morte fefellit;
si non pertaesum thalami taedaeque fuisset,
huic uni forsan potui succumbere culpae.
20 Anna (fatebor enim) miseri post fata Sychaei
coniugis et sparsos fraterna caede penatis
solus hic inflexit sensus animumque labantem
impulit. agnosco ueteris uestigia flammae.
sed mihi uel tellus optem prius ima dehiscat
25 uel pater omnipotens adigat me fulmine ad umbras,
pallentis umbras Erebo noctemque profundam,
ante, pudor, quam te uiolo aut tua iura resoluo.
ille meos, primus qui me sibi iunxit, amores
abstulit; ille habeat secum seruetque sepulcro.'
30 sic effata sinum lacrimis impleuit obortis.

∾ *Vergil,* AENEID *4.160–72*
The wedding in the cave

160 interea magno misceri murmure caelum
     incipit, insequitur commixta grandine nimbus,
     et Tyrii comites passim et Troiana iuuentus
     Dardaniusque nepos Veneris diuersa per agros
     tecta metu petiere; ruunt de montibus amnes.
165 speluncam Dido dux et Troianus eandem
     deueniunt. prima et Tellus et pronuba Iuno
     dant signum; fulsere ignes et conscius Aether
     conubiis summoque ulularunt uertice Nymphae.
     ille dies primus leti primusque malorum
170 causa fuit; neque enim specie famaue mouetur
     nec iam furtiuum Dido meditatur amorem:
     coniugium uocat, hoc praetexit nomine culpam.

∾ *Vergil,* AENEID *6.14–33*
Ecphrasis of the doors on the temple of Apollo

     Daedalus, ut fama est, fugiens Minoïa regna
15 praepetibus pennis ausus se credere caelo
     insuetum per iter gelidas enauit ad Arctos,
     Chalcidicaque leuis tandem super astitit arce.
     redditus his primum terris tibi, Phoebe, sacrauit
     remigium alarum posuitque immania templa.
20 in foribus letum Androgeo; tum pendere poenas
     Cecropidae iussi (miserum!) septena quotannis
     corpora natorum; stat ductis sortibus urna.

contra elata mari respondet Cnosia tellus:

hic crudelis amor tauri suppostaque furto

25 Pasiphae mixtumque genus prolesque biformis

Minotaurus inest, Veneris monimenta nefandae,

hic labor ille domus et inextricabilis error;

magnum reginae sed enim miseratus amorem

Daedalus ipse dolos tecti ambagesque resoluit,

30 caeca regens filo uestigia. tu quoque magnam

partem opere in tanto, sineret dolor, Icare, haberes.

bis conatus erat casus effingere in auro,

bis patriae cecidere manus…

❧ *Vergil*, Aeneid *6.179–82*
Felling of trees for Misenus' funerary pyre

itur in antiquam siluam, stabula alta ferarum;

180 procumbunt piceae, sonat icta securibus ilex

fraxineaeque trabes cuneis et fissile robur

scinditur, aduoluunt ingentis montibus ornos.

❧ *Vergil*, Aeneid *6.456–66*
Aeneas' encounter with Dido in the underworld

'infelix Dido, uerus mihi nuntius ergo

uenerat exstinctam ferroque extrema secutam?

funeris heu tibi causa fui? per sidera iuro,

per superos et si qua fides tellure sub ima est,

460 inuitus, regina, tuo de litore cessi.

sed me iussa deum, quae nunc has ire per umbras,

per loca senta situ cogunt noctemque profundam,

imperiis egere suis; nec credere quiui

hunc tantum tibi me discessu ferre dolorem.

465   siste gradum teque aspectu ne subtrahe nostro.

quem fugis? extremum fato quod te adloquor hoc est.'

∾ *Vergil, AENEID 8.625–34*
The shield of Aeneas

625   hastamque et clipei non enarrabile textum.

illic res Italas Romanorumque triumphos

haud uatum ignarus uenturique inscius aeui

fecerat ignipotens, illic genus omne futurae

stirpis ab Ascanio pugnataque in ordine bella.

630   fecerat et uiridi fetam Mauortis in antro

procubuisse lupam, geminos huic ubera circum

ludere pendentis pueros et lambere matrem

impauidos, illam tereti ceruice reflexa

mulcere alternos et corpora fingere lingua.

∾ *Vergil, AENEID 12.697–724*
Duel between Aeneas and Turnus

at pater Aeneas audito nomine Turni

deserit et muros et summas deserit arces

praecipitatque moras omnis, opera omnia rumpit

700   laetitia exsultans horrendumque intonat armis:

quantus Athos aut quantus Eryx aut ipse coruscis
cum fremit ilicibus quantus gaudetque niuali
uertice se attollens pater Appenninus ad auras.
iam uero et Rutuli certatim et Troes et omnes
705 conuertere oculos Itali, quique alta tenebant
moenia quique imos pulsabant ariete muros,
armaque deposuere umeris. stupet ipse Latinus
ingentis, genitos diuersis partibus orbis,
inter se coiisse uiros et cernere ferro.
710 atque illi, ut uacuo patuerunt aequore campi,
procursu rapido coniectis eminus hastis
inuadunt Martem clipeis atque aere sonoro.
dat gemitum tellus; tum crebros ensibus ictus
congeminant, fors et uirtus miscetur in unum.
715 ac uelut ingenti Sila summoue Taburno
cum duo conuersis inimica in proelia tauri
frontibus incurrunt, pauidi cessere magistri,
stat pecus omne metu mutum, mussantque iuuencae
quis nemori imperitet, quem tota armenta sequantur;
720 illi inter sese multa ui uulnera miscent
cornuaque obnixi infigunt et sanguine largo
colla armosque lauant, gemitu nemus omne remugit:
non aliter Tros Aeneas et Daunius heros
concurrunt clipeis, ingens fragor aethera complet.

∾ *Ovid, METAMORPHOSES 1.1–20*
Proem and description of chaos

in noua fert animus mutatas dicere formas

corpora; di, coeptis (nam uos mutastis et illa)

aspirate meis primaque ab origine mundi

ad mea perpetuum deducite tempora carmen.

5   ante mare et terras et quod tegit omnia caelum

unus erat toto naturae uultus in orbe,

quem dixere Chaos; rudis indigestaque moles

nec quidquam nisi pondus iners congestaque eodem

non bene iunctarum discordia semina rerum.

10 nullus adhuc mundo praebebat lumina Titan

nec noua crescendo reparabat cornua Phoebe

nec circumfuso pendebat in aere Tellus

ponderibus librata suis nec bracchia longo

margine terrarum porrexerat Amphitrite.

15 utque erat et tellus illic et pontus et aer,

sic erat instabilis tellus, innabilis unda,

lucis egens aer; nulli sua forma manebat

obstabatque aliis aliud, quia corpore in uno

frigida pugnabant calidis, umentia siccis,

20 mollia cum duris, sine pondere habentia pondus.

∾ *Ovid, Metamorphoses 1.89–112*

The golden age

aurea prima sata est aetas, quae uindice nullo,

90   sponte sua, sine lege fidem rectumque colebat.

poena metusque aberant, nec uerba minantia fixo

aere ligabantur, nec supplex turba timebat

iudicis ora sui, sed erant sine uindice tuti.

nondum caesa suis, peregrinum ut uiseret orbem,

95   montibus in liquidas pinus descenderat undas,

nullaque mortales praeter sua litora norant;

nondum praecipites cingebant oppida fossae;

non tuba derecti, non aeris cornua flexi,

non galeae, non ensis erat; sine militis usu

100   mollia securae peragebant otia gentes.

ipsa quoque immunis rastroque intacta nec ullis

saucia uomeribus per se dabat omnia tellus;

contentique cibis nullo cogente creatis

arbuteos fetus montanaque fraga legebant

105   cornaque et in duris haerentia mora rubetis

et quae deciderant patula Iouis arbore glandes.

uer erat aeternum, placidique tepentibus auris

mulcebant Zephyri natos sine semine flores.

mox etiam fruges tellus inarata ferebat,

110   nec renouatus ager grauidis canebat aristis.

flumina iam lactis, iam flumina nectaris ibant,

flauaque de uiridi stillabant ilice mella.

∾ *Ovid, METAMORPHOSES 4.706–39*
Perseus fights a sea-monster to rescue Andromeda

ecce, uelut nauis praefixo concita rostro

sulcat aquas iuuenum sudantibus acta lacertis,

sic fera dimotis impulsu pectoris undis.

tantum aberat scopulis quantum Balearica torto

710   funda potest plumbo medii transmittere caeli,

cum subito iuuenis pedibus tellure repulsa

arduus in nubes abiit. ut in aequore summo

umbra uiri uisa est, uisam fera saeuit in umbram;

utque Iouis praepes, uacuo cum uidit in aruo

715   praebentem Phoebo liuentia terga draconem,

occupat auersum, neu saeua retorqueat ora,

squamigeris auidos figit ceruicibus ungues,

sic celeri missus praeceps per inane uolatu

terga ferae pressit dextroque frementis in armo

720   Inachides ferrum curuo tenus abdidit hamo.

uulnere laesa graui modo se sublimis in auras

attollit, modo subdit aquis, modo more ferocis

uersat apri, quem turba canum circumsona terret;

ille auidos morsus uelocibus effugit alis,

725   quaque patet, nunc terga cauis super obsita conchis,

nunc laterum costas, nunc, qua tenuissima cauda

desinit in piscem, falcato uerberat ense.

belua puniceo mixtos cum sanguine fluctus

ore uomit; maduere graues aspergine pennae.

730   nec bibulis ultra Perseus talaribus ausus

credere conspexit scopulum, qui uertice summo

stantibus exstat aquis, operitur ab aequore moto;

nixus eo rupisque tenens iuga prima sinistra

ter quater exegit repetita per ilia ferrum.

735 litora cum plausu clamor superasque deorum

impleuere domos; gaudent generumque salutant

auxiliumque domus seruatoremque fatentur

Cassiope Cepheusque pater; resoluta catenis

incedit uirgo, pretiumque et causa laboris.

❧ Ovid, METAMORPHOSES 8.155–82
Cretan myths

155 creuerat opprobrium generis foedumque patebat

matris adulterium monstri nouitate biformis;

destinat hunc Minos thalami remouere pudorem

multiplicique domo caecisque includere tectis.

Daedalus ingenio fabrae celeberrimus artis

160 ponit opus turbatque notas et lumina flexa

ducit in errorem uariarum ambage uiarum.

non secus ac liquidis Phrygius Maeandros in undis

ludit et ambiguo lapsu refluitque fluitque

occurrensque sibi uenturas aspicit undas

165 et nunc ad fontes, nunc ad mare uersus apertum

incertas exercet aquas, ita Daedalus implet

innumeras errore uias uixque ipse reuerti

ad limen potuit; tanta est fallacia tecti.

quo postquam geminam tauri iuuenisque figuram

170 clausit et Actaeo bis pastum sanguine monstrum

tertia sors annis domuit repetita nouenis,

utque ope uirginea nullis iterata priorum

ianua difficilis filo est inuenta relecto,

protinus Aegides rapta Minoide Dian

175   uela dedit comitemque suam crudelis in illo

litore destituit. desertae et multa querenti

amplexus et opem Liber tulit, utque perenni

sidere clara foret, sumptam de fronte coronam

immisit caelo; tenues uolat illa per auras

180   dumque uolat gemmae nitidos uertuntur in ignes

consistuntque loco, specie remanente coronae

qui medius Nixique genu est Anguemque tenentis.

∾ Ovid, METAMORPHOSES 8.741–76
Erysichthon cuts down Ceres' tree

ille etiam Cereale nemus uiolasse securi

dicitur et lucos ferro temerasse uetustos.

stabat in his ingens annoso robore quercus,

una nemus; uittae mediam memoresque tabellae

745   sertaque cingebant, uoti argumenta potentum.

saepe sub hac Dryades festas duxere choreas,

saepe etiam manibus nexis ex ordine trunci

circuiere modum, mensuraque roboris ulnas

quinque ter implebat, nec non et cetera tantum

750   silua sub hac, silua quantum fuit herba sub omni.

non tamen idcirco ferrum Triopeius illa

abstinuit famulosque iubet succidere sacrum

robur et, ut iussos cunctari uidit, ab uno
edidit haec rapta sceleratus uerba securi:
755 "non dilecta deae solum, sed et ipsa licebit
sit dea, iam tanget frondente cacumine terram."
dixit et, obliquos dum telum librat in ictus,
contremuit gemitumque dedit Deoïa quercus,
et pariter frondes, pariter pallescere glandes
760 coepere ac longi pallorem ducere rami.
cuius ut in trunco fecit manus impia uulnus,
haud aliter fluxit discusso cortice sanguis
quam solet, ante aras ingens ubi uictima taurus
concidit, abrupta cruor e ceruice profundi.
765 obstipuere omnes aliquisque ex omnibus audet
deterrere nefas saeuamque inhibere bipennem;
aspicit hunc "mentis"que "piae cape praemia!" dixit
Thessalus inque uirum conuertit ab arbore ferrum
detruncatque caput repetitaque robora caedit.
770 redditus e medio sonus est tum robore talis:
"nympha sub hoc ego sum Cereri gratissima ligno,
quae tibi factorum poenas instare tuorum
uaticinor moriens, nostri solacia leti."
persequitur scelus ille suum, labefactaque tandem
775 ictibus innumeris adductaque funibus arbor
corruit et multam prostrauit pondere siluam.

ᴥ *Manilius, Astronomica 5.574–615*
Perseus fights a sea-monster to rescue Andromeda

    et, postquam poenae causam cognouit ab ipsa,

575   destinat in thalamos per bellum uadere ponti,

    altera si Gorgo ueniat, non territus illa.

    concitat aerios cursus flentisque parentis

    promissu uitae recreat pactusque maritam

    ad litus remeat. grauidus iam surgere pontus

580   coeperat ac longo fugiebant agmine fluctus

    inpellentis onus monstri. caput eminet undas

    scindentis pelagusque uomit, circumsonat aequor

    dentibus, inque ipso rapidum mare nauigat ore;

    hinc uasti surgunt inmensis torquibus orbes

585   tergaque consumunt pelagus. sonat undique Phorcus

    atque ipsi metuunt montes scopulique ruentem.

    infelix uirgo, quamuis sub uindice tanto

    quae tua tunc fuerat facies! quam fugit in auras

    spiritus! ut toto caruerunt sanguine membra,

590   cum tua fata cauis e rupibus ipsa uideres

    adnantemque tibi poenam pelagusque ferentem

    quantula praeda maris! quassis hic subuolat alis

    Perseus et semet caelo iaculatur in hostem

    Gorgoneo tinctum defigens sanguine ferrum.

595   illa subit contra uersamque a gurgite frontem

    erigit et tortis innitens orbibus alte

    emicat ac toto sublimis corpore fertur.

    sed, quantum illa subit, semper, iaculata profundo,

    in tantum reuolat laxumque per aethera ludit

600 Perseus et ceti subeuntis uerberat ora.

nec cedit tamen illa uiro, sed saeuit in auras

morsibus, et uani crepitant sine uulnere dentes;

ecflat et in caelum pelagus mergitque uolantem

sanguineis undis pontumque exstillat in astra.

605 spectabat pugnam pugnandi causa puella,

iamque oblita sui metuit pro uindice tali

suspirans animoque magis quam corpore pendet.

tandem confossis subsedit belua membris

plena maris summasque iterum remeauit ad undas

610 et magnum uasto contexit corpore pontum,

tum quoque terribilis nec uirginis ore uidenda.

perfundit liquido Perseus in marmore corpus

maior et ex undis ad cautes peruolat altas

soluitque haerentem uinclis de rupe puellam

615 desponsam, magna nupturam dote mariti.

✆ Lucan, *Bellum Civile* 2.1–15
Proem to Book 2

iamque irae patuere deum, manifestaque belli

signa dedit mundus legesque et foedera rerum

praescia monstrifero uertit natura tumultu

indixitque nefas. cur hanc tibi, rector Olympi,

5 sollicitis uisum mortalibus addere curam,

noscant uenturas ut dira per omina clades?

siue parens rerum, cum primum informia regna

materiamque rudem flamma cedente recepit,

fixit in aeternum causas, qua cuncta coercet,

10   se quoque lege tenens, et saecula iussa ferentem

fatorum inmoto diuisit limite mundum;

siue nihil positum est, sed fors incerta uagatur

fertque refertque uices et habet mortalia casus:

sit subitum quodcumque paras; sit caeca futuri

15   mens hominum fati; liceat sperare timenti.

✑ *Valerius Flaccus,* Argonautica *2.497–537*
Hercules fights a sea-monster to rescue Hesione

dat procul interea signum Neptunus, et una

monstriferi mugire sinus Sigeaque pestis

adglomerare fretum, cuius stellantia glauca

500   lumina nube tremunt atque ordine curua trisulco

fulmineus quatit ora fragor pelagoque remenso

cauda redit passosque sinus rapit ardua ceruix.

illam incumbentem per mille uolumina pontus

prosequitur lateri adsultans trepidisque ruentem

505   litoribus sua cogit hiems. non fluctibus aequis

nubiferi uenit unda Noti, non Africus alto

tantus ouat patriisque manus cum plenus habenis

Orion bipedum flatu mare tollit equorum.

ecce ducem placitae furiis crudescere pugnae

510   surgentemque toris stupet immanemque paratu

Aeacides pulsentque graues ut terga pharetrae.

ille patrem pelagique deos suaque arma precatus

insiluit scopulo motumque e sedibus aequor

horruit et celsi spatiosa uolumina monstri.

515   qualis ubi a gelidi Boreas conuallibus Hebri

tollitur et uolucres Rhipaea per ardua nubes

praecipitat, piceo necdum tenet omnia caelo,

illa simul molem horrificam scopulosaque terga

promouet ingentique umbra subit; intremere Ide

520   inlidique rates pronaeque resurgere turres.

occupat Alcides arcum totaque pharetrae

nube premit. non illa magis quam sede mouetur

magnus Eryx, deferre uelint quem uallibus imbres.

iam breuis et telo uolucri non utilis aer.

525   tum uero fremitus uanique insania coepti

et tacitus pudor et rursus pallescere uirgo.

proicit arma manu, scopulos uicinaque saxa

respicit, et quantum uentis adiuta uetustas

impulerit pontiue fragor, tantum abscidit imi

530   concutiens a sede maris. iamque agmine toto

pistris adest miseraeque inhiat iam proxima praedae.

stat mediis elatus aquis recipitque ruentem

Alcides saxoque prior surgentia colla

obruit. hinc uastos nodosi roboris ictus

535   congeminat. fluctus < ⏑⏑ — > defertur in imos

iam totis resoluta uadis. Idaeaque mater

et chorus et summis ulularunt collibus amnes.

∾ *Statius, THEBAID 1.401–27*
Duel between Polynices and Tydeus

ecce autem antiquam fato Calydona relinquens

Olenius Tydeus (fraterni sanguinis illum

conscius horror agit) eadem, sub nocte sopora,

lustra terit, similesque Notos dequestus et imbres,

405 infusam tergo glaciem et liquentia nimbis

ora comasque gerens subit uno tegmine, cuius

fusus humo gelida partem prior hospes habebat.

hic uero ambobus rabiem fortuna cruentam

attulit: haud passi sociis defendere noctem

410 culminibus; paulum alternis in uerba minasque

cunctantur, mox ut iactis sermonibus irae

intumuere satis, tum uero erectus uterque

exertare umeros nudamque lacessere pugnam.

celsior ille gradu procera in membra simulque

415 integer annorum; sed non et uiribus infra

Tydea fert animus, totosque infusa per artus

maior in exiguo regnabat corpore uirtus.

iam crebros ictus ora et caua tempora circum

obnixi ingeminant, telorum aut grandinis instar

420 Rhipaeae, flexoque genu uacua ilia tundunt.

non aliter quam Pisaeo sua lustra Tonanti

cum redeunt crudisque uirum sudoribus ardet

puluis; at hinc teneros caueae dissensus ephebos

concitat, exclusaeque expectant praemia matres:

425 sic alacres odio nullaque cupidine laudis

accensi incurrunt, scrutatur et intima uultus
unca manus penitusque oculis cedentibus intrat.

∾ *Statius*, THEBAID *6.84–117*
The Argive army goes logging in an uncut forest

parte alia gnari monitis exercitus instat
85   auguris aeriam truncis nemorumque ruina,
montis opus, cumulare pyram, quae crimina caesi
anguis et infausti cremet atra piacula belli.
his labor accisam Nemeen umbrosaque Tempe
praecipitare solo lucosque ostendere Phoebo.
90   sternitur extemplo ueteres incaedua ferro
silua comas, largae qua non opulentior umbrae
Argolicos inter saltusque educta Lycaeos
extulerat super astra caput: stat sacra senectae
numine, nec solos hominum transgressa ueterno
95   fertur auos, Nymphas etiam mutasse superstes
Faunorumque greges. aderat miserabile luco
excidium: fugere ferae, nidosque tepentes
absiliunt (metus urguet) aues; cadit ardua fagus
Chaoniumque nemus brumaeque inlaesa cupressus,
100 procumbunt piceae, flammis alimenta supremis,
ornique iliceaeque trabes metuendaque suco
taxus et infandos belli potura cruores
fraxinus atque situ non expugnabile robur.
hinc audax abies et odoro uulnere pinus

105   scinditur, adclinant intonsa cacumina terrae
      alnus amica fretis nec inhospita uitibus ulmus.
      dat gemitum tellus: non sic euersa feruntur
      Ismara cum fracto Boreas caput extulit antro,
      non grassante Noto citius nocturna peregit
110   flamma nemus. linquunt flentes dilecta locorum
      otia cana Pales Siluanusque arbiter umbrae
      semideumque pecus, migrantibus aggemit illis
      silua, nec amplexae dimittunt robora Nymphae.
      ut cum possessas auidis uictoribus arces
115   dux raptare dedit, uix signa audita, nec urbem
      inuenias; ducunt sternuntque abiguntque feruntque
      inmodici, minor ille fragor quo bella gerebant.

∾ Silius Italicus, PUNICA 1.1–28
Proem and foundation of Carthage

      ordior arma, quibus caelo se gloria tollit
      Aeneadum patiturque ferox Oenotria iura
      Carthago. da, Musa, decus memorare laborum
      antiquae Hesperiae, quantosque ad bella crearit
5   et quot Roma uiros, sacri cum perfida pacti
      gens Cadmea super regno certamina mouit
      quaesitumque diu, qua tandem poneret arce
      terrarum Fortuna caput. ter Marte sinistro
      iuratumque Ioui foedus conuentaque patrum
10   Sidonii fregere duces, atque impius ensis
      ter placitam suasit temerando rumpere pacem.

sed medio finem bello excidiumque uicissim

molitae gentes, propiusque fuere periclo,

quis superare datum: reserauit Dardanus arces

15   ductor Agenoreas, obsessa Palatia uallo

Poenorum, ac muris defendit Roma salutem.

tantarum causas irarum odiumque perenni

seruatum studio et mandata nepotibus arma

fas aperire mihi superasque recludere mentes.

20   iamque adeo magni repetam primordia motus.

Pygmalioneis quondam per caerula terris

pollutum fugiens fraterno crimine regnum

fatali Dido Libyes appellitur orae.

tum pretio mercata locos noua moenia ponit,

25   cingere qua secto permissum litora tauro.

hic Iuno ante Argos (sic credidit alta uetustas)

ante Agamemnoniam, gratissima tecta, Mycenen

optauit profugis aeternam condere gentem.

Commentary

ᛉ *Ennius*, ANNALES 34–50
Ilia's dream

Aeneas' daughter Ilia tells her sister and nurse about a dream, in which she encounters a "beautiful man" (the god Mars) by a riverbank and then looks for her father, who foretells her marriage to the river (Tiber). Ennius seems to have treated Mars' rape of the Vestal Virgin Ilia (= Rhea Silvia, mother of the twins Romulus and Remus) symbolically, by displacing it from the epic narrative into his character's dream. The report of a portentous dream to a confidant is a motif familiar from Greek tragedy, and Ennius' adaptation of the motif here suggests that he followed Apollonius of Rhodes' example in the *Argonautica* (which also adapts tragic conventions to epic narrative), of including Medea's report of her dream about an attractive stranger, Jason, to her sister Chalciope (*Arg.* 3.616–32). Homer includes an episode in which the princess Nausicaa dreams of marriage (*Odyssey* 6.25–40).

34   **citus, -a, -um** adj., "swift," used adverbially; cf. *tarda* (41)
      anus, -us f. Ilia's nurse

      artubus = *artibus*; cf. *lacrumans*, for *lacrimans* (49). The archaic spelling contributes to the ASSONANCE of *u* in the line.

34–35 **cum . . . tum . . .** "when . . . then . . . " When *cum* (rel. adv.) introduces one of two coordinate actions it is usually followed by *tum*, which indicates the more noteworthy.

35   **exterritus, -a, -um,** adj. "terrified"; Ennius does not signal the
      change of subject from the nurse to Ilia, who is awakened by
      her cries for her father, reported at the end of the passage.

36   **Eurydica** abl. of source or origin, dependant on *prognata*. Eu-
      rydica is the name of Aeneas' wife in the Greek epic cycle,
      though Vergil calls her Creusa in *Aeneid* 2.

      prognata vocative sing. f., addressed by Ilia to her sister, un-
      named in the passage

37   **uires uitaque** pl. subjects with sing. verb *deserit*; the verb
      agrees with the nearest noun, *uita*. Note the ALLITERATIVE
      and ASSONANTAL effects of the noun phrase.

      corpus meum scanned as if written *corpu' meum*; cf. *omnibu'*,
      78; *albu'*, 84. The suppression of final *-s* is pre-classical and felt
      as an archaism with rustic flavor already by the late republic.
      Catullus and the other neoterics avoid suppression of final *-s*
      in their verse and no later Latin poets admit it.

38   **uisus** Supply *est*, pf. pass. indicative, governing complemen-
      tary infinitive *raptare* in the following line; cf. *uidebar* gov-
      erning *errare* (40), *uestigare, quaerere,* and *posse* (41). Ennius
      occludes the violence of the rape in his word-choice.

      homo pulcer Mars, Ilia's divine rapist, appears as an attrac-
      tive man in her dream. The adj. *pulc[h]er* is drawn from the
      religious sphere and hints at the "man's" divinity.

39   **sola** nom. sing. f., of the speaking subject, Ilia

40   **postilla** archaic adv., "after that"

41–42 **neque posse | corde capessere** "nor could I reach you, though
      I desired to"; *corde*, abl. m. sing., is loosely dependant on
      capessere, complementary infinitive dependant on *posse*, and
      expresses the speaker's desire to find her sister; cf. *corde cupi-
      tus* (47). Note the continuing ALLITERATIVE play, here on *c*.

42   **semita nulla pedem stabilibat** The hexameter lacks a second-
      or third-foot CAESURA and thereby symbolically enacts the
      meaning of this sentence.

      stabilibat = *stabiliebat*, archaic impf.

43–44   **uoce uidetur | his uerbis** more ALLITERATION, on *u*

44   **tibi** dat. of agent with fut. pass. PERIPHRASTIC *sunt . . . gerendae | aerumnae*

45   **resistet** "will rise again," "will be fulfilled"

ex fluuio fortuna Ilia's destiny is "marriage" with the Tiber; note the ALLITERATION of *f*.

46   **ecfatus** The verb belongs to the poetic register and to solemn religious language.

48   **multa** acc. pl. n., used adverbially; "many times"

caerula templa acc. pl. n., object of *ad*, "to the heavenly abodes"

49   **blanda uoce** abl. of manner, "with a seductive voice"

uoce uocabam FIGURA ETYMOLOGICA, with more ALLITERATION; cf. *meo me* (50)

50   **aegro cum corde meo** abl. of manner, "sick at heart"

ᡄ *Ennius*, ANNALES *72–91*
Romulus and Remus take the auspices

The twins Romulus and Remus observe the heavens to ascertain which of them is destined to rule the newly founded city of Rome.

72   **curantes . . . cum cura** ETYMOLOGICAL WORDPLAY, with ASSONANCE and ALLITERATION

curantes . . . cupientes both nom. pl. m. pres. act. pple., describing Romulus and Remus

cum cura abl. of manner

73   **regni** objective gen. dependent on *cupientes*

dant operam . . . auspicio "take the auspices," a technical phrase

simul adv., of the twins, simultaneously observing the heavens

auspicio augurioque synonyms used for solemn effect, with ASSONANCE and ALLITERATION

74   **Murco** Skutsch (1985, 224 ad loc.) suggests that the transmitted reading *monte* (which is unmetrical) conceals the name of the spur on the Aventine hill, the Murcus, from which Remus observed the sky; Romulus watched from the Aventine proper.

      auspicio dat. of purpose, "to take the auspices"

      sedet is Skutsch's emendation, another durative pres. act. indicative like *dant* (73), *seruat* (75, 76), and *quaerit* (76).

75   **solus** The brothers take the auspices at the same time but not together; they sit alone on their separate hills.

      seruat "observe the heavens," the technical term. The final *a* retains its original (long) quantity in Ennius; in classical Latin epic it is usually short.

75   **Romulus pulcer** Like his father Mars (*Ann.* 38), Romulus is a "handsome" man; his beauty hints at his divine lineage and future deification.

76   **quaerit** used absolutely, without direct object; "seeks reply, makes enquiry"

      altiuolantum gen. of reference dependent on *genus*, "race of high-flying birds." The compound adj. is characteristic of epic high style.

77   "They were competing whether to call the city Rome or Remora" after Romulus or Remus.

      uocarent impf. act. subjunctive in indirect question introduced by interr. enclitic particle *-ne* and governed by *certabant*. Skutsch (1985, 226 ad loc.) observes that it seems natural to move into past tense narration in *Ann.* 77–78, after the vivid pres. tense verbs of the opening lines of the passage.

78   **omnibus** scanned as *omnibu'*, with suppression of final -s; cf. *corpus meum* above (37) and *sol albus recessit* below (84)

      omnibus cura uiris Supply *erat*, "it was a concern to all the men."

      uter esset induperator indirect question introduced by interr. *uter*, "which of the two would be the leader"

esset The final *e* retains its original (long) quantity here; in classical Latin epic it is usually short.

induperator = *imperator*; Ennius' archaizing coinage has the metrically convenient shape of dactyl-spondee (DS) at line end

79-83 A SIMILE, one of the characteristic features of epic style; cf. Lucr. 1.936–42; Cat. 64.61; Verg. *Aen.* 1.148–56 (all in this volume). Ennian SIMILES normally imitate Greek models, especially Homer and Apollonius of Rhodes, but here Ennius offers an anachronistically Roman scene of chariot racing in the Circus.

79-82 **expectant . . . spectant . . . expectabat** Threefold repetition of the same verb in four lines is avoided by classical Latin poets who prefer to vary their vocabulary.

79 **quom** = *cum*, "when"

mittere complementary infinitive, governed by *uolt* (= *uult*) in the following line

80 **uolt** = *uult*, in the temporal sense, "be about (to), on the point (of)"; see *OLD* s.v. 5d

auidus, -a, -um adj. used adverbially, "eagerly"

ora, -ae f. "border," hence "barrier" shutting off the "trap" (*carceris*) in which the chariots await the signal

81 **emittat** pres. act. subjunctive in indirect question introduced by *quam mox* and governed by *spectant* in the previous line

pictos . . . currus "painted chariots," indicating their faction by their color: see A. Cameron, *Circus Factions* (Oxford 1976), who argues that the Reds, Whites, Blues and Greens go well back in the republican period.

faucibus abl. of separation, "from the openings"

82 **populus** The final syllable is lengthened in the downbeat (i.e., the initial position of the foot, which is normally long); this feature of the dactylic hexameter is also called "lengthening in arsis" (i.e., in the "rise" or initial position of the foot).

ore timebat "the populace showed their apprehension on their faces"

83   **rebus** dat. pl. f., "for the future"

utri magni uictoria sit data regni "to which of the two brothers victory in the contest for the great kingdom was granted"; indirect question introduced by *utri* and governed by *ore timebat*

utri dat. of indirect object with *sit data*, pres. pass. subjunctive in primary sequence. Skutsch (1985, 231 ad loc.) suggests Ennius uses primary sequence because of "the present tense in the comparison; but sequences are known to be treated rather casually in early Latin."

magni . . . regni gen. sing. n., explained by Skutsch (1985, 281) as objective gen. with *uictoria*, but perhaps better interpreted as gen. of reference (i.e., "victory in the contest for the kingdom")

84   "Meanwhile the light of day gave way to the depths of night."

infera acc. n. pl., object of *in*, governing gen. sing. f. *noctis* = *noctem inferam*

85   **candidus, -a, -um** adj., "white," varies the synonymous *albus* in the preceding line

se radiis dedit icta foras lux "light struck out by the sun's rays presented itself"

lux Monosyllabic line-endings are generally avoided by the classical Latin poets, except as an archaism. Ennius employs monosyllabic endings in the *Annales* more than ten times as frequently as Vergil does in the *Aeneid* (but cf. *Aen.* 1.151, in this volume); see Skutsch 1985, 49–50. Lucretius employs monosyllabic line-endings more freely than the Augustans; cf. Lucr. 1.13, 33; in this volume.

86   **simul** conj., linking the verbs *dedit* and *uolauit*

ex alto "on high"

longe adv., "far away"

pulcerrima praepes another ALLITERATIVE collocation; the formula *pulcer praepes*, "favorable and swift," belongs to the technical terminology of bird-augury

praepes, adj., originally "flying," by extension "swift"; also applied (89) "to the place of good omen where the bird alights" (Skutsch 1985, 233–34)

87   **laeua** nom. sing. f. = *a laeua*, "on the left"

auis, -**is** f., used collectively, a "flight" of birds

simul adv. The birds appear at the very moment that dawn breaks. Sunrise was the most favorable time of day for augury.

sol another monosyllabic line-ending; cf. *lux* (85), *dant* (89)

88   **cedunt** = *decedunt*, "they leave the sky," with adverbial *de caelo*

quattuor scanned as a spondee with consonantal *u* (*qwat-twor*)

89   **auium** gen. of definition, dependent on *corpora sancta* in the preceding line and scanned as a spondee with consonantal *i*

praepetibus . . . pulcrisque locis Skutsch (1985, 236 ad loc.) observes that "the settling of the birds," in a place of good omen "foreshadows the settlement of Romulus and his followers."

90   **conspicit** = *intellegit*, introducing acc. + infinitive: *data . . . esse . . . stabilita scamna solumque* (90–91)

propritim adv., "as his very own"

91   **auspicio** abl. sing. n., governed by *stabilita*, "confirmed by the auspice"

stabilita acc. pl. n., pf. pass. pple. modifying *scamna solumque*; short final *a* is lengthened in the downbeat by the double consonant that begins the following word, *scamna*; contrast the lengthening of the final syllable of *populus* above (82).

regni . . . scamna solumque; "foundations and realm of the kingdom"

◯ *Ennius, ANNALES 175–79*
Felling of trees

The passage describes the felling of trees, probably for the cremation
of war dead on pyres in the aftermath of the Battle of Heraclea (280
BCE), where King Pyrrhus of Epirus defeated a Roman army but also
suffered great losses of his own. The felling of trees, often for the cremation of a hero, is a type-scene in classical epic and may perhaps be
traced back to the epic of Gilgamesh, where the felling of the wood-
spirit Humbaba presages the death of the hero's companion Enkidu.
Ennius here again reworks a Homeric model (*Il.* 23.114–20) and this
passage will, in turn, be closely imitated by Vergil (*Aen.* 6.179–182,
included in this volume).

175   **arbusta** acc. pl. n., object of prep. *per*, modified by *alta*. The
       passage begins and ends with the *genus*, pl. *arbusta* here, and
       sing. *arbustum* in 179, while the enclosed lines 176–78 offer
       a range of different species of trees, the artistic variety en-
       hanced by ASSONANCE (e.g., of *a* in 177), ALLITERATION (e.g.,
       of *p* in 178), and CHIASMUS (the pl. act. spondaic verbs, *per-
       cellunt* and *peruortunt*, framing the sing. pass. dactylic verbs,
       exciditur, frangitur, and *consternitur*). Quintilian exhorted his
       readers to "venerate Ennius just like groves sacred for their
       age" (*Ennium sicut sacros vetustate lucos adoremus, Inst. Or.*
       10.1.88), perhaps recalling this very scene.

       securibus instrumental abl. with *caedunt*; for the suppression
       of final *-s*, cf. 37 above and *fraxinus*, 177 below

       caedunt The pres. tense lends vividness to the description.
       This verb, like the other verbs of felling in the passage (*per-
       cellunt, exciditur, frangitur, consternitur, peruortunt*), is used
       in later Latin epic of battlefield killing. In this way Ennius
       personifies the trees as they are cut down and merges the pa-
       thos of the larger context (the battle dead, the loss to the com-
       munity) with the logging scene (preparation for the funerals
       of the battle dead).

176   **quercus, -us** f., an oak-tree. Note that tree-species are usually f. in Latin.

178   **pinus, -us** f., a species of pine-tree.

      sonabat The sound of the logging is also expressed in the onomatopoetic devices of the passage (e.g., ALLITERATION of *c*, *qu*, *x*, *g*, and plosive *p*; spondaic rhythm; etc.)

179   **fremitu** sums up the whole scene in its onomatopoetic evocation of the sound of the tree-cutting. Gratwick (1982, 71) suggests we hear as well here "the . . . continuous murmuring rustle of the leaves of the forest, commenting, as it were, on the destruction of the great lords of their community."

      siluai frondosai archaic gen. sing. f. ending *-ai*, scanned as a spondee. The spondaic rhythm contributes to the pathos of the scene while the double archaic ending combined with the elevated and emphatic *-osus* adj. draws attention to the solemnity of the whole passage.

Lucretius, De Rerum Natura 1.1–43
Invocation of Venus

In his opening lines, Lucretius invokes the goddess Venus, "mother of the Roman race," to assist him in his presentation of Epicurus' natural philosophy. This kind of proem is an epic convention, and is based on the openings of the epics of Homer, Hesiod, and Ennius, which all begin with an invocation of the Muses. But Lucretius recasts the conventional epic appeal to the Muses with an address to Venus, allegorized as "pleasure," the goal of the Epicurean life. The proem is in hymn form and draws on a number of earlier literary hymns, including the Homeric *Hymn to Aphrodite*, which celebrates the goddess' dominion over earth, sky, and sea. Greek tragedy and philosophy develop the goddess' cosmic associations, and the pre-Socratic philosopher Empedocles may even have opened his hexameter poem on the natural world, *Peri Physeôs* (of which Lucretius' title *De Rerum Natura* is a Latin translation), with a hymn to her. Lucretius' prayer is composed very much in the style of a cult hymn:

conventional features of the form include an invocation of the god
(1–2); an "aretalogy" (2–20), praise of the god that usually contains
a summary of the god's powers, in conjunction with repeated APOS-
TROPHE of the god in "*tu*-style" (4, 6, 7, 8, 12, 13, 16, 22, 24, 26, 31, 33,
36, 37, 38); and the speaker's requests, here to assist him in writing
poetry (21–28) and to persuade Mars to promote peace so that he
may write poetry and Memmius may study it (29–43).

1　　　**Aeneadum** gen. pl. m., patronymic "sons of Aeneas." The Ro-
　　　　mans traced their ancestry back to Troy through the union of
　　　　Aphrodite and Anchises, which is the subject of the Homeric
　　　　Hymn to Aphrodite. The family to which Lucretius' addressee
　　　　Memmius belonged, the *gens Memmia*, claimed descent from
　　　　the Trojan hero Mnestheus (cf. Verg. *Aen.* 5), who accompa-
　　　　nied Aeneas from Troy to Italy.

　　　　diuum gen. pl. m., archaic form appropriate to high epic style;
　　　　cf. Verg. *Aen.* 1.4 (in this volume). In combination with the
　　　　patronymic *Aeneadum*, and the parallel *hominum*, it lends an
　　　　elevated tone to the opening of the poem.

　　　　uoluptas In this key word, Lucretius expresses the moral
　　　　ideal of Epicurean philosophy (Greek *hêdonê*) and the Em-
　　　　pedoclean concept of love as the source of all creation. Lu-
　　　　cretius alludes to the latter concept in both *genetrix*, with its
　　　　etymological derivation from "birth," and *alma* in the next
　　　　line, from *alo* "foster." Epicurus was widely attacked for his
　　　　adoption of pleasure as the chief good (cf. 1.9, 1.945–47 in this
　　　　Reader).

2　　　**alma Venus** The cult of *Venus Physica*, which celebrated
　　　　the goddess in her role as a cosmogonic deity, was particu-
　　　　larly dear to the *gens Memmia*, whose moneyers traditionally
　　　　struck coins with her image.

　　　　subter = *sub,* prep. + acc. expressing direction

　　　　caeli . . . signa "constellations"

　　　　labentia acc. pl. n., pres. act. pple., "gliding"

2-3 **caeli . . . mare . . . terras** the triple division of the world is conventional

3 **nauigerum . . . frugiferentis** compound adjs. (here in *-ger* and *-fer*) were a feature of early Latin poetry, which Lucretius continues to use and invent (cf. *frondiferas*, 18; *suauiloquenti*, 945) as does Catullus (cf. *fluentisono*, Cat. 64.52, in this volume), but Vergil, a generation later, eschews. A five-syllable word at line-end is a metrical archaism avoided by the Augustan poets except for special effects; cf. 29.

frugiferentis, adj., "fruitful," here acc. pl. f., modifying *terras*, "the expanses of the earth"

4 **concelebras** Venus fills the world with both her presence and living things; cf. *OLD* s.v. *concelebro* 1, 1b.

animantum gen. pl. f., pres. act. pple. (for regular *animantium*), equivalent to *animalium*. A quadrisyllable at line-end is another archaism of meter avoided by the Augustan poets.

5 **concipitur uisit . . . exortum** Lucretius details the stages in the process of conception and birth.

lumina solis poetic pl., "light of the sun" = "light of life"; for the poetic pl. of *lumina*, cf. Ov. *Met.* 1.10, in this volume. Lucretius borrows the phrase *lumina solis* from Ennius in adaptation of the Homeric formula *phaos êelioio*.

6 Venus' arrival marks that of spring, when animals mate. Lucretius therefore attributes the flight of winter's winds and clouds to her presence.

7 **daedalus, -a, -um** adj., used here in active sense, "skillful"

7-8 **suauis . . . flores** acc. pl. m.

8 **summittit** "sends up"

aequora ponti "levels/plains of the sea"

9 **placatum** nom. sing. n., pf. pass. pple.; in this tranquility, which Epicurus identified as the most perfect pleasure, Lucretius figures the chief aim of the Epicurean life (Greek *ataraxia*); cf. *tranquilla pace* (1.31), *placidam pacem* (1.40), *aequo animo* (1.42).

diffuso lumine abl. absolute

10   **nam** "now," in a consecutive sense

species . . . uerna diei "the face of springtime"; nom. sing. f. adj. *uerna* is a transferred epithet, best taken with *diei*, which here bears the sense of *temporis* or *anni*.

patefactast = *patefacta est*, "is revealed." Although the *e* of *patefacta* is long by nature, Lucretius allows himself the metrical convenience of IAMBIC SHORTENING here.

11   **reserata uiget** "is unbarred and blows strong"

genitabilis aura nom. sing. f., "birth-favoring breeze"

fauoni gen. sing. m., the west wind. The Romans held that the west wind appeared at the end of the first week of February.

12   **aeriae . . . uolucris** nom. pl. f.

diua = *dea*, vocative sing. f.; cf. 1.28

13   **perculsae** "thrilled"

corda acc. pl. n., "in the heart"; internal or retained acc. with pf. pass. pple. *perculsae*

ui The monosyllabic hexameter line-ending is also avoided by the Augustan poets, except as an archaism; cf. Enn. *Ann.* 85, in this volume. Lucretius has another monosyllabic line-ending at line 33.

14   **inde** adv., "next"

ferae pecudes "wild beasts and cattle"; explained by Bailey (1947, 2.595 ad loc.) as a Lucretian ASYNDETON

laeta "rich" or "fruitful" as commonly in Lucretius; cf. 1.23

15   **capta** nom. sing. f., modifying the unexpressed subject of the verb *sequitur*, *quaeque*, which must be supplied from *quamque*, direct object in the rel. clause that follows. "Incorporation" of the antecedent in rel. clauses is a marked feature of Lucretius' style.

lepore "delight" or "pleasure," another reference to Epicurean *hêdonê*. Lucretius uses the word again at 1.28; cf. *cupide* (1.16, 20), *blandum amorem* (1.19)

17 **denique** adv., "then," following *primum* (1.12) and *inde* (1.14)

   rapacis acc. pl. m., "greedy"

19 **omnibus** dat. of interest/reference

   incutiens "instilling/inspiring"

20 **generatim** adv., "after their type"; Lucretius shows a preference for advs. with this termination.

   saecla = *genera*, "races"

21 **rerum naturam** "the nature of things," i.e., the subject of Lucretius' poem; cf. 1.25. Latin *natura* = Greek *physis*.

22 **dias in luminis oras** "into the bright borders of light"; the
   phrase *luminis oras*, an Ennian formula in the *Annales*, is
   used nine times by Lucretius and repeated also by Vergil.

22–23 **quicquam ... exoritur ... fit ... quicquam** CHIASMUS

24 **scribendis uersibus** dat. of purpose

25 **de rerum natura** The title of Lucretius' poem, "on the nature
   of things," translates the Greek phrase *Peri Phuseôs*, the title
   of many philosophical works of classical Greece. Of primary
   importance for Lucretius' project were a hexameter poem by
   the Sicilian pre-Socratic philosopher Empedocles (fifth century BCE) and a prose treatise by Epicurus in thirty-seven
   books (late fourth century BCE), both with this title.

   pangere Lucretius' standard word for poetic composition, earlier used by Ennius of his composition of the *Annales*. Bailey
   (1947, 2.597 ad loc) suggests the METAPHOR is from building.

26 **Memmiadae nostro** "for our son of the Memmii"; dat. sing.
   m., of an invented patronymic Memmiades, as the form *Mem-
   mio* will not scan in dactylic hexameter.

   C. Memmius, scion of an old aristocratic Roman family, was born in 98 BCE, married the daughter of the dictator
   Sulla in 72, held the office of praetor in 58, and was appoint-
   ed propraetor of Bithynia the following year. The patron of
   Catullus and his friend C. Helvius Cinna, who served on his
   staff in Bithynia (Cat. 10, 28), Memmius must have seemed

a potentially useful addressee to Lucretius in the mid-50s, but his subsequent career did not bear out his early promise. Although he opposed Caesar during his praetorship of 58 he supported him during his bid for the consulship of 54, which he failed to obtain and was prosecuted for bribery in the aftermath. As a result he went into exile, first to Athens, where in 52 he outraged the local Epicurean community by proposing to build on the remains of Epicurus' house, and then to Mitylene and Patrae, after which we hear nothing more of him. Cicero relates that he was well versed in Greek literature but contemptuous of Latin (*Brutus* 247), and speaks of him as dead in 46.

26–27   **omni | omnibus** POLYPTOTON, with ASSONANCE and ALLITERATION over the two lines

27   **excellere** "to excel, be conspicuous"

28   **quo magis** "all the more" reason for the goddess to grant everlasting delight to the poet's words, that the poem may be worthy of his patron

29   **moenera militiai** "works of war"; *moenera* (archaic spelling) = *munera* (also at 1.32). The line ends with a five-syllable word, with the archaic gen. sing. f. ending -*ai* scanned as a spondee (cf. *patriai*, 1.41).

30   **quiescant** pres. subjunctive in a jussive noun clause

32   **Mauors** archaic nom. sing. m. = Mars; cf. Verg. *Aen.* 8.630 (in this volume)

33   **armipotens** adj., another compound (cf. 1.3 above), extant in Accius and used again by Vergil (*Aen.* 2.425, 9.717)

35   **suspiciens** "looking up" into the goddess' face

    tereti ceruice reposta abl. absolute; "his shapely neck thrown back." The phrase is imitated by Vergil at *Aen.* 8.633 of the she-wolf tending Romulus and Remus (in this volume).

    reposta = *reposita*

36   **pascit . . . auidos . . . uisus** "feasts his greedy eyes"

    amore abl. with *pascit*

inhians lit. "gaping at"

37 **eque** = *et ex*

resupini spiritus "Mars' breath, as he reclines"; supply *Mauortis* with *resupini*, gen. sing. m.

38 **hunc . . . recubantem** of Mars, i.e., *resupinum*

corpore sancto may be construed with both *recubantem* (of Mars) and *circumfusa* (of Venus)

39 **circumfusa super** lit. "pouring herself round him," in middle sense; translate "enfolding him from above"

suauis . . . loquellas "sweet little words"; Lucretius, like his contemporary Catullus and the other neoteric poets, favors diminutives of this type (cf. Cat. 64.60, 88, in this volume). But the vogue for diminutives in Latin epic is short, as the Augustans eschew the practice and their successors follow their example.

41 **agere hoc** "set about this task"

patriai tempore iniquo "at this cruel time for the fatherland"; i.e., in the 50s BCE when Caesar was building up an army in Gaul, in the first half of the decade with the support of Pompey and Crassus in opposition to the Senate, in the latter half of the decade (after the deaths of Crassus and his own daughter Julia) in opposition to Pompey and the Senate in the run-up to the civil war of the 40s. For the archaic gen. form *patriai*, cf. *militiai*, 29.

42–43 **nec . . . saluti** "nor in such events <can> the illustrious scion of Memmius fail the safety of the state." Strictly speaking, Epicurean ethical principles required abstention from politics.

42 **Memmi clara propago** an epic PERIPHRASIS, designed to lend dignity to the addressee; with *propago*, cf. *propagent*, 1.20 above.

Memmi sing. for pl. *Memmiorum*, which does not scan

43 sc. *potest*

communi . . . dat. with *desse* (= *deesse*)

∾ *Lucretius, De Rerum Natura 1.936–50*
The honey round the cup

The mythological machinery of the invocation is not typical of the poem's contents, but functions instead like a rhetorical *captatio beneuolentiae*, designed to gain the audience's attention and goodwill for Lucretius' exposition of Epicurean philosophy. Lucretius explains this principle in a famous SIMILE later in the first book, which figures poetry as a sweetener that sugarcoats the bitter medicine of Epicurean philosophy and entices the audience to swallow it. The image is conventional and can be paralleled in both Greece (Plato, *Laws* 2.659e) and Rome (Horace, *Sat.* 1.1.25).

936 **absinthia taetra** acc. pl. n., "nauseating tincture of wormwood"

medentes = *medici*, pres. act. pple. employed as substantive

937 **dare** "to dose" or "administer"

oras pocula circum "the rims around the cups"; *pocula* is acc. pl. n. object of postponed prep. *circum*

938 **contingunt** "touch"; also at 947. Bailey (1947, 2.760) suggests that the spondaic rhythm of the line evokes the stickiness of honey.

939 **improuida** "unsuspecting," causal in sense

ludificetur pres. subjunctive in result clause introduced by *ut*; so also *perpotet* (940), *non capiatur* (941), and *ualescat* (942)

940 **labrorum tenus** "up to the lips"; prep. *tenus* normally follows its object and the construction with abl. is regular in prose authors but verse authors often employ gen., as here, perhaps on the analogy of Greek *mekhri*.

interea adv., in ASYNDETON with the previous clause and in the same construction; i.e., before they realize what they are drinking

perpotet pres. subjunctive of *perpoto* (1); "drink up," i.e., drain the cup

941   **absinthi** gen. of definition

       decepta nom. sing. f., modifying the subject *aetas* (939)

       decepta . . . capiatur "and though deceived, be not caught"; Bailey (1947, 2.760) offers "and though charmed be not harmed," transforming Lucretius' ETYMOLOGICAL WORDPLAY into an English pun.

942   **tali pacto** "by such a method"

943   **haec ratio** "this system," i.e., Epicureanism (cf. 946)

944   **tristior** nom. sing. f., pred. adj. in the comparative degree, "rather bitter"; cf. *amarum . . . laticem* (940–41)

       quibus = *eis a quibus*, with rel. pron. ATTRACTED into the case of the antecedent

       tractata "practiced"

945   **uulgus abhorret** Strict Epicureanism was an ascetic philosophy, but Cicero (a contemporary of Lucretius) speaks of the widespread popularity of Epicureanism in Italy (*Tusc.* 4.6–7) and it seems to have been the sect's reputation for indulgence in pleasure that interested the masses rather than the disciplined asceticism Epicurus espoused.

       suauiloquenti abl. sing. n., modifying *carmine Pierio* (946), instrumental abl. In form, it is another compound adj. with a participial ending; cf. *frugiferentis* (1.3).

947   **musaeo dulci . . . melle** abl. sing. m., "with the sweet honey of poetry"

948   **tali ratione** = *tali pacto* (942)

948–49   **si . . . possem** "in the hope that I could . . ."; impf. subjunctive in the protasis of a mixed condition (pres. contrary-to-fact in the protasis, past general in the apodosis, *uolui* 945) in secondary sequence

949   **dum** conj., "until"; often used idiomatically with pres. indicative as here

950   "with what shape the whole universe has been shaped and framed"

> **qua . . . figura** instrumental abl., introducing indirect question depending on *perspicis*
>
> **compta** nom. sing. f., pf. pass. pple. from *como*; lit. "taken together," modifying the unexpressed subject (of pres. subjunctive *constet*) *natura*, understood from earlier in the line.

‍ *Catullus,* CARMEN *64.50–93*
Ariadne in love

Catullus (ca. 84–54 BCE) is best known for his development of Latin lyric but his short epic "Peleus and Thetis" (poem 64), part of the neoteric experimentation with Alexandrian poetic forms, was widely imitated by later Roman poets of epic. This selection illustrates his artistic refinement of the hexameter and the neoteric predilection for pathos and unrequited love, as well as mythological and geographical erudition, in poetic subject matter. The opening lines of the passage turn from the frame narrative of the wedding of Peleus and Thetis to the inset narrative, with Catullus' description of the tapestry on the wedding couch of Peleus and Thetis, detailing Theseus' desertion of Ariadne after she saved him from the Minotaur.

50–51   The unhappy love of Ariadne and Theseus is the subject of an inset ECPHRASIS, which inverts the happy love of Peleus and Thetis celebrated in the framing narrative.

50   **priscis hominum uariata figuris** "decorated with figures of men of old"

> **priscis** instrumental abl. modifying *figuris*, by HYPALLAGE (transferred epithet) for *hominum priscorum*

51   **heroum . . . uirtutes** "the heroes' glorious deeds"; Catullus may pun on the derivation of *uirtus* from *uir* in the conjunction of Greek *heroum* with Latin *uirtutes*. Despite this characterization of the pictures on the tapestry, it is difficult to see anything heroic in Theseus' clandestine affair with Ariadne and subsequent desertion of her.

mira ... arte abl. of manner; the phrase hints at Catullus' own artistry in the poem.

52 **fluentisono** compound adj. appearing only here in all of Latin literature, where it modifies *litore*, separative abl.

Diae Catullus follows Homer (*Od.* 11.321–25) in setting Ariadne on Dia, an island identified with Naxos by the Hellenistic period.

53 **Thesea** Greek acc. sing. m.; cf. *Minoa*, 85

cedentem celeri cum classe ALLITERATION of *c* and ASSONANCE of *e*

54 **indomitos ... furores** "unmastered passions"; note the artful word order with adj. at line-beginning and the noun it modifies at line-end. *Furor* (again at Cat. 64.94) is the passion of love, a frequent subject of neoteric verse; cf. the erotic passion of the Carthaginian queen Dido in Verg. *Aen.* 4.1–2, in this volume.

55 **sese ... uisere** acc. + infinitive in indirect statement, depending on *credit*

uisit uisere The collocation is an example of ADNOMINATIO, in which two different forms of the same verbal root are juxtaposed side by side.

56 **utpote ... quae** "no wonder, since she"; the construction introduces an explanatory clause with subjunctive verb (*cernat*, 57).

58 **immemor** adj., used absolutely here, and applied to Theseus again at 64.123, 135, 248; the adj. implies not just forgetfulness but ingratitude.

at conj., redirects attention from one part of the tapestry to another

pellit uada remis The strong CAESURA in the fifth foot extends the conflict between the metrical beat and word accent very late in the hexameter line, where they normally coincide. The rare cadence, in conjunction with the series of dactyls, evokes the sound of the rowers splashing the waves with their oars.

59   A golden line with the mannered arrangement of two adjs. (a, b) and two nouns (A, B) around a central verb (V). This kind of verbal artistry was much prized by the neoteric poets; cf. 72, 89, 90.

60   **ex alga** "from the seaweed" at the edge of the shore; separative abl.

       Minois Greek nom. sing. f. patronymic, "daughter of Minos"

       ocellis The diminutive lends notes of intimacy and pathos to the scene. Catullus and his contemporaries admitted diminutives, which belonged to the colloquial idiom, to high poetry, particularly for sentimental effect (cf. 88, 93, and Lucr. 1.39, in this volume), but the mannerism was not continued by the Augustan poets, except for highly localized special effects (e.g., *Aen.* 4.328, *paruulus Aeneas*, not in this volume).

61   **saxea ut effigies bacchantis** The comparison of Ariadne to a Bacchant coheres with Catullus' (and the other neoteric poets') interest in the psychopathology of love.

61–62   **prospicit, eheu | prospicit** Repetition of a word from one line to the next (EPANALEPSIS) is one of Catullus' favorite figures in this poem (cf. 64.26, 132, 259, 285, 321, 403), here employed for pathos along with the interjection *eheu*. The figure is found already in Homer but Catullus seems to have had a special fondness for it, and particularly for EPANALEPSIS after the bucolic DIAERESIS (Wills 1996, 132–43).

62   **fluctuat** "seethes"; for the METAPHORICAL use, see *OLD* s.v. 3

63–65   **non . . . non . . . non** Repeated *non* (in ANAPHORA) underlines the parallelism of the lines, each containing pple. with direct object and abl. construction (local in 63, instrumental in 64–65) in artfully varied word order.

63   **flauo** The heroes and heroines of classical mythology conventionally have blonde hair.

       mitram a piece of cloth worn by Greek women to tie up their hair; if the Greek word also carried Bacchic associations,

Catullus here anticipates Ariadne's later rescue by Bacchus
(64.251–64; cf. 61 above).

64–65 **uelatum pectus . . . lactentis . . . papillas** internal acc., construed respectively with *contecta* and *uincta*, each past pple.
used in the middle voice to express an action performed in
relation to the agent (here in relation to Ariadne's body)

65 **tereti** "shapely"; cf. Lucr. 1.35 (in this volume).

67 **alludebant** A fifth-foot spondee appears occasionally in Homeric hexameters but was especially cultivated by the poets of
Hellenistic Alexandria. Catullus reproduces the mannerism
in poem 64, which has 30 "spondaic" lines (*spondeiazontes*);
cf. 74, 78–80, 83, 91.

68 **sed neque tum . . . neque tum** ANAPHORA

68–69 **neque . . . mitrae . . . uicem curans** "and not worrying about
the plight of her headband . . ."

69 **ex te . . . Theseu** rhetorical second person address (APOSTRO-
PHE) by the poet to his character. The device appears in Homeric epic and was further developed in Alexandrian poetry
to impart a subjective, emotional cast to the narrative.

69–70 **pectore . . . animo . . . mente** Catullus emphasizes Ariadne's
emotional distress with the repetition of forms of *totus* but
varies its expression with the use of synonyms for the "heart"
as the seat of the feelings.

71 **a** The exclamation, favored by the neoterics, expresses the
poet's sympathy and underlines the pathos of the scene.

72 **Erycina** epithet of Venus, alluding to her ancient cult on Mt.
Eryx in western Sicily; cf. Verg. *Aen.* 12.701 (in this volume).
A (near) golden line of the form abVBA; for the term, see note
on 59 above.

73 **illa tempestate . . . quo ex tempore** PLEONASTIC temporal
abl. with *tempestas* and *tempus* used as synonyms; lit. "at that
time . . . from which time," i.e., "ever since the time that"

74 **Piraei** the harbor of Athens; another spondeiazon

75 **iniusti regis** = Minos, unjust from the Athenian perspective

Gortynia templa "Cretan sanctuary," of Minos' palace, which was traditionally located at Cnossus (*Od.* 19.178) rather than Gortyn; cf. *Gnosia litora* at 64.172.

76   **perhibent olim** Catullus sets the scene in the romantic mythological past with both adv. (*olim*, "once upon a time") and verb (*perhibent*, "they say"), the latter used as an "Alexandrian footnote" (Hinds 1998, 1–5) to emphasize the traditional source of the story, a characteristic mannerism of Catullus in poem 64 (124; cf. *dicuntur*, 2; *ferunt*, 212).

Minos' son Androgeos was killed on a visit to Athens, and Minos blamed the Athenians, sacking their city (already devastated by plague) and imposing as his terms the cruel tribute of youths (traditionally seven of each sex, due every nine years), whom he fed to the Minotaur (hence *dapem*, 79), Pasiphaë's monstrous offspring, which he kept hidden away in the Labyrinth constructed by the archetypal craftsman of classical myth, Daedalus (on whom see my note on Verg. *Aen.* 6.14). The Minotaur was finally killed by Theseus, helped by Minos' daughter Ariadne out of love for the Athenian stranger. Vergil tells the story at *Aen.* 6.20–30 and Ovid at *Met.* 8.169–82, both in this volume.

76–79 **crudeli peste coactam . . . poenas exsoluere . . . Cecropiam solitam esse . . . dare** "the city of Cecrops [a mythological king of Athens], compelled by cruel plague to pay the penalty, was accustomed to give"; complementary infinitive *exsoluere* depends on *coactam*, modifying subject acc. (*Cecropiam*) in indirect statement (with verb *solitam esse*, which takes another complementary infinitive, *dare*) depending on *perhibent*.

77   A four-word hexameter, a rare feature of exquisite neoteric artistry.

Androgeoneae . . . caedis objective gen. The possessive adj. (instead of gen.) is a metrical convenience and a mark of high epic style (cf. Verg. *Aen.* 6.14, Manil. *Astr.* 5.594, both in this volume).

78–80   Three successive spondaic lines, another tour-de-force of neoteric artistry found only here in Latin poetry. The heaviness of the meter suggests the terrible burden of the penalty on the Athenians.

80   **quis** = *quibus*, connective rel. with *malis*

     angusta Catullus alludes to the small size of Athens, before Theseus' "synoecism" (union) of Attica; a piece of Hellenistic erudition.

82   **proicere optauit** "elected to hazard"

     quam = *quam ut* + subjunctive; the idiomatic construction is ante-classical, with abundant parallels in Plautus, Terence, and Cicero.

83   **funera . . . nec funera** "living corpses"; Catullus imitates the Greek construction with the alpha-privative (e.g., *taphos ataphos, gamos agamos, dôra adôra*).

     portarentur The heavy quadrisyllable underpins a spondaic line; cf. 67, 74, 78–80, 91.

84–85   Two quasi-golden lines, each with two noun-adj. pairs disposed round a central verb.

85   **Minoa** Greek acc. m. sing. of Minos; cf. *Thesea*, 53

86ff.   Ariadne (the *uirgo regia* of 86–87) falls in love with Theseus at first sight, a convention of Hellenistic poetry. Catullus here reworks Apollonius' description of Medea (whom Apollonius had compared to Ariadne in love with Theseus) falling in love with Jason (*Arg.* 3.275ff.).

86   **lumine** sing. for pl., "eyes"

87–88   **suauis exspirans castus odores | lectulus** "her chaste little bed, emitting sweet scents"; note the diminutive (*lectulus*) and the parallelism of two noun-adj. pairs in acc. and nom. respectively. Catullus has a Homeric model in Helen's "sweet-scented bedchamber" (*Od.* 4.121).

89   **quales Eurotae praecingunt flumina myrtus** "such as the myrtles which gird Eurotas' streams"; a quasi-golden line of the form abVBA.

quales = *tales quales*. The *suauis odores* of 87 are like myrtle, which was sacred to Venus; the SIMILE is conventional (cf. Cat. 61.22).

90   Another (near) golden line of the form abVAB.

auraue = *uel quales aura*

colores = *flores*, "flowers of varied (*distinctos*) hue"

91   **declinauit** another spondaic line; cf. 83 *portarentur*. Thomson (1997, 406) suggests "spondees for reluctance (to tear the eyes away)."

91–92   **non prius . . . quam** Take *non* with the main clause in 91; *priusquam* introduces the subordinate clauses in 92–93.

92–93   Note the ALLITERATION of *c* and *f*. The METAPHOR of love as a fire is conventional, and can be paralleled in the Alexandrian poets (Call. *Epigr.* 43.5, Ap. Rhod. 3.287); Vergil uses it to great effect in his account of Dido's love for Aeneas (cf. *Aen.* 4.2, in this *Reader*).

93   **imis . . . medullis** "her innermost marrow"; Catullus reuses the phrase at 64.196 and elsewhere in his poetry (35.15, 66.23), and Vergil imitates his usage in the *Aeneid* (4.66–67, 8.379–80).

⚘ *Vergil,* AENEID *1.1–11*

Proem

Vergil introduces the controlling themes of the *Aeneid* in the opening words of the poem—"arms and a man." The two keywords, along with the invocation of the Muse (8), are designed to set Vergil's epic in the context of their Homeric models, the *Iliad* and *Odyssey*, and to situate the time of the action as the Trojan War and its aftermath. Out of this Homeric material, Vergil fashions his account of the origins of the Roman people.

1   **arma** = *bella*, by METONYMY for the "wars" in which Aeneas fought, both at Troy (the subject of *Aeneid* 2 as well as Homer's *Iliad*) and in Italy (the subject of *Aeneid* 7–12).

uirum Aeneas is unnamed, like Odysseus in the opening line of the *Odyssey* (*andra moi ennepe Mousa*, "tell me of a man, Muse . . .").

qui rel. pron. (nom. sing. m.) standing second in its clause, after *Troiae*

2   **Italiam** The meter requires the first syllable to be lengthened in the metrical downbeat; cf. Enn. *Ann.* 82 (in this volume).

fato profugus Aeneas is commissioned by destiny to go into exile from Troy and found the Roman race in Italy. In this regard, Vergil's hero differs significantly from the resourceful hero of the *Odyssey*, who overcomes the obstacles he encounters on his journey home to Ithaca by devising stratagems but who is driven by no larger purpose than his personal return from Troy.

Lauinia the second *i* is treated as consonantal by SYNIZESIS (*Lauinja*). Tradition held that Lavinium was Aeneas' first foundation in Italy. From there his son Ascanius founded Alba Longa and thence the Italianized Trojans subsequently moved to Rome (cf. 7).

Italiam . . . Lauinia . . . | litora acc. of motion toward, without prep. Vergil greatly extends this usage of the acc. with verbs of motion.

3   **multum** adverbial with *iactatus*, "much tossed"

4   **superum** = *superorum*, archaizing Latin 2nd declension gen. pl. m. (cf. *diuum*, Lucr. 1.1, in this volume). With *Iunonis* later in the line, Vergil particularizes the deity responsible for the relentless hostility to Aeneas and the Trojans' mission in the epic.

memorem . . . ob iram Wrath is the traditional theme of Greek epic, and Vergil's reference here recalls the opening of the *Iliad*, "anger be now your song, goddess" (*mênin aeide thea*, *Il.* 1.1, of Achilles), and the *Odyssey* (1.20–21, of Poseidon). Juno's remembering anger is a central theme of the epic.

5   **dum conderet** "until he could found"; purpose clause

urbem = Lavinium

6   **inferretque** parallel to *conderet* in the previous line

Latio dat. of direction, a poetic usage much favored by Vergil and his successors; cf. Ov. *Met.* 4.722, 8.179 (in this volume).

genus unde Latinum sc. *ortum est*; so also in the next line, sc. *orti sunt*.

7   **altae** possessive gen. modifying *Romae*, by HYPALLAGE (transferred epithet) for *moenia alta*

8   **Musa** vocative sing. f., conventional epic address to the Muse. Vergil invokes the Homeric Muse (cf. *Il.* 1.1; *Od.* 1.1) in his proem to signal the central importance of Homeric epic to his poem. Contrast Lucretius' invocation of Venus, the ancestress of the Roman people (Lucr. 1.1–2, in this volume), to convey the central theme of his epic, *viz.* the application of Epicurean philosophy (with its emphasis on pleasure) to contemporary Rome.

quo numine laeso "for what affront to her dignity"; abl. absolute expressing the ground for Juno's animus against Aeneas, elaborated in an indirect question (*impulerit*, 11).

9   **deum** archaic 2ⁿᵈ declension gen. pl. m.

uoluere infinitive with subject acc. *uirum* (10) and direct object acc. *casus* (9); the construction depends on *impulerit* (11).

10   **pietate** causal abl. with *insignem*, characterizing *uirum* (= Aeneas). With this word, Vergil introduces the distinguishing feature of his hero, his "devotion to duty." The concept of *pietas* gives a very Roman context to Aeneas' scrupulous observance of his responsibilities towards gods, family members, friends, and allies. Greek mythology celebrates Aeneas' rescue of his aged father Anchises and the city's tutelary gods from the sacked city of Troy in archaic art and poetry, and Vergil makes these acts the basis of his Roman renovation of Aeneas' character.

11   **tantaene animis caelestibus irae** sc. *sunt*; *animis* is dat. of possession

∞ *Vergil, Aeneid 1.148–56*

First simile, Neptune calms the sea

This famous SIMILE, the first in the poem, gives further Roman color to Vergil's account of the Trojans' wanderings in the Mediterranean after the sack of Troy, as Aeneas' *pietas* is implicitly reflected in the Roman statesman's magisterial calming of the masses. In addition to the anachronism of the Roman civic setting, which finds a model in Ennius' circus SIMILE in *Annales* 1 (79–82, included in this *Reader*), the SIMILE is unusual in illustrating nature (a storm at sea) by comparison to culture; Homer characteristically illustrates human group behavior by reference to nature.

148   **ac ueluti** Vergil frequently introduces a SIMILE with this formula; cf. *ueluti* at Enn. *Ann.* 79 (in this volume).

      ac ueluti . . . cum saepe "and as often happens when"

149   **animis** locative abl.

      ignobile uulgus "the common masses"; not pejorative so much as pitying

150   **faces** Fires were a frequent danger in a city like ancient Rome, in which buildings were characteristically constructed of wood.

      furor Another central theme of the *Aeneid* is the danger of unchecked passion, often *furor* (as here) but also *amor* (as in the Dido-narrative); note the reappearance of *arma* and *ui-rum* (from the proem) in 150–51.

151   **pietate . . . meritis** both causal abl., with *grauem* "venerable"

      quem = *aliquem*; for the effect of the monosyllabic line-ending, cf. Enn. *Ann.* 85 (in this volume)

152   **conspexere** = *conspexerunt*, pl. because of the collective sing. *populo* (148) and *uulgus* (149)

      arrectis . . . auribus abl. of manner

154   **sic** correlative with *ueluti* (148)

      aequora acc. pl. n., direct object of *prospiciens* (155)

155   **genitor** = Neptune

caelo . . . aperto abl. of place where

156 flectit . . . dat historic pres. tense

curru = *currui*, archaic dat. sing. m., indirect object

secundo "willing" or "obedient"

∾ *Vergil,* AENEID *1.338–68*
Dido's family background

Shipwrecked in Libya, Aeneas explores the countryside with his
faithful companion Achates and encounters his mother Venus, dis-
guised as a Tyrian huntress, who tells them where they are and explains the history of Dido and the city of Carthage. Scholars have
compared Venus' recital of Dido's past to the prologue of a Euripid-
ean tragedy such as the *Hippolytus,* in which Aphrodite explains the
background to the plot of the play; this is an attractive interpretation of Venus' speech, since Vergil's account of Dido's story has many
points of contact with the genre of tragedy. But it also has many
points of contact with recent Roman history, for both Julius Caesar
and Mark Antony had spent time in Egypt at the wealthy court of
Alexandria and interfered in the dynastic politics of the Ptolemies
by favoring Cleopatra's claim to the throne.

338 Punica regna . . . Tyrios . . . Agenoris urbem Latin *Punicus,
-a, -um,* adj. ("Carthaginian") is related to Greek *phoinikeios*
(cf. *Phoenicum,* 344 below) and connects the city of Carthage
(= *Agenoris urbem*) and her inhabitants with Phoenicia, whose
legendary king Agenor was Neptune's son by a nymph named
Libya, and whose inhabitants were known as Tyrians from the
name of their most prominent city, Tyre.

339 sed fines Libyci "but the territory is Libyan"; sc. *sunt*

genus in apposition with the Libyans, implied by *Libyci*

intractabile bello Vergil characterizes the North Africans as
"unmanageable in war" (*bello* = abl. of respect), to underline the
danger posed by Dido and her city to Aeneas and the Trojans.

340 **imperium** "rule," cognate acc. with *regit*. Vergil's use of *imperium* here introduces another Roman anachronism into the Trojan legend (cf. *Aen.* 1.148–56, in this volume), since the Latin word denotes the supreme Roman administrative power (cf. English "empire"), which by Vergil's day had been extended over the whole of the Mediterranean basin.

Dido The Greek historian Timaeus (ca. 350–260 BCE) recorded that Dido, originally called Elissa in Phoenician, was the sister of Pygmalion (a king of Tyre) and the founder of Carthage. After her brother killed her husband Sychaeus she fled with the latter's wealth and a company of Tyrian citizens to Libya where, after many hardships and wanderings, she founded the city of Carthage. When her citizens pressured her to accept an offer of marriage from a local Libyan king, she killed herself by throwing herself on a pyre in order to maintain the vow of chastity she had sworn to her dead husband. As a result, she received the alternate name Dido (= Latin *uirago*, "a woman with the qualities of a man"). Vergil follows a different version of the myth (perhaps that of Naevius in his early Latin *Carmen belli poenici,* written in Saturnians) that linked Dido with Aeneas and offered a mythological explanation for the historical enmity between Rome and Carthage.

Tyria . . . urbe abl. of place from which, with *profecta*

341 **germanum fugiens** Vergil puts the essence of Dido's story up front; the intrafamilial feud is the ANTITHESIS of Roman *pietas* and so contrasts Dido with *pius Aeneas* from the outset.

longa est iniuria = *longum est narrare iniuriam*

342 **ambages** "a complicated tale," i.e., one of many twists and turns

summa . . . fastigia "main points"

343 **huic** = *Didoni*, dat. of possession

Sȳchaeus The -*y*- is scanned as long here, but short at 348, an example of prosodic variation.

auri gen. of definition, with *ditissimus*

344   **magno . . . amore** Vergil characterizes Dido throughout the
       epic as lovelorn, initially, as here (cf. 350, 352), for Sychaeus
       but by the end of the first book and throughout the fourth for
       Aeneas (cf. *Aen.* 4.28–29, in this volume).

       miserae dat. of agent. Vergil conveys his sympathy for Dido
       in the use of an adj. that draws Dido into a long line of mytho-
       logical heroines destroyed by love; cf. Ariadne at Cat. 64.57
       (in this volume). Myths of heroines who suffered from love-
       sickness were particularly popular subjects with the poets of
       Hellenistic Alexandria (e.g., Cydippe in Call. *Aet.* 3) and late
       republican Rome (e.g., Ariadne in Cat. 64).

345   **intactam** sc. *Didonem*; she was a virgin

       iugarat = *iugauerat*

345–46 **primis . . . | ominibus** "in her first marriage," instrumental
       abl. The phrase emphasizes the solemnity of the marriage
       ritual, hallowed by the customary consultation of the omens.

347   **Pygmalion** in apposition to *germanus* (346). He and his sis-
       ter Elissa were named as co-heirs by their father, a situation
       that would have reminded a Roman audience of the Egyp-
       tian custom of brother-sister rule and, especially, that of
       Ptolemy xiii and Cleopatra vii (51–48 bce), culminating in
       a civil war settled by Julius Caesar in Cleopatra's favor in 47
       bce, with her younger brother Ptolemy xiv as her husband
       and consort.

       scelere abl. of respect with *immanior*

       ante alios . . . omnis pleonastic with *immanior*, "more mon-
       strous in wickedness before all the rest"

348   **quos inter** = *inter Pygmalionem et Sychaeum*

       medius translate adverbially, "in their midst"

       furor on the theme, cf. 1.150

349   **impius ante aras** Throughout the poem Vergil characterizes
       the Carthaginians and their ancestors, the Phoenicians, as
       impious—in sharp contrast to Aeneas and the proto-Roman
       band of Trojan exiles. Pygmalion's murder of Sychaeus at the

altar encapsulates the impiety of the Phoenicians and, by extension, the Carthaginians, with whom the Romans waged three bitter wars in the course of the republic.

auri objective gen., dependent on *amore*, causal abl. Vergil links Dido's erotic passion (*amore*, 344; *amorum*, 350) with the Carthaginians' excessive wealth (1.14, not in this volume, and elsewhere) and implicitly contrasts both with Aeneas' loss of wife and possessions in the sack of Troy.

350–51   **securus amorum | germanae** "indifferent to his sister's love"; *amorum* is objective gen. with adj. *securus*

351   **aegram** acc. sing. f. modifying *amantem* (= *Didonem*) in the next line; the adj. is often used of "lovesickness" (cf. *Aen.* 4.35, of Dido's love for Aeneas).

353   **in somnis** "in a dream"; the dream-motif goes back to Homeric epic, where Patroclus' ghost appears to ask for burial in a dream to Achilles (*Il.* 23.62ff.). In Latin epic, the motif appears in Ennius, whose account of Ilia's dream (*Ann.* 34–50) is included in this volume.

353–54   **ipsa . . . inhumati . . . imago | coniugis** "the very likeness of her unburied husband"

354   **modis . . . miris** abl. of manner with *pallida*, "strangely pale"

355   **crudelis aras** "the altar at which the cruel crime took place"

356   **domus** gen. sing. f. Domestic murder might also have reminded Vergil's contemporary audience of the Ptolemaic dynasty's history of kindred bloodshed, especially Cleopatra's murders of her successive brother-husbands, Ptolemy XIII and XIV.

357   **celerare . . . excedere** both complementary infinitives expressing purpose with *suadet* (instead of *ut* + subjunctive)
     patria abl. of separation

358   **auxilium** in apposition to *thesauros*
     uiae objective gen. with *auxilium*, "an aid for the voyage"
     tellure abl. of separation

360   **his** sc. *dictis*, instrumental abl.

361   **quibus** dat. of reference with *erat*, "who felt"

        odium crudele tyranni "savage hatred for the tyrant"; *tyranni* is objective gen. with *odium* and *metus*

362   **nauis** acc. pl. f., direct object with *corripiunt onerantque*

        quae forte paratae sc. *sunt*

364   **pelago** "over the sea"; local abl.

        dux femina facti Vergil's EPIGRAM encapsulates Dido's heroism and establishes her as the female counterpart of Aeneas.

365   **deuenere** = *deuenerunt*

        locos acc. of motion toward, without prep.

366   **nouae Karthaginis** Servius explains that in the Punic tongue, Carthage meant "new city," and Vergil here shows his familiarity with the ETYMOLOGY by glossing the name with an "etymological epithet"; on Vergil's interest in etymology, see O'Hara 1996.

367   **mercati** sc. *sunt*

        Byrsam in apposition to *solum*; the Greeks associated the Phoenician name for the citadel of Carthage, *Bosra*, with the Greek word for "bull's hide," thereby giving rise to the aetiological tale Vergil here relates.

368   **quantum** sc. *mercati tantum solum quantum possent circumdare taurino tergo*

        possent impf. subjunctive, depending on the oral contract implied in *mercati sunt*; Vergil refers to the conditions of the bargain the Carthaginians negotiated for the purchase of the land.

ᚱ Vergil, AENEID 4.1–30
Dido in love

After the encounter with his mother, Aeneas proceeds with Achates to Carthage where he sees the city walls rising, is reunited with the other shipwrecked Trojan survivors and meets Queen Dido. She welcomes the Trojans, especially Aeneas, to her city and invites them to a banquet in her palace that evening. There Aeneas captures her heart during his narration of Troy's fall (*Aen.* 2) and the Trojans' subsequent travels around the Mediterranean (*Aen.* 3). By the opening of the fourth book, Dido has fallen deeply in love with the Trojan hero. Vergil strikes a note of ominous foreboding, with the description of Dido's love in the METAPHORICAL terms of wound and fire, and in the literary echoes of Catullus' account of Ariadne's doomed love for Theseus (Cat. 64, included in this volume) and Apollonius' of Medea's for Jason (*Arg.* 3–4).

1   **at regina** The opening words focus attention on the Carthaginian queen, who is the dominant figure of the book. The adversative *at* points up a strong contrast between Aeneas, the focus of *Aen.* 2–3, and Dido, the focus of *Aen.* 4; between the past sufferings of the Trojans and the new sufferings of Dido, consumed by love for the Trojan leader; between his silence in this book, and her speeches.

    graui . . . cura lovesick (*saucia*), Dido is beset "with grievous passion"; abl. of attendant circumstance. The collocation *saucia cura* recalls Catullus' description of Ariadne (Cat. 64.250, *multiplices animo uoluebat saucia curas*) and sets Dido in the long line of mythological heroines abandoned by their lovers, thereby anticipating Aeneas' departure from Carthage at the end of the book.

2   **uulnus alit uenis** "nourishes the wound with her lifeblood"; *uenis* is instrumental abl. Vergil will transform the METAPHORICAL wound from which Dido suffers here into the literal wound that kills her at the end of *Aen.* 4, when she mounts a funerary pyre and kills herself on Aeneas' sword.

    caeco carpitur igni "she is consumed by the unseen fire within"; *caeco . . . igni* is instrumental abl.

3   "The man's abundant heroism and his family's plentiful glory return to her mind again and again." The repetition *multa . . . multus* emphasizes not only the extent of Aeneas' heroism and familial glory, but also the frequency with which Dido's thoughts turn to the Trojan leader.

uiri uirtus Vergil's *FIGURA ETYMOLOGICA* draws our attention to the derivation of *uirtus* from *uir*.

4   **honos** nom. sing. m.; Vergil always uses this nom. form of the noun, but his contemporaries Horace and Ovid avoid it as an anachronism, preferring the classical form *honor*.

4–5   **haerent infixi pectore uultus | uerbaque** "his features and words stick fast, stamped in her heart"

5   **placidam . . . quietem** Dido and her court, with their pleasure-loving aspect on display at the luxurious banquet of *Aen.* 1, bear some resemblance to the popular view of the Epicurean sect as pleasure-loving profligates. Vergil continues this characterization of Dido in his application of the Lucretian language of Epicurean tranquility to her (cf. Lucr. 1.9, in this volume), even as she succumbs to passion.

6   **Phoebea . . . lampade** = the sun

6–7   "Next day's Dawn (*postera . . . Aurora*) was moving over the earth with Phoebus' torch"; a good example of Vergilian high style. Note the mannered word arrangement of these two lines.

8   **unanimam . . . sororem** With these words, Vergil introduces Dido's loving sister and confidante, Anna. We know that she appeared in Naevius' version of the Dido-episode, though we do not know what role she played in it. In Vergil's account, she plays the part of a tragic confidante, who encourages the tragic hero in a disastrous course; she is also modeled in part on Medea's sister Chalciope in Apollonius' *Argonautica* 3.

male sana of Dido, lit. "badly sane," i.e., "beside herself"; in colloquial usage the adv. *male* negates the adj. it modifies. Vergil elevates this colloquial usage to epic high style.

9   "What dreams terrify me, uncertain!" Vergil here translates into Latin a line from Apollonius' epic (*Arg.* 3.636).

quae exclamatory = *qualia*; so also *quis* (= *qualis*) in 10, *quem* (= *qualem*) and *quam* in 11

10 "What a distinguished man is this stranger who has come un-
    der our roof!" For *nouus* in the sense of "newly arrived," see
    OLD s.v. 12c.

11 "How well he bears himself in his demeanor, how brave in
    breast and arms!"

    ore . . . pectore . . . armis abl. of quality

12 **credo** introduces indirect statement, with acc. (*genus*) + in-
    finitive (*esse*).

    nec uana fides "nor is my confidence misplaced"

12–13 **genus . . . | degeneres** FIGURA ETYMOLOGICA, inviting us to
    take *degeneres*, "degenerate," with reference to *genus* in the
    previous line. Aeneas has proven his fearlessness in his ac-
    count of his bellicose role in the sack of Troy in *Aen.* 2.

14 **iactatus** Aeneas is "buffeted" by fate; cf. 1.3 (in this volume).

    quae bella exhausta canebat "What wars he was saying he
    had borne!" Aeneas, like Vergil, is a poet of war; cf. 1.1 (in this
    volume).

15 **animo** local abl.

    sederet impf. subjunctive in the protasis of pres. contrary-to-
    fact condition; the subject of the verb is Dido's resolution, ex-
    pressed in *ne . . . iugali* in the next line.

16 The first three feet are spondees, Vergil's metrical gravity
    matching Dido's purposeful resolution.

    cui indef., "to anyone"

    ne . . . uellem subjunctive in noun clause, subject of *sederet*
    (15)

    uinclo . . . iugali "in the bond of matrimony"

17 **primus amor** = Sychaeus

    deceptam morte fefellit "failed me, deceived by his death"

18 **pertaesum fuisset** plpf. pass. subjunctive of impers. *pertae-
    det*, which governs gen. *thalami taedaeque*

    thalami taedaeque METAPHORS for marriage

19   **huic uni . . . culpae** dat. with compound verb; as the line de-
      velops, we expect *huic uni* to refer to Aeneas and it is a shock to
      reach the end of the line and realize that this is how Dido char-
      acterizes the consummation of her love for the Trojan hero. Cf.
      Vergil's characterization of the wedding in the cave, later in the
      book, as Dido's "fault" (*culpam*, 4.172, in this volume).

      potui pf. act. indicative in the apodosis of the condition be-
      gun in 15 and continued in 18. The indicative mood is normal
      with modal verbs such *potui* and *debui* (in place, e.g., of *potu-
      issem succumbere* or *succubuissem*), although in prose *forsan*
      requires the subjunctive.

      succumbere The Latin word, like English "succumb," carries
      an erotic charge and is used in contemporary Latin love elegy
      of the physical act of intercourse.

20   **fata** = *mortem*

21   Venus tells Aeneas the story of the murder of Dido's husband
      Sychaeus by her brother Pygmalion in *Aen*. 1.338–68 (in this
      volume).

      fraternus, -a, -um adj. modifying *caede*, equivalent to a sub-
      jective gen.

22   **hic** = Aeneas. The pron. is here scanned short, the original
      quantity of the vowel.

      inflexit sensus "has turned my feelings"

22–23 **animumque labantem | impulit** "and moved my wavering
      heart"; *labantem*, pres. act. pple., describes the confusion of
      Dido's mind and expresses the consequences of Aeneas' im-
      pact on her feelings.

24   **mihi** dat. with compound verb, *dehiscat*

      optem potential subjunctive, on which depend two noun
      clauses (indirect wishes), introduced by *uel . . . uel . . .* , both
      with subjunctive verbs (*dehiscat*, 24; *adigat*, 25).

      tellus . . . ima subject of *dehiscat*

      prius taken up by *ante* (27) with *quam* (27)

25 **ad umbras** i.e., to the Underworld, as is clarified in the next line

26 **Erebo** local abl., "in Erebus"

27 **pudor** vocative in APOSTROPHE (direct address); *Pudicitia*, "Chastity," was worshipped by Roman women as a goddess. *Pudor* is a more difficult word, conveying the ideas of both modesty and sensitivity to what is right. Vergil uses it here in the sense of "conscience."

28 **ille** = Sychaeus

29 Dido's oath to remain faithful to her first husband and not to remarry is in accordance with republican Roman custom and sentiment, which esteemed the once-married woman (*uniuira*). Augustus' marriage legislation of 18 and 16 BCE required widows to remarry if they were of childbearing age, but there is evidence of public resistance to the legislation and the laws had to be repromulgated a generation later in 9 CE.

habeat . . . seruetque jussive subjunctives

∾ *Vergil, AENEID 4.160–72*
The wedding in the cave

At Dido's invitation, Aeneas and the Trojans remain in Carthage and enjoy the queen's hospitality while the goddesses Juno and Venus plot to save their respective protégés from one another. To this end Juno proposes to Venus that the royal pair marry during a storm on a hunting expedition, though Venus is skeptical that a marriage between the two could be consistent with Aeneas' destiny to establish the Roman race in Italy. The supernatural setting of the "wedding" and its elemental witnesses also undermine its validity. Later in the book, moreover, Aeneas will repudiate any intention of having married Dido, denying that he had ever held the torches of a bridegroom (4.338–39). Apollonius supplies an epic model for the doomed union of the lovers in Medea's rushed marriage to Jason in a cave on Phaeacia (*Arg.* 4.1130–55).

160   ALLITERATION and ASSONANCE mark this onomatopoetic line.

      magno . . . murmure abl. of manner

161   **commixta grandine** abl. absolute

163   **Dardanius . . . nepos Veneris** = Ascanius; in myth, Dardanus was a son of Zeus and Electra, the founder of Dardania in the Troad, and an ancestor of the Trojan king Priam.

163–64   **diuersa per agros | tecta . . . petiere** "sought cover at scattered points throughout the fields"

164   **metu** causal abl.

165   **speluncam . . . eandem** acc. of motion towards without prep.; cf. *Lauinia . . . litora*, 1.1–2 (in this volume). The heavy rhythm of the line suggests the portentousness of the leaders' encounter.

      dux et Troianus "and the Trojan leader"

166–68   The witnesses of the union are the Elements (Earth, Fire, Air), Juno, and the mountain Nymphs. Each plays a part in the wedding ritual: Juno (Dido's divine patroness and the Roman goddess of marriage) is the matron (*pronuba*) who gives the bride to her husband; the Nymphs sing the wedding chant (*ulularunt*); lightning stands in for the wedding torch; and the ether is witness (*conscius*).

168   **conubiis** dat. with adj. *conscius*. The prosody of the noun is much debated (see *OLD* s.v.); in republican Latin poetry, it seems to be scanned *cōnūbium* by SYNIZESIS (i.e., with the *-i-* at the end of the stem treated as consonantal): *cōnūbjīs*. It is the technical term in Latin for a wedding ceremony.

      ulularunt by SYNCOPE for *ululauerunt*. Vergil suggests the Nymphs' howling by eliding the verb with the preceding enclitic, *-que*, with the result that the line has only one CAESURA (in the second foot). Vergil normally employs the verb and its related noun *ululatus* of the shrieks of (female) lamentation (cf. 2.487–88 and 4.667, at the end of the book, when Dido's household mourns her death). The ill-omened sound anticipates the fatal outcome of her union with Aeneas.

169   **primus** adverbial (cf. 1.1, in this volume); "that day first was the cause of her death, first the cause of her ills"

170   **specie famaue** "by appearance or report"

171   **furtiuum . . . amorem** Vergil's application of the adj. *furtiuus* to Dido's love recalls the usage of *furtum* in Catullus and the Roman elegists for a clandestine love affair.

172   **coniugium** the technical term for the condition of being lawfully married at Rome; the poet states unequivocally that Dido was wrong to call her union with Aeneas by that name.

    culpam cf. Dido's refusal at the opening of the book to countenance marriage with Aeneas, which she herself labels *culpa* (4.19, also at line end, in this volume).

⌘ *Vergil, AENEID 6.14–33*
Ecphrasis of the doors on the temple of Apollo

Upon his arrival in Cumae, Aeneas seeks a prophecy from the Sibyl but stops briefly to admire the sculptures Daedalus crafted on the doors of the Temple of Apollo before consulting her. The sculptured doors commemorate the gratitude of the archetypal Greek artist and inventor for his escape from Crete, where he had been imprisoned by the Cretan king Minos, either because he helped the king's wife Pasiphaë consummate her desire for a bull (an affliction implanted in her by Venus, who persecuted the female descendants of the Sun, among them Pasiphaë, because he had revealed her affair with Mars to her husband Vulcan), or because he helped Ariadne save Theseus from the Minotaur. Daedalus' art commemorates the terrible crimes and dark passions of the Cretan royal house and establishes a tone of solemn mystery for Aeneas' encounter with the Sibyl and subsequent journey to the Underworld. The story of Pasiphaë and her daughter Ariadne were popular with the Latin poets, including Catullus, who told it in poem 64 (cf. 64.51–93, in this volume) and Ovid, who told it in the *Metamorphoses* (cf. *Met.* 8.159–82, in this volume): see Armstrong 2006.

14   **Daedalus** legendary artist, craftsman, and inventor associ-
      ated with Crete already in Homer, who credits him with Ari-
      adne's dancing-ground (*Il.* 18.590ff.). Linear B tablets from
      Cnossos seem to confirm the association in their reference to
      "Daedalus' place." Later authors ascribe to him the ingenious
      devices of the Labyrinth, in which Minos concealed the Mi-
      notaur; the spool of thread, which Ariadne gave to Theseus
      to escape from the Labyrinth; and the wooden cow, in which
      Pasiphaë coupled with the bull. Ovid gives the fullest account
      of Daedalus' career in Latin literature at *Met.* 8.152–259 (par-
      tially included in this volume).

      ut fama est "as the story goes," an Alexandrian footnote (for
      the term, see my note on Cat. 64.76). With this phrase, Vergil
      acknowledges that his tale is traditional and that he will re-
      count it allusively.

      Minoïa regna The use of an adj. derived from a proper name
      is characteristic of high epic style and takes the place of the
      gen. of Minos' name; cf. Cat. 64.77, Manil. *Astr.* 5.594 (both in
      this volume).

15   **praepetibus** instrumental abl. For the sense ("swift") of the
      word, which also belongs to high epic style, cf. Enn. *Ann.* 86
      (in this volume).

      caelo dat. with verb (*credere*)

16   **insuetum** "novel, new"

      enauit "flew out"; Vergil's epic predecessors Ennius and Lu-
      cretius also use the verb of flying.

17   **Chalcidica . . . arce** "the citadel of Euboean Cumae"; the his-
      torical foundation of Cumae was by settlers from Chalcis in
      Euboea, a piece of geographical erudition typical of Vergil's
      antiquarian interests.

      leuis best translated adverbially, "lightly"

19   **remigium alarum** lit. "the oarage of his wings"; upon return-
      ing to land and retiring from flying, Daedalus dedicates the
      wings that propelled him through the air.

posuit "he established"; the temple is part of Daedalus' dedication to the god in gratitude for his escape. In Vergil's day, a temple of Apollo stood near the entrance to the Sibyl's cave, and the topography of Vergil's mythological Cumae reflects that of contemporary Augustan Cumae.

20-30 Vergil describes the Cretan scenes represented on the doors of Apollo's temple in a brief ECPHRASIS, as Catullus describes in a lengthy ECPHRASIS the myth of Ariadne and Theseus pictured on a tapestry in poem 64 (partially included in this volume).

20 **Androgeo** Greek gen. sing. m.; on Androgeos, a son of Minos killed by the Athenians, see Cat. 64.77 (in this volume).

pendere poenas "to pay as recompense"; cf. Cat. 64.77 *poenas exsoluere* (in this volume).

21 **Cecropidae** nom. pl. m. patronymic, "descendants of Cecrops," a legendary king of Athens; cf. Cat. 64.79, 83.

(miserum!) exclamatory acc. Vergil interjects a sympathetic comment on the cruelty of Minos' punishment.

21-22 **septena . . . | corpora natorum** lit. "seven bodies of sons," i.e., seven living sons. *Septena corpora* is in loose apposition to *poenas* (20).

22 **ductis sortibus** abl. absolute

23 **contra** "opposite," i.e., on the other side of the folding door

elata mari "rising from the sea"; pf. pass. pple. *elata* modifies *Cnosia tellus* ("the Cretan land"), nom. sing. f., at line end, with *mari* abl. of separation

respondet "balances"

24 **hic** "here," i.e., on this side of the folding door; so also at 27

tauri objective gen.

supposta = *supposita*, "fraudulently introduced," nom. sing. f. modifying Pasiphaë (Greek nom. sing. f.) in the next line. Daedalus built a wooden cow covered with cowhide, in which to hide Pasiphaë, thereby enabling her to consummate her passion for the bull. The syncopated form (*supposta*) is archaic, but was favored by Catullus and the neoteric poets.

furto "by a trick"; for the undertone of sexual infidelity, cf. Dido's description of her *furtiuus amor* with Aeneas as marriage (*Aen.* 4.171–72, in this volume).

25   **mixtumque genus prolesque biformis** "the mixed birth and biform offspring," of the Minotaur (26). Double *-que* in POLYSYNDETON is another feature of high epic style.

26   **Veneris** = *amor*, by METONYMY

       monimenta "a memorial," poetic pl.

27   **labor ille domus** "that famous labor of the house," i.e., the Labyrinth, commissioned by Minos to conceal the Minotaur and built by Daedalus. Vergil seems to derive *labyrinthus* (which he describes but does not identify by name) from *labor . . . domus*: see O'Hara (1996), 166.

       inextricabilis error "the intricate maze"; Vergil imitates Catullus' description of the Labyrinth as *inobseruabilis error* (Cat. 64.115).

28   **reginae** = Minos' daughter Ariadne, whose great love for Theseus led her to ask for Daedalus' aid in saving him from the Minotaur. Catullus tells the story in poem 64 (included in this volume).

       sed enim "but indeed," an archaism that Vergil made a feature of high epic style

29   **dolos tecti ambagesque resoluit** "unraveled the trick of the dwelling, its winding ways"

30   **caeca regens filo uestigia** "directing [Theseus'] uncertain steps with a thread"; Vergil imitates Catullus again here (cf. *errabunda regens tenui uestigia filo*, Cat. 64.113).

30–31   Daedalus could not bring himself to represent the death of his son Icarus, who flew too close to the sun and so melted the wax that held the feathers on the frame of his wings and drowned in the Icarian Sea. Ovid tells the story in *Ars* 2 and *Metamorphoses* 8.

31   **sineret . . . haberes** impf. act. subjunctive in present contrary-to-fact condition; *si* is omitted from the protasis with *sineret*.

32–33 **bis . . . | bis** ANAPHORA; the rhetorical figure heightens the emotion of the passage. The subject of the verb in 32, *conatus erat*, is Daedalus (*sc. pater*, from *patriae . . . manus* in 33).

32 **casus** acc. pl. m., poetic pl., for Icarus' "fall." The noun is cognate with the verb *cado*, from which *cecidere* in the next line is derived; an example of ADNOMINATIO or PARONOMASIA (ETYMOLOGICAL WORDPLAY).

33 **patriae**: adj. for gen. case of the noun, *patris.*

∾ *Vergil, AENEID 6.179–82*
Felling of trees for Misenus' funerary pyre

The passage describes the felling of trees for the funeral pyre of Misenus, Aeneas' Trojan trumpeter killed by Triton after he challenged the sea-god to a musical contest. Vergil imitates his Ennian model closely (*Ann.* 175–79, included in this volume), though he has transformed the context from communal to individual loss, reversing Ennius' imitation of Homer: the funeral is once more for an individual, as in Homer, rather than a community. Nonetheless, the site of Misenus' pyre will bear his name (Misenum): the act of cremation is closely associated with the whole Trojan-Roman communal enterprise, with the community taking possession of the land by naming it.

179 **itur** idiomatic Latin impersonal use of the pres. pass. sing. form, best translated as pres. act. pl. in English, "they go"

siluam Alexandrian Greek poets and their Roman successors often signal an allusion to a poetic source by repeating at the opening of their imitation a word or phrase that concludes the modeling passage; so here Vergil picks up *siluai*, from the last line of the Ennian model (*Ann.* 179). Hinds (1998, 12) notes that the noun *siluam* "is used METAPHORICALLY in various contexts in Latin to represent Greek *húlê*, in the sense 'matter', 'mass of material', 'raw material' . . ." and he argues (1998, 12–13): "It is precisely as *antiqua silua,* in this sense, that the Ennian passage is laid under contribution by Virgil here in

Aen. 6.179–82 . . . the *tour de force* of allusion to poetic material from the *Aeneid*'s archaic predecessor, the *Annales*, is figured as a harvest of mighty timber from an old-growth forest . . ."

stabula alta acc. pl. n., in apposition to *siluam*, referring to the "lairs" of the wild animals rather than actual buildings housing domestic ones (English "stable"). Vergil reuses Ennius' *alta* (*Ann.* 175, 177) but only once; this "streamlined" imitation of the Ennian model suggests that the Augustan poet was concerned to "trim" the exuberance of Ennius' sound effects, in accordance with the contemporary stereotype of Ennius as "shaggy" (Prop. 4.1.61, Ov. *Tr.* 2.259); in this connection it is probably also significant that he has trimmed Ennius' five lines to four.

180   **picea, -ae** f., a "spruce" tree. Vergil has specified Ennius' *pinus* (*Ann.* 178).

sonat . . . securibus ilex three more lexical borrowings from the Ennian source. While Vergil has retained the case usage of Ennius' *securibus* and the metrical *sedes* of *ilex* (at line end in both poets), he has regularized the verb tenses to pres. throughout the passage.

181   **fraxineus, -a, -um** adj., "made of ash wood." Vergil has varied Ennius' noun (*fraxinus*, *Ann.* 177) with an adj. derived from it, modifying *trabes*. Commentators normally supply *sonant* with *trabes* from *sonat* in the preceding line.

cuneis The use of wedges to split the tree is old technology, normally preceding the invention of axes. Ennius' historical characters have good stout modern axes (*securibus*) and no need of wedges, while Vergil's Trojans have got axes but still use wedges as well to weaken the wood.

fissile robur a mild OXYMORON, since *robur* is hard wood par excellence and not naturally *fissile*, but made so by the preceding *cuneis*

182   **ingentis . . . ornos** acc. pl. f., "huge mountain-ashes"

montibus abl. of separation, "from the mountains"

❧ *Vergil*, AENEID 6.456–66
Aeneas' encounter with Dido in the underworld

As Aeneas journeys through the Underworld with the Sibyl as his guide he encounters different groups of people—the unburied; mythological heroines who killed themselves for love; Greek heroes; and famous sinners. The catalogue of mythological heroines Vergil offers here is modeled on Homer's Catalogue of Women in *Odyssey* 11, but Vergil refines the earlier catalogue by particularizing its members as women who died for love and by locating them in the "Mourning Fields." The focus on unhappy love reflects the taste of the Hellenistic Greek and neoteric Latin poets for psychological and emotional extremes of passion. In this company, Aeneas meets Dido, who had cursed Aeneas and the Roman race on her deathbed after he abandoned her at the end of *Aeneid* 4. At the very center of the sixth book, the poet thus brings the former lovers together for a final encounter, which simultaneously recalls and reverses their last meeting in *Aeneid* 4.

456 **infelix Dido** The phrase occurs like a refrain throughout *Aeneid* 4 (68, 450, 529, 596) and characterizes her, already in *Aeneid* 1 (712, 749), as ill-fated, destined to die unhappily.

457 **exstinctam . . . secutam** pf. pass. pples. (in middle and act. senses respectively) in indirect discourse, dependent on the idea of reporting in *nuntius* (456)

  extrema = *mortem*

460 **inuitus, regina, tuo de litore cessi** Aeneas' words recall his statement to Dido on his departure in Book 4 (*Aen.* 4.361, *Italiam non sponte sequor*).

462 **loca senta situ** "places rough with decay"

  noctemque profundam The same phrase appears in the same *sedes* at 4.26 (in this volume).

464 **me . . . ferre** subject acc. and pres. act. infinitive in indirect discourse dependent on *credere* in the previous line (463), with *hunc tantum . . . dolorem* acc. direct object

discessu causal abl.

465 **aspectu** = *aspectui*, dat. indicating separation with the compound verb *subtrahe*; for the irregular form, cf. *curru* (1.156, in this volume)

subtrahe negative command with *ne* instead of *nolle*

466 **quem fugis?** Aeneas echoes Dido's words at their last meeting, *mene fugis* (4.314), where Dido spoke and Aeneas withdrew; here Aeneas speaks and Dido withdraws.

467 **extremum . . . hoc est** "This is the last time by destiny that I address you." Note the heaviness of the line (DSSSDS) and monosyllabic ending.

❧ Vergil, AENEID 8.625–34
The shield of Aeneas

Homer provides a description of Achilles' shield, made at the request of his mother Thetis by the divine craftsman Hephaistos, in *Iliad* 18 before Achilles re-enters the war. Vergil follows his model with an ECPHRASIS describing Aeneas' shield, made at the request of his mother Venus by her husband Vulcan, before Aeneas returns to the Trojan camp from an embassy to Rome and Etruria to seek allies in the war with the Italians. Containing scenes of mostly peaceful life, the shield of Achilles shows what the Greek hero consciously foregoes by returning to war (since he knows he will die at Troy). By contrast, the shield of Aeneas records important moments in the history of the Roman people and thus documents the continuity between the hero's dutiful acceptance of his mission to establish the Trojans in Italy and his descendants' achievements. The scenes on the shield of Aeneas eschew Greek mythology (unlike the ECPHRASIS of the doors to Apollo's temple in *Aeneid* 6, included in this volume) to relate stories of Roman historical and political import that fall into three broad categories: early Roman legends, the Battle of Actium, and the triple triumph of Augustus. The Shield of Aeneas thus brings the narrative of the *Aeneid* into its closest contact with events of the poet's own day as the poet reflects on the significance of the refoundation of Rome and her empire by Aeneas' descendant, the emperor Augustus.

625   The grammatical construction of the line depends on 8.619, [Aeneas] *miratur . . . et . . . uersat*: "Aeneas admires the weapons and turns them in his hands . . . ," including helmet, sword, breast-plate, greaves, spear, and the marvelous shield.

     et clipei non enarrabile textum "and [he admires] the indescribable fabric of the shield"; the marvelous artistry of Vulcan's shield reflects that of Vergil's poem.

626   **res Italas . . . triumphos** both acc., direct object of *fecerat* two lines later (628); the Shield focuses on Rome's political history and acquisition of an empire.

627   **ignarus . . . inscius** nom. sing. m. with *ignipotens* (= Vulcan) in the next line; both adjs. take gen. (*uatum, uenturi . . . aeui*).

     -que disjunctive, "or"

628–29   **futurae | stirpis ab Ascanio** "of the offspring that was to descend from Ascanius"

630–31   **fecerat . . . | procubuisse lupam** *Fecerat* introduces acc. + infinitive (631–34), "he had represented the she-wolf as having thrown herself down."

630   **fetam** "newly delivered," of the she-wolf

     Mauortis = *Martis*, gen. of the archaic form *Mauors*; cf. Lucr. 1.32 (in this volume).

     in antro = the Lupercal; the association of the she-wolf with a cave implies the cave called the Lupercal on the Palatine hill, where tradition held that the she-wolf nursed the twins Romulus and Remus (cf. *geminos . . . pueros*, 631–32).

631–32   **geminos . . . | ludere pendentis pueros** acc. + infinitive depending on *fecerat*; "the twin boys hanging and playing"

631   **huic ubera circum** "around her teats"; *huic* is dat. of possession with *ubera*, object of prep. *circum*

633   **tereti ceruice reflexa** "her shapely neck bent back"; abl. absolute. Vergil imitates Lucr. 1.35 (in this volume).

634   **mulcere . . . fingere** "she stroked and fashioned," like a cat licking her kittens into shape

∾ *Vergil, Aeneid 12.697–724*
Duel between Aeneas and Turnus

At the beginning of *Aeneid* 12 Turnus agrees to face Aeneas in single combat for the right to marry King Latinus' daughter Lavinia, but the compact is broken and a general mêlée breaks out. Turnus wreaks havoc on the sidelines while Aeneas marshalls his troops to invest the Latin city, and his assault causes Queen Amata to kill herself. When a messenger reports the city's danger to Turnus, he returns to fight with Aeneas before their assembled armies in the poem's final scene.

697   **pater Aeneas** As victor, Aeneas will be the father of the Roman people.

       audito nomine abl. absolute, "when he heard the name of Turnus"

699   **praecipitat** "he forestalls"

       moras omnis acc. pl. f.

       rumpit "he breaks off"

700   **laetitia** causal abl. with *exsultans*

       horrendum adverbial acc.

701–3 **quantus Athos aut quantus Eryx aut . . . | . . . quantus . . . | . . . pater Appenninus** Aeneas is compared to Mount Athos in Greece or Mount Eryx in Sicily (cf. Cat. 64.72, in this volume), or the Apennine mountain range, which runs down the center of the Italian peninsula. Vergil passes swiftly over Athos and Eryx to focus on the Italian range.

701   **Athōs** Greek nom. sing. m., with long final vowel

ipse take with *pater Appenninus* in 703. The word order in these lines is highly interwoven.

702   **fremit** "roars"

703   **se attollens . . . ad auras** The image of Aeneas, like the Apennine range, rising up towards the sky, implies his victory in the contest to come and contrasts strongly with the immediately preceding description of Turnus plunging down a mountain like a landslide (12.684–90). Pöschl (1962, 131) explains the thematic significance of the two SIMILES: "The plunging rock [= Turnus] which leaves a downward path of destruction is contrasted with the majestic power of the enduring mountains [= Aeneas] . . . darkness with light, falling with rising, defeat with victory, 'barbarian' with 'Roman,' wild violence with cosmic order."

704   **Troes** Greek nom. pl. m., with short final vowel

704-5 **et Rutuli . . . et Troes et omnes | . . . Itali** "The Rutulians and Trojans, and all the Italians . . ." All the warriors, on both sides, watch the contest that will decide the war and the marriage.

705-6 **quique . . . | . . . quique** "both those who . . . and those who"; i.e., both the Italians who were defending their city and the Trojans who were besieging it.

706   **ariete** instrumental abl. The form is scanned as a dactylic trisyllable with consonantal *i* (*ar-jete*). The battering "ram" was a long, thick log fashioned from a tree-trunk, with a mass of metal affixed to one end, which caused it to resemble a ram's head.

707   **umeris** abl. of separation

       stupet introduces acc. (*ingentis . . . uiros*, 708-9) + infinitive (*coiisse, cernere*, 709).

708   **genitos** acc. pl. m., in apposition to *ingentis uiros*

       diuersis partibus local abl.

       orbis partitive gen.

709 **coiisse** pf. act. infinitive of *coeo*, "come together, meet in battle"

    cernere = *decernere* "settle the issue"

710 **atque illi** Vergil turns from describing the audience to focus on the combatants.

    ut "when"

    uacuo . . . aequore "with the plain clear"; abl. absolute

711 **procursu rapido** abl. of manner

    coniectis . . . hastis abl. absolute

712 **inuadunt Martem** "they plunge into battle"; *Martem* = *pugnam*, by METONYMY

    clipeis atque aere sonoro "with shields of resonant bronze"; HENDIADYS

714 **fors . . . unum** "chance and courage are mixed together"; *fors* and *uirtus* apply equally to both Turnus and Aeneas.

715-24 Vergil had adapted a brief bull SIMILE from Apollonius of Rhodes (*Arg.* 2.88–89) in a description of bulls fighting over a heifer at *Georgics* 3.217–36; here he returns georgic reality into epic SIMILE.

715 **Sila . . . Taburno** both local abl., recalling Vergil's description in *Georgics* 3 of the fighting bulls on Sila, a mountain range in Bruttium in southwestern Italy. Taburnus was also a mountain in southern Italy, located between Campania, Samnium, and Apulia.

715-16 **ac uelut . . . | cum** "and just as when," introducing the SIMILE

716 **conuersis** "leveled," abl. absolute with *frontibus* in the next line

717 **magistri** nom. pl. m., "herdsmen"

718 **mussant** "low faintly"; the verb introduces two indirect deliberative questions, with subjunctive verbs, in the next line (*imperitet . . . sequantur*).

720 **multa ui** abl. of manner. The heavy rhythm of the line (all spondees except for a dactyl in the fifth foot), along with clash

of metrical beat and accent in the first four feet, effectively conveys the struggle.

721 **obnixi** nom. pl. m., of the bulls struggling "with all their might"

infigunt "drive deep"

722 **gemitu nemus omne remugit** ALLITERATION and ASSONANCE convey the grove's echo of the bulls' struggle. Vergil is fond of the device of "pathetic fallacy," in which the natural world reflects the travails of its inhabitants, as here; cf. 12.928–29 *consurgunt gemitur Rutuli totusque remugit | mons circum.*

723 **Daunius heros** = Turnus, whose father is named Daunus.

724 **clipeis** instrumental abl.

aethera Greek acc. sing. m.

ꙮ *Ovid, METAMORPHOSES 1.1–20*
Proem and description of chaos

Ovid's response in the *Metamorphoses* (in circulation ca. 8 CE) to Vergil's achievement in the *Aeneid* inaugurates the proliferation of epic poetry in early imperial Rome. The proem (*Met.* 1.1–4) and opening description of Chaos (*Met.* 1.5–20) show Ovid addressing some of the most elevated themes of the genre in an invocation of the gods and a brief cosmogony. Vergil's influence is omnipresent, but Homer, Lucretius, and even Catullus, also contribute significantly to Ovid's reorientation of epic from Roman national themes to cosmic mythological themes.

1–4 The poet appeals to all the gods, rather than to the Muses, for his inspiration and sets out the controlling themes of his poem—change and transformation, novelty and innovation— in one of the shortest and thematically densest epic proems to survive from classical antiquity.

1 **in noua** The prepositional phrase is completed with the first word of the following line, *corpora*, "into new bodies." But the words can also be read initially as standing alone, and thereby

function as an alternative title to the *Metamorphoses* (just as the *Aeneid* can be evoked by the alternate title *arma*, from its opening word). Read autonomously, the phrase suggests Ovid's commitment to innovation, evident throughout his literary career but perhaps especially in the *Metamorphoses*, his only work written in dactylic hexameters. The phrase is imitated by Manilius, at the opening of the third book of his *Astronomica*.

fert animus The poet's mind is as much the source of inspiration for the poem as the gods whom he invokes in the following line. Verb and subject, on a first reading, appear to give complete sense, like the opening HEMISTICHS (lit. "half-verses") of Homer's epics and Vergil's *Aeneid* (*arma uirumque cano*, 1.1, included in this volume). Lucan treats the phrase as a programmatic unit in the proem of his *Bellum Ciuile* (*BC* 1.67, included in *A Lucan Reader*), and Statius deploys it in the context of epic combat (*Theb.* 1.416, in this volume).

dicere *sc. me*, unexpressed direct object of *fert* and acc. subject of pres. act. infinitive *dicere*

mutatas . . . formas direct object of *dicere*; in the exile poetry, Ovid refers to his poem by this phrase (*Tr.* 1.1.117, 1.7.13, 3.14.19), which translates (and sounds remarkably similar to) the Greek word *metamorphoses*, the title of the poem.

2   **coeptis** dat. with compound verb *adspirate* in the next line, "undertakings," i.e., new poetic enterprise. Vergil had used *coepta* of his new poetic project at the outset of the *Georgics* (1.40), where all the gods are also invoked (*dique deaeque omnes, Geo.* 1.21).

illa picks up *coeptis*, with reference to Ovid's new meter. All Ovid's extant earlier poetry is composed in elegiac couplets, and up to the parenthesis, which starts at the main CAESURA of the line, this line too could still be a pentameter; but the four long syllables that open the parenthesis leave no doubt that the second line of the poem is another dactylic hexameter.

The first metamorphosis the poem thus records is that of the poet from an elegist into an epic poet.

3 **adspirate** The METAPHOR is nautical, and likens the epic's course to that of a sea-voyage. Ovid borrows the METAPHOR from Vergil (*Aen.* 9.525).

primaque ab origine mundi This theme opens the poem, immediately following the proem. The phrase is Lucretian (3.331, 5.548, 5.678), picked up by Vergil (*Geo.* 3.48, 4.286).

4 **ad mea . . . tempora** The *Metamorphoses* ends with the death and apotheosis of Julius Caesar (*Met.* 15.843–51) and the rise of Augustus (*Met.* 15.860–70) in the poet's own lifetime, and predicts Ovid's own immortality (*Met.* 15.871–79).

perpetuum . . . carmen "a continuous song"; the phrase emphasizes the chronological continuity of Ovid's poem and IRONICALLY adapts Callimachus' tendentious refusal in the *Aetia* prologue to produce "one continuous song" (*Aet.* 1, fr. 1.3 Pf.). Yet despite the fluidity of Ovid's transitions from tale to tale in the *Metamorphoses*, his poem has most often been read as a highly episodic narrative, very like Callimachus' *Aetia*. The adj. also testifies to Ovid's ambition that his *magnum opus* may last forever.

deducite a verb with a multiplicity of meanings, several of which seem to be in play here. In its literal meaning of "bring down," *deducite* makes sense; but the nautical METAPHOR (of bringing a ship in to port) continues that in *adspirate* from the line before, while the spinning METAPHOR ("spin a fine thread of continuous song") implicitly imparts Callimachean refinement to Ovid's project. The latter METAPHOR is introduced into Latin in Vergil's adaptation of Callimachean poetics in his pastoral poetry, where he employs the phrase *deductum carmen* (*Buc.* 6.5) to contrast the bucolic poet's "finespun song" with the fat sheep pastured by the shepherd.

5 **quod tegit omnia** The rel. clause precedes its "antecedent," *caelum*.

7 **quem** The antecedent is best taken as *uultus* rather than *orbe*.

dixere = *dixerunt*, an Alexandrian footnote emphasizing the traditional source of the story; cf. my note on Cat. 64.76.

Chaos Greek acc. sing. n.; the noun first appears in Hesiod's *Theogony* and is derived from a Greek verb *khaskein* meaning "yawn, gape." Ovid uses it here in the sense of a "formless state of primordial matter," i.e., *rudis indigestaque moles*.

indigesta "shapeless"; note the negative prefix *in-*. The word appears first here in extant Latin.

8 **pondus iners** "useless weight"; *iners* < *in-* (negative prefix) + *ars* implies that artistry will be required to shape the universe. As the passage develops, Ovid defines the state of Chaos by negative enumeration, i.e., by referring to all that it is not: *nec . . . nisi . . . non . . . nullus . . . nec . . . nec . . . nec* (8–13).

congesta "crowded together," pf. pass. pple (modifying *discordia semina* in the next line) from the same root and placed in the same metrical position as *indigesta* in the immediately preceding line. Ovid's own language thus begins to shape the universe.

9 **non bene** = *male*

discordia The METAPHOR of conflict returns in 17–20. Ovid alludes to Empedocles' doctrine of the birth of the universe through the interaction of Strife and Love; on Empedocles' epic cosmogony, *Peri Physeôs*, see the headnote to Lucr. 1.1–43, in this volume.

semina rerum "the seeds of things," a Lucretian expression for "atoms"; Ovid uses it here for the four elements—earth, air, water, and fire.

10 **adhuc** "yet"

Titan Greek nom. sing. m., modified by *nullus* at the beginning of the line; used here of Helios, the Sun, a son of the Titan Hyperion. With the introduction of the Titans in this line and the next, Ovid mingles mythology and natural science.

11 **noua ... cornua** acc. pl. n., direct object

crescendo gerund in instrumental abl.

Phoebe Greek nom. sing. f.; a daughter of Earth and Heaven (a Titanness), associated by Ovid with the goddess Diana in her capacity as a moon-goddess.

12 **aere Tellus** Personified "Earth" is juxtaposed with the element of air.

13 **ponderibus librata suis** "balanced by her own weight," i.e., her own gravitational forces; *librata* is nom. sing. f. pf. pass. pple., modifying *Tellus.* Ancient scientific theory held that the earth remained balanced in the center of the universe by the weight of all else pressing on it.

13-14 **longo | margine** abl. of place where. Ovid refers to the common ancient view that the ocean encircled the earth.

14 A four-word spondaic line is a tour-de-force of technical skill (cf. *Met.* 4.737, in this volume); for the spondaic ending, cf. Cat. 64.67, in this volume. Catullus also supplies the model for later Latin hexameter poets of a four-word spondaic line in 64.15; for another four-word line (though not spondaic) cf. Cat. 64.77 (in this volume).

Amphitrite Greek nom. sing. f. Daughter of Nereus and wife of Neptune, she stands here for "the ocean."

15 Ovid reprises the three elements of earth, water, and air from 5.

15-16 **utque ... | sic** "but although ... yet"

16 **instabilis** adj. formed from negative prefix *in-*; cf. *indigesta*, 7, *innabilis* at line end. Translate in passive sense, "not able to be stood on."

innabilis an Ovidian coinage, to match *instabilis*, "not able to be swum in"; the adj. is a *hapax.*

17 **lucis** gen. sing. f. with *egeo*

nulli dat. of (dis)advantage or interest; sc. *elemento*

18   **aliis** dat. pl. n., with compound verb; note the POLYPTOTON
      in *aliis aliud*, which recalls Lucretian usage and is appropri-
      ate to the cosmogonic theme Ovid adumbrates here. Strictly
      speaking, both adjs. should be either pl. or sing.; the asym-
      metry serves Ovid's purpose in suggesting the disorder that
      characterizes Chaos.

      corpore Chaos is described as a single body because no part of
      what exists at this point is distinct from any other.

19   **calidis . . . siccis** dat. pl. n., with *pugnabant*, a poetic usage.
      Prose prefers *cum* + abl., which Ovid supplies in the next line
      (*cum duris*), or another prepositional phrase.

19–20 **frigida . . . umentia . . . | mollia . . . habentia** nom. pl. n., sub-
      jects of *pugnabant*

20   **sine pondere** "those without weight"

      pondus acc. sing. n., direct object of *habentia*, "elements hav-
      ing weight"

ᴗ *Ovid, Metamorphoses 1.89–112*
The golden age

Ovid's description of the golden age is indebted to the descriptions
of the generations of men by Hesiod (*Works and Days* 106–201) and
Aratus (*Phaenomena* 96–136), and to famous treatments of the gold-
en age by his elder contemporaries Vergil (*Buc.* 4) and Horace (*Iambi*
16). The passage is formally structured in two parts of twelve lines
(1.89–100, 101–12), each developed by negative enumeration (for the
term, see the note on *Met.* 1.8) and concluding with a "golden line"
(for the term, see the note on Cat. 64.59).

89   **uindice nullo** abl. of attendant circumstance or absolute,
      "with no defender/avenger"

91–92 **nec . . . | . . . nec** ANAPHORA of *nec* heralds a sequence orga-
      nized by negative enumeration (cf. 94–99).

      fixo | aere In ancient Rome laws were engraved on bronze tab-
      lets and set up in public.

92   **ligabantur** Ovid seems to derive the word for "laws," *leges*, from the verb *ligo*, "bind," with "the *binding* nature of the laws" appropriately figured in the indelibly carved bronze tablets (Lee 1953, 82 ad loc.).

94–96   A common theme in ancient literature is the impiety of sea-travel, whose purposes (commerce and war) were often represented as misfortunes for mankind.

94   **caesa** nom. sing. f., modifying *pinus* (in the next line), a common METONYMY for "ship"

   suis abl. pl. m., modifying *montibus* in the next line; abl. of place where

   uiseret 3rd sing. impf. act. subjunctive in a purpose clause introduced by *ut*

96   **norant** = *nouerant*, by SYNCOPE

97   **praecipites . . . fossae** "steep ditches"

98   **derecti . . . flexi** both gen. of description, modifying *aeris*; used to distinguish the straight horn from the curved, both instruments for military signaling

99   **sine militis usu** "without the need of soldiers"; *militis* poetic sing. for pl., gen. dependent on *usu*.

100   a golden line of the form abVAB

101   **ipsa . . . immunis . . . intacta** nom. sing. f., modifying *tellus* at the end of the next line; note the formation of the adjs. *immunis* and *intacta* from negative prefix *in-*, and Ovid's characteristic technique of negative enumeration in this line. *Ipsa* = *sponte sua* (cf. 90), reinforced by *per se* in the next line. *Immunis* of the land means both "unworked" and "untaxed" (the latter an idiomatic contemporary usage).

101–2   **rastro . . . | . . . uomeribus** both instrumental abl., modifying *intacta* and *saucia* respectively

103   **contenti** nom. pl. m., adj. used predicatively with unexpressed *sunt*; subject of *legebant* in the next line

   nullo cogente abl. absolute with concessive force, surrounded by another abl. *cibis creatis* dependent on *contenti*

104-6 **arbuteos fetus montanaque fraga . . . | cornaque et . . . mora . . . | et . . . glandes** all acc. pl., direct object of *legebant*. These fruits and berries are traditionally held to be the simple food of primitive man (Lucr. 5.939–42) and are also conventional features of Vergil's quasi-golden age pastoral landscape, though they are characterized as poor fare, indeed nearly inedible, by ancient authors.

106 **patula Iouis arbore** The oak-tree, sacred to Jupiter, is characterized by a spreading canopy of foliage. Ovid's pleasant pastoral image is undermined when we recall that acorns were fed to pigs and cattle in his day.

108 **Zephyri** poetic pl.; the west wind prevails in the Mediterranean spring (cf. my note on *fauoni*, Lucr. 1.11)

109 **inarata** another adj. modifying *tellus* and formed on negative prefix *in-*; cf. *immunis, intacta,* 101

110 **nec renouatus** = *et non renouatus*

111 **flumina iam . . . iam flumina** CHIASMUS. Streams of milk and honey (1.112) are traditional features of utopia, but nectar is conventionally the food of the gods and here evokes the quasi-divine life of ease enjoyed by mortals in the golden age.

112 A (near) golden line of the form abVBA, with abundant ALLITERATION and ASSONANCE, concludes the passage effectively.

॰ *Ovid, METAMORPHOSES 4.706–39*
Perseus fights a sea-monster to rescue Andromeda

The hero Perseus fights a duel with a sea-monster, sent by Neptune to avenge Cassiope's disparagement of the Nereids' beauty by comparison to that of her daughter Andromeda. Their combat furnishes an exemplary model of the epic type-scene of a contest between an epic hero and a bestial monster menacing the beautiful woman loved by the hero. The hero's duel with the monster also varies the type-scene of combat between two warriors for the same woman (e.g., in *Aen.* 12.697–724, in this volume).

706 **ecce** With this interjection, Ovid turns our attention to the approach of the sea-monster.

uelut nauis . . . concita "just like a rapidly moving ship . . . " SIMILES conventionally compare ships to sea-monsters. Vergil, in the ship-race of *Aen.* 5, gives one of the ships the name *Pristis*, "Sea-Monster" and another "Scylla." Ovid delights in overturning the convention with his anachronistic comparison of the sea-monster to an enemy warship.

praefixo . . . rostro abl. absolute, "beak fixed to prow"

707 **acta** nom. sing. f., pf. pass. pple., modifying *nauis* in the preceding line

708 **sic fera** sc. *uenit*; "so the beast approached"

dimotis . . . undis abl. absolute

pectoris subjective gen. with *impulsu*, abl. of manner

709 **scopulis** abl. of separation with *aberat*

709-10 "The monster was as far away from the rocks as (much as) the extent of air a Balearic sling can traverse when its lead shot is propelled."

Balearica . . . | funda The "Balearic sling" was the characteristic weapon of the Balearic islanders, who wielded it formidably in formation in Rome's imperial armies. Ovid's reference to the weapon is another anachronism.

torto | . . . plumbo abl. absolute

710 **medii . . . caeli** partitive gen. with *quantum*

711 **cum** with an indicative verb in a *cum-inversum* clause

tellure repulsa abl. absolute

712 **arduus, -a, -um** adj. modifying *iuuenis* in the preceding line; best translated adverbially, "when suddenly the youth shot high into the clouds"

713 **umbra . . . uisa est, uisam . . . in umbram** chiasmus with POLYPTOTON, ASSONANCE, and ALLITERATION—all rhetorical devices much favored by Ovid. The reversible structure of the line reflects its sense—Perseus' image reflected in the water's

surface—and thematizes the hero's mastery of the reflected image, as evidenced by his murder of Medusa, accomplished while gazing at her reflection in his shield.

714 **utque Iouis praepes** "and like Jove's bird," i.e., the eagle, introducing another SIMILE (of an eagle hunting a snake) in the grand epic style. For *praepes*, cf. Enn. *Ann.* 86, in this volume.

715 **Phoebo** by METONYMY for the Sun; dat. of indirect object with *praebentem*

liuentia terga acc. n. pl. (poetic), direct object of *praebentem*

716 **auersum** acc. sing. m., modifying *draconem* in the preceding line. Ovid ingeniously compares Jove's (flying) son Perseus to an eagle, which seizes its prey unawares (from behind), just as Perseus had caught Medusa, in order to avoid her deadly gaze.

neu = *et ne*, introducing a negative purpose clause

717 a golden line

718 **celeri . . . uolatu** abl. of manner

missus praeceps nom. sing. m., modifying *Inachides* (720) = Perseus, a descendant of Inachus, the Argive river-god

719 **ferae . . . frementis** gen. (of possession), exhibiting ASSO-NANCE and ALLITERATION. Ovid's anatomical precision in the phrase *dextro . . . in armo* recalls the physical details of epic battle scenes.

720 **curuo . . . hamo** abl. with prep. *tenus*. The short sword with a sickle-shaped hook projecting partway up the blade is Perseus' characteristic weapon; cf. 727, *falcato . . . ense.*

721-29 Rosati (2007, 341 ad loc.) notes that Ovid's vivid and violent description of the beast's death agonies is indebted to contemporary amphitheatrical displays of animal hunts.

721 **laesa** Supply *fera.*

sublimis nom. sing. m. adj., best translated adverbially, "high/aloft" (cf. Man. *Astr.* 5.597, in this volume), with *in auras* acc. pl. f., indicating motion towards

721-22   **modo ... | ... modo ... modo** The monster tries first one ap-
         proach then another in an effort to escape Perseus' onslaught;
         the triple *nunc* of 725–26, of Perseus' continuing attack on the
         monster, responds to this triadic series.

722   **aquis** dat. of direction with compound verb

722-23   Another comparison, this time of the sea-monster to a wild
         boar. The image of the beast cornered by a pack of baying
         hounds recalls the myth of Actaeon, hunted and killed in the
         form of a deer by his own hounds, which Ovid tells in the
         previous book (*Met.* 3.206–51).

723   **circumsona** compound adj., coined by Ovid in the highest epic
         style; its meaning, "resounding," is reinforced by the sound
         effects in this line full of ALLITERATION and ASSONANCE.

724   **ille** = Perseus

         auidos morsus acc. m. pl., direct object of *effugit*

725   **quaque patet** "and where there is an opening"; Perseus presses
         his advantage.

         terga cauis super obsita conchis "his back, overgrown with
         hollow shells"

729   **ore** abl. of separation with *uomit*

         maduere graues aspergine pennae The hero's winged san-
         dals grow heavy and drip with the foam coughed up by the
         sea-monster.

730   **bibulis ... talaribus** dat. n. pl. with *credere*, complementary
         infinitive with pf. act. pple. *ausus*

731   **uertice summo** instrumental abl.

732   **stantibus exstat** Ovid favors this type of *FIGURA ETYMOLOGICA*.

         stantibus ... aquis abl. of separation with *exstat*; the cliff stands
         out "from the calm waters" but "is covered by rough seas."

         ab aequore moto Ovid often uses abl. of agent with inanimate
         objects where prose usage requires an instrumental abl.

733   **eo** abl. m. sing. (of the cliff, *scopulum* 731), with pf. act. pple. of
         deponent verb *nitor*

735   **cum plausu** abl. with otiose prep. *cum* (cf. abl. of agent above 732). The spectators' applause and cries (*clangor*) comprise the pl. subject of the verb *impleuere* (736). The spectators applaud Perseus' killing of the sea-monster, just like the audience applauds at the animal hunts in the Roman amphitheater.

736   **impleuere** alternate ending for *impleuerunt*, 3rd pl. pf. act. indicative. The verb governs two direct objects, *litora* in the preceding line, and *domos* (modified by *superas deorum* in the preceding line).

736-37 **gaudent ... salutant | ... fatentur** The subjects of these verbs are Andromeda's parents, Cassiope and Cepheus, named at 738.

737   **domus** objective gen. with both *auxilium* and *seruatorem*

738   **Cassiope** Greek nom. sing. f.

      catenis abl. of separation with pf. pass. pple. *resoluta*, nom. sing. f. modifying *uirgo* in the next line

739   **pretium ... causa** both nom. in apposition to *uirgo*

      laboris objective gen. with both *pretium* and *causa*. The word *labor* underlines Perseus' heroic stature and recalls the celebrated labors of Hercules; cf. also those of Aeneas (Verg. *Aen.* 1.10, in this volume).

∾ Ovid, METAMORPHOSES 8.155–82

Cretan myths

In this passage, Ovid rehearses the body of Cretan myths treated by Catullus and Vergil before him, from Pasiphaë's adulterous liaison with the bull and birth of the Minotaur, through Daedalus' construction of the Labyrinth and Theseus' killing of the Minotaur and his escape with Ariadne's help, to Dionysus' rescue of the abandoned princess and her subsequent transformation into the constellation of the Crown. The selection offers an exemplary case study of Ovid's intertextual relations with his predecessors in Latin epic.

155 **opprobrium generis** "the family's disgrace," i.e., the Minotaur. Ovid uses abstract for concrete; cf. *pudorem*, 157.

156 **matris adulterium** = Pasiphaë's adultery; cf. *Veneris monimenta nefandae, Aen.* 6.26 (in this volume).

monstri . . . biformis cf. 169; the Minotaur was traditionally represented with the head of a bull on the body of a man; cf. *Aen.* 6.25, *proles biformis* of the Minotaur (in this volume).

nouitate causal abl. Ovid frequently uses this noun, and related forms, to signal a metamorphosis; certainly the monstrous Minotaur is an appropriate subject for a poem about *mutatae formae* (cf. Ovid's proem, *Met.* 1.1–4, in this volume).

157-58 **remouere . . . | . . . includere** both complementary infinitives, depending on *destinat*

158 **multilplici . . . domo caecis . . . tectis** abl. of place where or dat. with compound verb; Ovid imitates Vergilian style, with the second half of his line, amplifying the first (cf., e.g., *Aen.* 6.25, 27, both in this volume). He also imitates Vergil's description of the Labyrinth's dark paths, *caeca uestigia* (*Aen.* 6.30, in this volume).

159 **ingenio** causal abl. with *celeberrimus*

fabrae . . . artis gen. of definition, depending on *ingenio*; "most famous for his talent in the craftsman's art," i.e., for his skill as an architect

160 **ponit** historic pres.; for *ponere* in the sense of "build, construct," cf. *Aen.* 6.19 (in this volume), also of the Labyrinth.

notas marks to indicate the way to the exit

160-61 **lumina flexa | ducit in errorem** "He bends the eye and leads it into error." Ovid recalls the poetic descriptions of Catullus and Vergil of the Labyrinth as a "maze," *error* (Cat. 64.115; Verg. *Aen.* 6.27, in this volume); cf. 167 below.

161 **uariarum . . . uiarum** The WORDPLAY suggests the intricate interplay of paths in the Labyrinth.

ambage instrumental abl. The word recalls Vergil's characterization of the Labyrinth at *Aen.* 6.29 (in this volume).

162   **non secus ac** "not otherwise than"; the phrase introduces a
       SIMILE that concludes with the clause beginning with *ita* at
       166.

       Maeandros Greek nom. sing. m. The Meander river in Phry-
       gia was celebrated already in antiquity for its "meandering"
       course.

163   **ambiguo lapsu** "in uncertain motion," abl. of manner; note
       the echo of *ambage* in 161

       refluitque fluitque Ovid figures the river's confused and
       winding course with the juxtaposition of the compound verb
       before *simplex*.

164   **sibi** dat. with *occurrens*

167   **reuerti** pres. infinitive of deponent verb, complementary with
       potuit in the next line, here used intransitively, in the sense
       of "return"; i.e., he could scarcely find his own way back out
       again

168   **tanta est fallacia tecti** a characteristic Ovidian clausula with
       tanta, filling the second half of the line and drawing the im-
       age to a pointed close

169   **quo** connective rel. adv., lit. "where"; translate "there"

170   **Actaeo bis pastum sanguine monstrum** "the monster which
       had fed twice on Attic blood." *Monstrum* is acc. sing. n. direct
       object of *domuit* in the next line, and *sanguine* is instrumental
       abl. with *pastum*, acc. sing. n. pf. act. pple. of deponent verb
       pascor, modifying *monstrum*. Ovid compresses the details of
       the myth to move swiftly from Daedalus' construction of the
       Labyrinth to the third delivery of Athenian youths to the Mi-
       notaur: see my note on Cat. 64.76.

171   **tertia sors** The Athenians selected youths for the Minotaur by
       lot, but on the occasion that the third installment fell due the
       Athenian King Aegeus' son Theseus volunteered for inclusion
       in the tribute; cf. Verg. *Aen.* 6.22 (in this volume).

       annis . . . nouenis "in nine years"; temporal abl.

172   **utque** = *ut* + *que*, "and when"

ope uirginea "with a maiden's help," instrumental abl. The maiden is Ariadne, not named in Ovid's allusive version of the myth. She is the "ravished daughter of Minos" referred to in the next line (*rapta Minoide*). This PERIPHRASTIC style of description is typical of high epic verse.

nullis dat. of agent (with pf. pass. pple. *iterata*) on which **priorum** (partitive gen.) depends, "by none of the earlier youths"

iterata nom. sing. f., modifying *ianua difficilis* in the next line; lit. "repeated," but better translated here "revisited"

173 **filo . . . relecto** abl. absolute; on Daedalus' advice, Ariadne gave Theseus a spool of thread to unwind as he journeyed into the Labyrinth to meet the Minotaur and gather back up again on his way out; cf. Cat. 64.113–15, Verg. *Aen.* 6.27–30 (in this volume).

174 **Aegides** Greek nom. sing. m., patronymic of Theseus, "son of Aegeus"

rapta Minoide abl. absolute with another patronymic, of Ariadne "daughter of Minos," also used by Catullus in 64.60 (in this volume)

Dian Greek acc. sing. f.; as a small island, Dia takes acc. of motion toward without prep. For the identification of the island with Naxos, see my note on Cat. 64.52.

175 **crudelis** nom. sing. m. modifying *Aegides*, best translated adverbially here as "cruelly"

176 **desertae . . . querenti** dat. sing. f., indirect object; Ovid uses both pples. (pf. pass. and pres. act. respectively) of Ariadne, who remains unnamed throughout the passage.

multa internal acc. with *querenti*; Catullus' Ariadne laments her plight at length in 64.132–201, and Ovid rehearses her lament in *Heroides* 10.

177–82 Bacchus rescues the deserted Ariadne and as they speed through the air in the god's chariot, he takes off her crown (a gift of Aphrodite) and throws it into the sky where it is transformed into the constellation of the Northern Crown

(*Corona Borealis*). Metamorphosis into a star or constellation ("catasterism") was a popular theme of Hellenistic Greek poetry and supplies the climax of Ovid's version of the myth of Ariadne and Theseus in the *Metamorphoses.*

177   **amplexus et opem** both acc., direct objects of *tulit*. Anderson (1972, 350, ad loc.) observes a "naughty ZEUGMA" here. "One or the other of the nouns must dominate, and it is easy to think of Liber [= Bacchus] as the typical lecherous deity, all too eager to offer embraces."

      utque = *ut* + *que*, "and in order that," introducing a purpose clause

177–78   **perenni | sidere** descriptive abl. with *clara* (178), characterizing Ariadne's crown (*coronam*, 178)

179   **caelo** dat. of direction with *immisit*

181   **specie remanente** abl. absolute

182   Ovid situates Ariadne's Crown between the constellations of the Kneeler (usually identified with Hercules) and the Snake-Holder (Ophiuchus), though it is actually to be located between Bootes and the Kneeler.

      medius governs both gen., *Nixi* (pf. act. pple. of deponent verb *nitor*) and *tenentis* (pres. act. pple.)

      Nixi . . . genu "of the man resting on his knee," i.e., the constellation of the Kneeler

      Anguem . . . tenentis "of the man holding the snake," i.e., the constellation of the Snake-Holder (Ophiuchus)

∾ *Ovid,* METAMORPHOSES *8.741–76*
Erysichthon cuts down Ceres' tree

This selection describes Erysichthon's felling of an oak-tree sacred to the goddess Ceres (Greek Demeter). Ovid introduces Erysichthon as a man "who spurned the gods' divinity and burned no incense on the altars" (*qui numina diuum | sperneret et nullos aris adoleret odores, Met.* 8.739–40) and he repeatedly emphasizes his impiety throughout the passage, which adapts the tree-felling scenes of Ennius (*Ann.* 175–79) and Vergil (*Aen.* 6.179–82), both included in this *Reader*, to draw out undertones of impiety latent in their scenes. The adaptation shows Ovid as a particularly sensitive reader of the nuances of earlier Roman epic.

741–42   **ille . . . | dicitur** "The notorious Erysichthon is reported . . ." The myth was the subject of Callimachus' *Hymn to Demeter* and Ovid acknowledges the literary tradition as his source for the myth with *dicitur*, here used as an "Alexandrian footnote" (for the term, see my note on Cat. 64.76).

741   **Cereale nemus** "Ceres' grove"; for the use of the possessive adj. (instead of gen.), see my note on Cat. 64.77 and cf. Verg. *Aen.* 6.14 and Manil. *Astr.* 5.594 (both in this volume).

      uiolasse = *uiolauisse*, by SYNCOPE; the verb emphasizes the impiety of Erysichthon's action. The sentiment is very old: a third-century BCE Latin inscription forbids the felling of trees in a grove (Warmington 1967, 4.154).

742   **temerasse** = *temerauisse*, again by SYNCOPE. The verse reiterates the sense of the preceding line, with the addition of the detail that the grove was old, in markedly Vergilian fashion (cf. my note on *Met.* 8.158), characteristic of Ovid in high epic style.

743   **ingens annoso robore quercus** "a huge oak of many years' strength"; *annoso robore* is descriptive abl.

744   **una nemus** "a grove in and of itself"; an example of the rhetorical figure of HYPERBOLE

744–45 Woollen fillets, votive tablets (recording the discharge of a vow or the grant of a wish), and garlands were conventional elements in the worship of the classical gods and were traditionally hung in temples, though there is some evidence that they also adorned trees in the sacred grove of the goddess Diana at Aricia (Ov. *Fast.* 3.268). The point here is that the oak-tree's accoutrements plainly showed its sanctity and should have been respected by Erysichthon.

745   **uoti argumenta potentum** The final word in the line is a con-
jecture by a renaissance humanist for the transmitted *poten-
tis*. Hollis (1970, 135 ad loc.) translates "proofs of men who
had gained their desire," and explains *uoti* as objective gen.,
depending on *potentum*.

746–47   **saepe . . . | saepe** Ovid emphasizes the sanctity of the oak-tree
with the rhetorical device of ANAPHORA as well as by the Dryads' attendance on the tree.

746   **Dryades** Greek nom. f. pl.

duxere = *duxerunt*; cf. *circuiere* for *circuierunt*, 748

747   **manibus nexis** abl. absolute, "they linked hands"

ex ordine "in order"

747–48   **trunci | circuiere modum** "they encircled the tree-trunk's ex-
tent," i.e., the Dryads embraced the tree's circumference

748–49   **ulnas | quinque ter** an "ell" was a poetic measure of length,
defined by the *OLD* (s.v.) as the span of the outstretched arm;
i.e., from elbow (Latin *ulna*) to fingertip, about eighteen inch-
es. "Thrice five ells" would therefore yield a circumference for
the oak-tree of about twenty-two and a half feet, as Hollis suggests (1970, 135 ad loc).

749   **nec non et** = *et*, a Varronian phrase that Vergil elevated to
grand epic style in the *Aeneid*.

749–50   **cetera tantum | silua sub hac, silua quantum fuit herba sub
omni** "There was as much of the rest of the forest beneath this
tree as there was grass beneath the whole forest." Ovid com-
presses into these lines three rhetorical figures: HYPERBATON
(interlocking word order), CHIASMUS of case (*silua . . . hāc,
siluā . . . herba*) and the formally balanced cola *silua sub hāc
. . . herba sub omnī*.

751   **ferrum** = the axe of 741 (cf. 742), since *securis* is difficult to
put into dactylic hexameter

Triopeïus = Erysichthon, "son of Triopas"

illa abl. of separation with *abstinuit* in the following line

752–53 **iubet ... | ... iussos** Ovid favors this kind of verbal play (AD-NOMINATIO); cf. 4.732, another play with pple. and verb.

753 **ab uno** abl. of separation with abl. absolute *rapta securi* in the following line

754 **sceleratus, -a, -um** adj. modifying Triopeïus, subject of *edidit*; best translated adverbially, "wickedly." Ovid continues to emphasize Erysichthon's impiety.

755 **deae** dat. of agent with the pf. pass. pple. *dilecta*

licebit introduces a subordinate clause with subjunctive (*sit*, 756), but is best translated concessively as "though"

755–56 "Though she be not only beloved by the goddess but even the goddess herself, she will now touch the ground with her leafy summit." Erysichthon's blasphemous words are truer than he realizes: the tree is beloved by the goddess and she will avenge his impiety.

757 **obliquos dum telum librat in ictus** "while he balances his weapon for transverse blows"

in prep. + acc., here indicating purpose

758 **contremuit gemitumque dedit** Note the anthromorphism of the tree's response. Ovid continues to emphasize both the sanctity of the tree and the blasphemy of Erysichthon in the details with which he describes the tree's response to the assault.

Deoïa "of or belonging to Demeter"; nom. f. sing. adj. derived from Demeter's Greek byname *Dēō*

759 The ANAPHORA of *pariter* underlines the parallelism of the growing pallor of the tree's foliage and acorns.

pallescere complementary infinitive with *coepere* (= *coepe-runt*) in the following line, which also governs *ducere*

760 Entirely spondaic except for the fifth foot, the line effectively conveys the spectators' tension and the gravity of Erysichthon's offence.

761 **cuius** connective rel., of the tree; translate as *quercūs* with *in trunco*

762-63   **haud aliter ... | quam** "by no means otherwise ... than," introducing a grand epic SIMILE

762   **discusso cortice** abl. of separation

763-64   **quam solet ... | ... abrupta cruor e ceruice profundi** "than blood is accustomed to gush forth from the ruptured neck"; *profundi*, pres. pass. infinitive, lit. "to be poured forth"

    ante aras ingens ubi uictima taurus | concidit "when a huge bull falls, a sacrificial victim, before the altars." Such bull SIMILES are a convention of the highest epic style (cf. *Il.* 20.403–5, *Aen.* 2.223–24). Ovid represents Erysichthon's felling of the tree as a corrupted sacrifice in its sacrilegious blasphemy.

765   **obstipuere omnes** Ovid contrasts the appropriate, god-fearing reaction of Erysichthon's attendants with their master's impiety. The verb (= *obstipuerunt*) is a favorite of Vergil's in the *Aeneid*, often used to describe Aeneas' astonishment at a supernatural event. Ovid enhances the Vergilian pedigree of the verb by giving the line a characteristically Vergilian shape: Hollis (1970, 136–37) comments "-*ēre* + (e.g.) *omnes*, + -*que* is a Vergilian pattern," comparing *Aen.* 2.1 *conticuere omnes, intentique ora tenebant.*

    omnes ... omnibus The rhetorical device of POLYPTOTON is a favorite of Ovid's: see Wills 1996, 222–42.

    aliquis ... ex omnibus The contrast of one vs. many is another epic commonplace, popularized in Latin epic by Vergil and enthusiastically taken up by his successors: see Hardie 1993, 19–56.

766   **nefas** Ovid continues to insist on the theme of Erysichthon's blasphemy.

    bipennem "axe," another synonym for *securis*

767   **-que** One of Ovid's favorite mannerisms is to connect a new clause containing direct discourse by attaching the enclitic conj. -*que* to the first word of the speech rather than to the verb of speaking (here *dixit* at line end), which is, strictly speaking, coordinate with *aspicit* at the beginning of the line.

mentis ... piae objective gen. with *praemia*

768   **Thessalus** Erysichthon was Thessalian, a people notorious in myth for barbarism.

769   **detruncat ... caedit** Ovid employs verbs with connotations of battlefield slaughter to describe not only Erysichthon's murder of his attendant but also his felling of Ceres' sacred tree; for the verb *caedit*, cf. *caedunt*, also of felling trees, at Enn. *Ann.* 175, in this volume. Ovid seems to pun on *truncus* (used of the tree-trunk at 747, 761) in his use of *detruncat*.

771   **Cereri** dat. with adj.

772   **tibi** dat. with compound verb

       factorum ... tuorum objective gen. with *poenas*

773   **nostri ... leti** objective gen. with *solacia*, which is in apposition to the acc. + infinitive construction in 772

774   **persequitur** prefix *per-* emphasizes Erysichthon's determination to pursue his criminal impiety in the face of every warning; cf. *scelus* here and *sceleratus* of Erysichthon above, 754.

774-75   **labefacta ... | ... adducta** both nom. sing. f. pf. pass. pple., modifying *arbor*. Erysichthon is so determined to fell the tree that he uses both an axe and ropes to pull the tree down.

774-76   The sound effects of the passage recall those in the tree-felling scenes of Ennius (*Ann.* 175–79) and Vergil (*Aen.* 6.179–82), though Ovid has condensed the treatment of the actual felling of the tree still further, from Ennius' five lines and Vergil's four to two and a half.

❧ *Manilius, ASTRONOMICA 5.574–615*
Perseus fights a sea-monster to rescue Andromeda

The shadowy figure of Manilius, apparently a younger contemporary of Ovid who wrote an *Astronomica* at the end of the reign of Augustus and outset of that of Tiberius, offers an interesting and understudied example of didactic epic in the early Principate. While his didactic subject and form align him with the model of Vergil in the *Georgics*, the passage included here illustrates his considerable debt to Ovidian epic in subject-matter, theme, and literary style.

574   **cognouit ab ipsa** The subject of the verb is Perseus, who learns from Andromeda herself (= *ipsa*) the reason for her exposure in chains on the cliff.

575   **in thalamos . . . uadere** lit. "enter the marriage chamber," by METONYMY for "enter marriage"; *uadere* is complementary infinitive with *destinat* (cf. Ov. *Met.* 8.157–58, in this volume).

      per bellum . . . ponti "through war with the sea"; *ponti* is objective gen. depending on *bellum*.

576   **altera si Gorgo ueniat** "even if another Gorgon should come"; protasis of fut. less vivid condition. Perseus has already proven his heroic mettle by killing Medusa and so is confident that he could win another such contest.

      illa causal abl. with *territus*, describing Perseus; "not frightened at that prospect"

577   **flentis . . . parentis** acc. pl. m., direct object of *recreat*

578   **pactusque maritam** "and having negotiated for his bride"; *maritam* is direct object of pf. act. pple. of deponent *paciscor*.

579   **remeat** pres. act. indicative of *remeo* (1), "return"

580   **longo . . . agmine** descriptive abl.

581   **caput** subject of both *eminet* and *uomit*; the latter verb recalls Ov. *Met.* 4.729 (in this volume).

582   **scindentis** gen. sing. f. pres. act. pple., of the sea-monster "cleaving" the waves, with direct object *undas*

pelagus Greek acc. n. sing., direct object of *uomit*; acc. again and direct object at 585, 591, 603

582–83 **circumsonat aequor | dentibus, inque ipso rapidum mare nauigat ore** "The sea sounds from the gnashing of the beast's teeth, and the swift sea floats in its very mouth." Manilius' HYPERBOLE recalls Ovid's description of the sea-monster greedily trying to catch Perseus in its teeth (*Met.* 4.724, in this volume).

584 **immensis torquibus** descriptive abl.

585 **Phorcus** = "the sea," by METONYMY. The father of the Gorgons and the Graeae, Phorcus was said to have been transformed into a sea-god; his association with Medusa gives Manilius' use of his name for "ocean" extra point.

586 **ruentem** of the sea-monster

587 **infelix uirgo** The phrase recalls the emotional intensity of neoteric poetry (cf. Verg. *Aen.* 6.456 of Dido, in this volume) and invites our sympathy with the "unhappy maiden."

sub uindice tanto "under the protection of such a hero"; cf. 606 *pro uindice tali*

588 **quae tua tunc fuerat facies!** "What then was your demeanor!" The Latin poets seem to use the plpf. not infrequently as an aorist, especially in the report of a rapid succession of events.

quam exclamatory use of the rel. adv., "how!"

589–92 "How your limbs lost all their strength when from the hollow rocks you saw with your own eyes your destiny, the avenging monster swimming toward you bearing the sea before him! How small a prize for the sea were you!"

589 **ut** exclamatory use of the interr. adv., "how!"

toto . . . sanguine abl. of separation with *caruerunt*

591 **tibi** dat. with *adnantem*, pres. act. pple. of compound verb

poenam abstract (punishment) for concrete (the sea-monster sent to punish Cassiope's pride)

592 **quassis . . . alis** abl. absolute, "flapping his wing(ed sandal)s"

593   **semet** = *se*, strengthened with intensifying suffix -*met*; acc.
      m. sing. of the reflex. pron., direct object of deponent *iaculor*
      caelo abl. of place from which, without prep.

594   "burying the sword stained with the Gorgon (Medusa)'s
      blood" in the sea-monster; a golden line.
      Gorgoneo abl. sing. n. adj. modifying *sanguine*; for the use of
      an adj. derived from a proper name, characteristic of high epic
      style, cf. Cat. 64.77, Verg. *Aen.* 6.14 (both in this volume). The
      adj. first appears in extant Latin in Vergil's *Aeneid* of the Fury
      Allecto's poison (*Aen.* 7.341) and next in Ovid's *Metamorpho-
      ses* of the Gorgons' house (*Met.* 4.779).

595–97 "The monster comes up to meet him, turns and raises its face
      from the deep and, supporting itself on twisted coils, it leaps
      into the air and bears itself aloft along its whole length."

595   **illa** = *belua* (608); cf. 598, 601. Manilius specifies the sea-
      monster as a "whale," *cetus* (Greek *kêtos*), at 600.

596   **tortis . . . orbibus** dat. pl. m., with compound verb *innitor*

597   **sublimis** nom. sing. f. adj., modifying *illa*; cf. Ovid's wounded
      and rearing sea-monster at *Met.* 4.721

598–600 "But as far as the monster comes up, having launched itself
      from the deep, Perseus always flies back up just as much and
      through the yielding air he mocks the monster and lashes its
      face as it comes up."

598   **profundo** abl. of place from which, without prep.

599   **reuolat . . . ludit** Perseus is the subject.

600   **ceti subeuntis** possessive gen.
      uerberat Manilius recalls Ovid's use of the same verb at *Met.*
      4.727 (in this volume).

602   **uani** nom. pl. m., best translated adverbially: the beast's teeth
      gnash "vainly" without inflicting a wound.

603   **ecflat** < *ex* + *flo* (1), "breathe out," taking *pelagus* as direct
      object
      uolantem acc. sing. m., of Perseus

604   **exstillat** < *ex* + *stillo* (1), "let fall in drops," taking *pontum* (= *pelagus*) as direct object and in CHIASTIC word order with *ecflat . . . pelagus* in the preceding line

605   **pugnam pugnandi** FIGURA ETYMOLOGICA

       pugnandi causa cf. Ov. *Met.* 4.739 *causa laboris*, also of Andromeda (in this volume)

       puella = Andromeda, nom. sing. f. in apposition to *causa*

606   **sui** gen. sing. f. with *oblita*, "forgetting herself"

607   **animoque magis quam corpore pendet** "she hangs in more suspense in her mind than in her body," i.e., she is more worried about Perseus' fate than her own because she has fallen in love with the hero; a witty epigram (SENTENTIA) worthy of Ovid

       animo . . . corpore both abl. of respect

608   **confossis . . . membris** abl. absolute, "its limbs fatally pierced"

609   **maris** gen. with *plena*

610   near golden line of the abVBA variety

       uasto . . . corpore instrumental abl., "with its huge body"; *corpus* verges on our sense of its English cognate, "corpse"

611   **terribilis . . . uidenda** nom. sing. f., modifying *belua*

       ore instrumental abl. with gerundive *uidenda*

612   **marmore** = sea

613   **maior** a "greater" hero now because he has just dispatched a second monster

614   **uinclis** = *uinculis* by SYNCOPE; instrumental abl.

615   **desponsam . . . nupturam** acc. sing. f., pf. pass. pple. and fut. act. pple. respectively, both modifying *puellam* in the preceding line; Andromeda was betrothed to Perseus and will be able to marry him because of his wedding gift to her of her life.

       magna . . . dote = *uita*, instrumental abl.

∾ *Lucan*, BELLUM CIVILE 2.1–15
Proem to Book 2

The proem to the second book of Lucan's "anti-Vergilian" civil war poem takes up the language and themes of the proem to the epic as a whole and well illustrates Lucan's opposition to the institution of the principate under the Julio-Claudian dynasty. (The poem was published posthumously as a result of Nero's ban on its circulation during the poet's lifetime.) The passage included here shows the rhetorical quality of Lucan's poetry, censured by Quintilian, in his use of pointed EPIGRAMS (*SENTENTIAE*) and other figures of speech, and is of particular interest in the adaptation of Stoic cosmological theory to Latin epic; in this regard, it offers an illustrative counterweight to Lucretius' Epicurean proem (1.1–43, in this volume).

1–4   **iamque . . . manifestaque . . . legesque . . . indixitque** the book opens with four clauses, each connected by *-que*. The first three clauses increase in length, a neat example of the rhetorical figure of *TRICOLON CRESCENDO* (in which the three cola increase in length); but the fourth clause abruptly deflates this familiar pattern, as it is both extra to and shorter than the preceding clauses.

belli | signa . . . | . . . nefas these words connect the proem of the second book to the opening lines of the work as a whole, where Lucan undertakes to narrate "wars more than civil in the fields of Thessaly" (*bella per Emathios plus quam ciuilia campos*, 1.1), "worldwide guilt" (*commune nefas*, 1.6), and "standards facing hostile standards" (*infestisque obuia signis | signa*, 1.6–7). See *A Lucan Reader*.

1   **irae . . . deum** for wrath as the traditional theme of epic, see my note on Verg. *Aen.* 1.4. In the hyperbolic world of Lucan's epic, anger animates all the gods, not just a single deity as in Vergil's *Aeneid* or Homer's *Odyssey*. Although Lucan does not deploy the gods as characters in his epic, he often reports supernatural events as portents of divine favor or disfavor. In this, his poem is consistent with Stoic philosophical beliefs,

which held that the gods sent omens to warn men when they embarked on wrongdoing and to deter them from it.

3   A golden line of the form abVAB. Paradoxically, Lucan employs a line-type remarkable for the symmetry of its order to describe the overthrow of order into monstrous chaos.

monstrifero compound adj. in the highest epic style; for the suffix *-fer* in Latin epic, see my note on Lucr. 1.3.

tumultu instrumental abl. The noun was idiomatic for "civil riot" in Latin usage; here Lucan figures Roman political upheaval as infecting the universe.

4   **indixit . . . nefas** the verb is regularly employed in formal Roman declarations of war, but Lucan strains its sense when he has Nature "proclaim wickedness."

tibi dat. of interest with *uisum* [supply *est*] . . . *addere* (5). The verb *uideo* is used idiomatically in the passive with dat. + infinitive (*addere*); translate "why did you decide to add . . . "

rector Olympi = Jupiter. Lucan frequently employs APOSTROPHE (*rector* is vocative, *Olympi* objective gen.) for emotional effect.

5   **sollicitis . . . mortalibus** dat. of indirect object with *addere*

6   **noscant** subjunctive in an explanatory clause introduced by *ut*, with the subject supplied from *sollicitis . . . mortalibus* in the previous line: "Why have you resolved to add this concern—that they know . . .—to the anxieties of men?"

7–13   **siue . . . siue** Lucan offers two alternatives, each inflected through contemporary philosophy: 7–11 rehearses the Stoic view of the universe as ordered by a benevolent deity while 12–13 sets out an Epicurean view of the world in which everything is contingent and events happen purely by chance.

7   **parens rerum** The phrase inevitably recalls Lucretius' *alma Venus* (Lucr. 1.2, in this volume) in her guise as a cosmogonic deity who governs the universe (cf. Lucr.1.21 *quae quoniam rerum naturam sola gubernas*, in this volume); but it is also conventional in Stoic discussions of Nature.

8   **materiamque rudem** acc. of direct object with *recepit*, coordinate with *informia regna* in the preceding line. The phrase recalls Ovid's description of Chaos as *rudis indigestaque moles* (*Met.* 1.7, in this volume).

  flamma cedente abl. absolute. The phrase alludes to the Stoic conception of the birth of the world out of universal conflagration, which recedes to the edge of the atmosphere and then, after the prescribed number of generations (cf. *saecula iussa* below, 10), returns to destroy the world again (*ekpyrosis*).

9–10   **qua cuncta coercet | . . . lege** the antecedent (*lege*, instrumental abl.) follows its relative clause; *qua* is also instrumental abl.

10–11   **saecula iussa ferentem | . . . mundum** *Ferentem* goes with *mundum* (acc., direct object) and governs *saecula iussa*, also acc., direct object.

11   A near golden line; note the position of *diuisit* at the CAESURA, underlining its meaning.

  fatorum: construe with *saecula iussa* in the preceding line

  inmoto . . . limite instrumental abl., "unmovable limit"; negative pf. pass. pple. *immoto* is used here with gerundive force.

12–13   **fors incerta uagatur | fertque refertque uices** *Fors* is the subject of all three verbs, *uices* is acc., direct object, only of the latter two.

13   **fertque refertque** paired verbs are coordinated by paired epic *-que*, an Ovidian touch (cf., e.g., Ov. *Met.* 8.163, in this volume).

  habet "controls"

14–15   Lucan offers three variations on his theme, in another TRICOLON but this time an isocolon (three clauses of equal length).

  sit . . . sit . . . | . . . liceat 3rd sing. pres. act. jussive subjunctives

14   **quodcumque paras . . . subitum** the relative clause is the subject of the first *sit*; *subitum* is predicate nom.

  caeca = *nescia*; predicate nom. taking objective gen. *futuri . . . fati* (14–15)

15   **timenti** = *menti hominum*; dat. with *liceat*

∾ *Valerius Flaccus, ARGONAUTICA 2.497–537*
Hercules fights a sea-monster to rescue Hesione

Quintilian commented that Valerius' death deprived Rome of a promising talent, and the passage included here bears out his judgment. The selection shows Valerius adapting Ovid's Perseus episode to the myth of Hercules' rescue of Hesione, the daughter of Laomedon exposed to a sea-monster. Valerius' innovation is particularly clear by comparison with Manilius' more pedestrian retelling of the Ovidian myth.

497   **dat . . . signum Neptunus** Valerius characterizes the sea-god anachronistically as the Roman magistrate who gives the signal for the chariot race to start; for the anachronism, cf. Enn. *Ann.* 79–81 (in this volume).

498   **monstriferi . . . sinus** nom. pl. m., subject of *mugire*, historic infinitive. Valerius attributes the monster's bellowing to the gulf that it crosses to reach the exposed princess. For compound adj. in *-fer*, cf. 506 and see my note on Lucr. 1.3.

         Sigea . . . pestis nom. sing. f., "the plague of Sigeum," of the sea-monster. Sigeum is a promontory in the Troad.

499   **adglomerare** "rolled [the channel's waters] into a mass"; historic infinitive

499–502 Valerius describes the sea-monster with its terrifying attributes: flashing eyes, threatening teeth, long tail, and high neck.

499–500 **stellantia glauca | lumina nube tremunt** "its starry eyes flicker in a blue-grey cloud"; *glauca . . . nube* is an unusual abl., perhaps best taken as abl. of attendant circumstance, describing the sea-spray that the beast generates as it moves through the waves.

500–501 **ordine curua trisulco | fulmineus quatit ora fragor** "and a thundering crash shakes its mouth, curved with triple rank" of teeth; *trisulco*, lit. "three-forked," suggests the sea-monster's affinity with the monstrous snakes of classical myth (e.g., Ladon, the dragon that guards the apples of the Hesperides).

501   **pelagoque remenso** abl. absolute

502   **passos . . . sinus rapit ardua ceruix** "the high neck moves
        the extended coils along," after the tail has returned to its
        starting point and the coils lie flat. The sea-monster's prog-
        ress across the channel is described in terms of that of a
        snake over land.

503   **illam** = *pestem*; cf. *illa*, of the sea-monster (518, 522).

        incumbentem sc. *ponto* (dat.); the sea-monster is "leaning
        over" the sea.

503–4   **pontus | prosequitur** The "sea accompanies" the monster like
        an escort.

        lateri dat. with compound verb *adsultans*

504–5   **trepidisque ruentem | litoribus sua cogit hiems** "and its own
        storm drives it headlong to the apprehensive shores"

        trepidis . . . | litoribus dat. of direction with *ruentem*

505   **sua . . . hiems** The monster generates a storm in and of itself
        as it moves across the sea.

505–8   Valerius compares the storm generated by the sea-monster
        to the winds Notus (a south wind) and Africus (a southwest
        wind), and to the waves Orion causes.

506–7   **non Africus alto | tantus ouat** "the African wind does not
        exult so greatly over the high sea"; *tantus*, nom. sing. m. modi-
        fying *Africus*, is best translated adverbially.

        alto = *mari*, local abl.

507–8   **patriisque manus cum plenus habenis | Orion bipedum
        flatu mare tollit equorum** "or when Orion, with his hands
        full of his father's reins, raises the sea at the breath of the two-
        footed horses"

507   **patriis . . . habenis** abl. with adj. *plenus*

        -que disjunctive; translate "or."

        manus acc. of respect with *plenus*, nom. sing. m. adj. modify-
        ing *Orion* in the next line

        cum temporal subordinating conj.

508   **Orion** Greek nom. sing. m. In myth, Orion is Poseidon's son and so Valerius extends the application of the image of Poseidon driving his chariot over the sea to his son. Also relevant to Valerius' description is the setting of the constellation Orion in November at the beginning of the stormy winter season.

      bipedum . . . equorum = *hippocampi*, "sea-horses"; mythical marine creatures, with the front legs of a horse and a fish tail behind

      flatu instrumental abl.

509–11   Valerius turns from the sea-monster to describe Hercules' excitement at the prospect of combat with the monster, as seen through the eyes of Hercules' squire, Telamon.

509   **ducem** = Hercules, acc. subject with pres. act. infinitive *crudescere* ("grow fierce/savage"), depending on *stupet* ("is amazed/astonished") in the next line (510); the subject of *stupet* is *Aeacides* (511), Aeacus' son Telamon.

      placitae furiis . . . pugnae "out of frenzy for his chosen combat"; *furiis* is abl. of cause, *placitae pugnae* subjective gen.

510   **surgentem . . . immanem** acc. sing. m., direct object of *stupet* (supply *ducem*), describing Hercules "swelling" with muscles and "huge" under arms; *toris* and *paratu* are abl. of respect with *surgentem* and *immanem* respectively.

511   **pulsent . . . ut** The *ut* clause is also governed by *stupet*, in an extension of that verb's usage; translate "and how the heavy quiver strikes his back."

513   **scopulo** dat. of direction with compound verb *insiluit*; cf. Perseus' movements at Ov. *Met.* 4.730–35 (in this volume).

      motumque e sedibus aequor acc. sing. n., direct object of *horruit* in the next line; "the sea stirred up from the bottom." Hercules is the subject of *horruit*.

515–17   Another SIMILE, this time comparing the sea-monster to Boreas (the north wind). Boreas is the subject of the verbs *tollitur* (516), *praecipitat* (517), and *tenet* (517); the sea-monster (*illa*, 518) is the subject of the verbs *promouet* and *subit* (519).

515   **qualis ubi** "just as when"

a . . . conuallibus abl. of separation

516   **tollitur** "rises"; translate as a middle form rather than passive.

        Rhipaea per ardua a mythical mountain range in the extreme
        north

516–17 **uolucres . . . nubes | praecipitat** "sends the clouds flying"; *uo-
        lucres*, acc. pl. f., is used predicatively of *nubes*.

517   **piceo . . . caelo** "in a pitch-black cloud"

518   **illa** = *pestis*, of the sea-monster; cf. 522 below.

        simul molem horrificam scopulosaque terga The sea-monster
        advances its "terrifying mass and rock-covered back" together,
        as it propels itself through the waves.

519   **ingenti . . . umbra** "with his huge shadow"

        subit The motion of Valerius' sea-monster imitates that of
        Manilius' (cf. *Astr.* 5.595, in this volume).

519   **Ide** Greek nom. sing. f., subject of *intremere*, historic infini-
        tive; Ida was the name of a mountain range in Phrygia, a
        center of worship of Cybele (the Idaean mother; cf. 536). The
        sea-monster's approach causes land and sea to shudder with
        fear and therefore shake to their foundations.

520   **inlidi** historic infinitive (pres. pass. in form), with nom. pl. f.
        subject *rates*; "ships were dashed," *sc.* "against the rocks"

        pronae . . . turres nom. pl. f. subject of historic infinitive *re-
        surgere*; the sea-monster's approach causes the towers to tilt
        forward and then sway back.

521–22 "Hercules seizes his bow and closes in with a whole cloud of
        arrows."

521   **Alcides** Greek nom. sing. m., of Hercules; cf. 533. In myth,
        Alcaeus was the son of Perseus and father of Amphitryo,
        the mortal father of Hercules; both the name Alcaeus and
        the patronymic Alcides are derived from the Greek word for
        "strength/prowess/courage" (*alkê*).

        pharetrae lit. "quiver," by METONYMY for the arrows it contains

522   **illa** = *pestis*, nom. sing. f. subject of *mouetur*

sede abl. of separation with *mouetur*; the monster's home is the sea.

523   The sea-monster's unshakable mass is compared to Mt. Eryx in Sicily, a frequent comparandum for heroic stature in Latin epic: cf. Verg. *Aen.* 12.701–3 (in this volume).

uelint potential subjunctive in rel. clause

uallibus dat. of direction with compound *deferre*

524   **telo uolucri** dat. of purpose with *utilis*, "for a flying weapon"; Hercules has to shift tactics as the sea-monster nears the shore.

aer "expanse of air" = "space"

525–26 **fremitus . . . insania . . . | et tacitus pudor** three subjects, with the verb *sunt* understood. Hercules groans, recognizes the madness of his vain undertaking, and is silently ashamed.

526   Valerius models Hesione's response to Hercules' danger on Andromeda's reaction to Perseus' plight at Man. *Astr.* 5.587–92 (in this volume).

pallescere historic infinitive

uirgo = Hesione, daughter of the Trojan king Laomedon, a byword for perjury in classical myth. After he refused to pay Apollo and Poseidon for building the Trojan walls, Poseidon sent the sea-monster to ravage Troy, but the exposure of Hesione saved the city.

527   **manu** abl. of separation

527–28 **scopulos . . . | respicit** Valerius' Hercules imitates Ovid's Perseus (*conspexit scopulum*, Ov. *Met.* 4.731, in this volume).

528   **quantum** "as big a piece" of the rock; acc. sing. n., direct object of *impulerit* in the next line (529). The antecedent is *saxa* in the previous line; cf. *saxo* at 533.

528–29 **uentis adiuta uetustas | . . . pontiue fragor** "age, helped by the winds, or the roar of the sea"; *uetustas* and *fragor* are alternate subjects of *impulerit*. Both wind and sea are commonly adduced in classical literature as causing the erosion of rocks over time.

529   **impulerit** potential subjunctive in a correlative clause of comparison introduced by *quantum*

      ponti subjective gen. with *fragor*

529–30 **tantum . . . imi | . . . a sede maris** "so big a piece from the bottom of the deep ocean"

530   **concutiens** *sc.* Hercules

      agmine toto abl. of manner; Valerius is indebted to Manilius' description of the sea-monster that menaces Andromeda, *Astr.* 5.580 (in this volume).

530–31 **iam . . . | . . . iam** While Hercules provides himself with a weapon for close combat, the sea-monster is nearly upon Hesione.

531   **pistris** = *pristis*, a Greek word denoting a large fish but frequently employed in Latin epic in the sense of "sea-monster"; cf. my note on Ov. *Met.* 4.706.

      miseraeque inhiat iam proxima praedae "And the monster opens its mouth now very close to its pitiable prey." The adj. *proxima* modifies *pistris* and is best translated predicatively.

      praedae = Hesione; cf. Manilius' characterization of Andromeda (*Astr.* 5.592, in this volume).

532   **mediis . . . aquis** abl. of separation with *elatus*; the subject is Alcides (= Hercules) in the next line. "Hercules stands high in the midst of the waters."

      recipit "awaits"

533   **prior, prius** adj., modifying Alcides; best translated adverbially, "first"

      surgentia colla poetic pl., direct object of *obruit* in the next line

534   **nodosi roboris** Hercules' "gnarled club" is his characteristic weapon in myth.

535   The line does not scan as transmitted by the MSS; something is missing before or after *defertur*. The editor of the Stuttgart Teubner text (Ehlers 1980) records *praeceps defertur*

and *defertur belua* in his apparatus criticus, and the latter is an attractive possibility since Manilius refers to the sea-monster that menaces Andromeda as *belua* at *Astr.* 5.608 (in this volume).

536   **totis . . . uadis** abl. of place where; translate *uadis* "at the bottom of the sea."

resoluta "outstretched," of the sea-monster; nom. sing. f. subject of *defertur* in the previous line

536   **Idaea . . . mater** = Cybele

537   **chorus** = Cybele's worshippers, the Corybantes

summis . . . collibus local abl.

ulularunt = *ululauerunt*, by SYNCOPE; best taken in the unusual sense, "howl for joy." Cybele and her attendants celebrate the death of the sea-monster that has threatened her home near Troy.

∾ *Statius, THEBAID 1.401–27*
Duel between Polynices and Tydeus

Statius wrote extensively in the genre of epic, composing both a *Thebaid* and an unfinished *Achilleid*, and, as his birthday poem to Lucan reveals (*Silvae* 2.7), he was a connoisseur of the genre. His account of the duel between Oedipus' son Polynices (exiled from Thebes) and Oeneus' son Tydeus (exiled from Calydon) outside the Argive King Adrastus' palace draws on earlier epic, especially Vergilian, treatments of heroic combat but varies the commonplace scene significantly in the outcome, in which the two heroes become best of friends and brothers-in-law. The two heroes are driven to seek shelter from stormy weather on the porch of Adrastus' palace.

401   **fato** instrumental abl., characterizing Tydeus by reference to Aeneas. Vergil characterizes the latter as commissioned by destiny to go into exile (*fato profugus*, Verg. *Aen.* 1.2, in this volume), while Statius here describes the mythical Greek hero

Tydeus, son of Oeneus the King of Calydon and his second
wife Periboia, going into exile after killing his brother Agrius
(cf. *fraterni sanguinis* in the next line). Tydeus went to Argos
where he was welcomed by the Argive king Adrastus and
married his daughter Deipyle.

Calydona Greek acc. sing. m., direct object of *relinquens* (to
be construed with Olenius Tydeus in the next line); the Aeto-
lian city of Calydon

402   **Olenius, -a, -um** adj. Olenos was the name of a town in Aetolia, from which Statius derives an ornamental epithet for his
hero.

fraterni sanguinis objective gen. with *conscius horror* in the
next line

403–4 **eadem . . . | lustra terit** Tydeus "traverses the same rough
country" as Polynices.

404   **dequestus** The compound occurs first in imperial Latin epic
and intensifies the emotional pitch of the simplex, *queror*; like
queror, dequeror takes acc. of direct object, here *similes . . .
Notos . . . et imbres.*

405–6 **glaciem et . . . | ora comasque** acc., direct objects of pple. *ge-
rens* (406)

405   **tergo** dat. of direction with pple. of compound verb *infusam*
liquentia "dripping"; acc. pl. n. with *ora* in the next line

406   **uno tegmine** abl. of place with *subit*, "the sole shelter" from
the storm, i.e., describing the Argive king Adrastus' porch
cuius partitive gen. with *partem* in the next line; *tegmine* is
the antecedent

407   **fusus** nom. sing. m., pf. pass. pple., modifying *prior hospes*.
Oedipus' son Polynices, exiled from Thebes by his brother
Eteocles, is the "earlier stranger."
humo gelida local abl.

408   **ambobus** dat. of indirect object; lit. "but here Chance brought
bloody rage to both," i.e., to Polynices and Tydeus.

409 **passi** Supply *sunt*; "they did not tolerate [the idea of] warding off the night with a shared roof."

defendere pres. act. infinitive, complementary with *passi sunt*, used here in its primary sense of "ward off"

409–10 **sociis . . . | culminibus** instrumental abl. in poetic pl.

410–13 Statius articulates the stages of the brawl with temporal advs.: *paulum*, "briefly"; *mox*, "soon"; *tum*, "then."

410 **alternis** adv., "one after the other, by turns"

in uerba minasque prep. *in* + acc. of purpose, "for shouts and threats"

411 **ut** temporal subordinating conj., "when"

iactis sermonibus abl. absolute with temporal force, lit. "after taunts had been flung"

412 **intumuere** 3ʳᵈ pl. pf. indicative act., alternate form

413 **exertare . . . lacessere** both historic infinitives; "they expose their shoulders and challenge [one another] to naked combat."

414 **ille** = Polynices

gradu abl. of respect with *celsior*

in prep. + acc. (*procera . . . membra*), expressing proportion (*OLD* s.v. A5); lit. "in proportion to his long limbs"

415 **annorum** gen. with adj. *integer*, "young in years"

uiribus abl. of respect

infra adv., lit. "inferior in quality"

416 **Tydea** Greek acc. sing. m., direct object of *fert*

fert animus cf. Ov. *Met.* 1.1 (in this volume)

infusa nom. sing. f., pf. pass. pple., with *maior . . . uirtus* in the next line

417 A golden line of the type abVBA; for the term, see my note on Cat. 64.59. Statius' remark about Tydeus' small stature but large fighting spirit recalls Homer (*Il.* 5.801), where Athena tells Tydeus' son Diomedes how Tydeus slew the fifty men Eteocles sent to ambush him after his embassy to the Theban court on behalf of Polynices (recounted by Statius in *Theb.* 2).

418   **crebros ictus** acc. pl. m., direct object of *ingeminant* in the next line

circum prep. + acc.; unusually **circum** follows both its objects, *ora* and *caua tempora*

419   **obnixi** nom. pl. m., describing Polynices and Tydeus as they fight; cf. Verg. *Aen.* 12.721 (in this volume), the bull SIMILE in the context of the duel of Aeneas and Turnus, where the bulls, like the heroes, are struggling "with all their might"

instar defective n. sing. noun, appearing only in the nom. and acc. (as here); "likness, size." It often takes the gen. case and is normally used in apposition, as here; translate "like darts or Rhipaean hail."

420   **Rhipaeae** gen. sing. f., modifying *grandinis* in the previous line; for the mountain range, see my note on Val. Fl. 2.516.

flexo ... genu instrumental abl. n. sing. for pl., of both heroes

uacua ilia "bare flanks"

421–22   **non aliter quam ... | cum** "not otherwise than when ... ," introducing a wrestling SIMILE that will become a reality in the funeral games of *Theb.* 6, where Tydeus defeats Agylleus.

421   **Pisaeo ... Tonanti** dat. of indirect object; the "Pisaean Thunderer" is Jupiter of Elis near Olympia, hence Olympian Zeus

sua lustra nom. pl. n., subject of *redeunt* in the next line; of Zeus' own festival that takes place every four years, i.e., the Olympics. Distinguish between the homonyms *lustra*, "wild place" (404 above) and "lustral period" (i.e., an event that recurs once every fixed number of years).

422   **crudis ... sudoribus** instrumental abl., "with fierce sweat"

423   **caueae dissensus** "disagreement in the audience," i.e., among the spectators

424   **exclusae ... matres** Women were not permitted to view the athletic contests at the Olympic games.

425–26   **sic alacres ... | accensi** "so the heroes, eager ... and ... roused"

425   **odio nullaque cupidine** both causal abl., with *alacres* and *accensi* respectively

      laudis objective gen. with *cupidine*

426   **intima** acc. n. pl. of the adj., used substantively, "the inmost part of the face"

427   **unca manus** lit. "the hooked hand" = the nails

      oculis cedentibus dat. with *intrat*, a post-classical usage; "and enters deep within their yielding eyes"

∾ Statius, THEBAID 6.84–117
The Argive army goes logging in an uncut forest

Although the Argive army sets out for Thebes in Book 4, determined to support Polynices' claim to the Theban throne by warfare, a drought in Nemea stalls their march through the Argolid. There the Argive leaders meet Hypsipyle, nursemaid to the Nemean princeling Opheltes, and she guides the army to water. In doing so, however, she abandons her infant charge and he is killed by a snake. The bereaved parents celebrate funeral games for their dead son, renamed Archemorus ("beginning of delay") as the first casualty of the war against Thebes. In this passage, the Argive army harvests wood for his funeral pyre, in expiation for his death. Statius imitates Ennius (*Ann.* 175–79, in this volume), Vergil (*Aen.* 6.179–82, in this volume), Ovid (*Met.* 8.741–86, in this volume), and Lucan (*BC* 3.399–452, in *Silver Latin Epic*).

84   **parte alia** local abl. Statius moves from the actions of the parents to those of the army.

84–5 **gnari . . . | auguris** subjective gen. with *monitis*, causal abl.

84–86 **exercitus instat | . . . aeriam . . . | . . . cumulare pyram** "the army presses on to raise an airy pyre"; for *insto* + complementary infinitive see *OLD* s.v. 8b.

85   **truncis . . . ruina** both abl. of material; take *nemorum*, gen. pl., with **ruina**, "with the collapse of groves."

86   **montis opus** "the size of a mountain," in apposition to *aeriam pyram*, suggesting the height of the structure; for the idiomatic usage of *opus* + gen. in this sense, see *OLD* s.v. 9d.

86–87   **quae . . . | . . . cremet** rel. clause of purpose, with pres. act. subjunctive in primary sequence

    crimina . . . | . . . atra piacula acc. pl. n., direct object of *cremet*; an example of the rhetorical figure of HENDIADYS, the use of two nouns connected by a conj. in place of noun + adj. Translate "dark expiatory offerings for the crime of the slaughtered snake and for the accursed war."

87   **infausti . . . belli** Statius characterizes the war of the Seven against Thebes as "accursed" because it is fratricidal; at its climax, Oedipus' sons Eteocles and Polynices kill one another. In *Bellum Civile*, Lucan develops the parallels between the fratricidal war of the Seven against Thebes and the fratricidal wars of Roman myth and history (Romulus and Remus, Caesar and Pompey, Antony and Octavian).

88–89   **his labor accisam Nemeen . . . | praecipitare . . . ostendere** "They labor to cut down Nemea, hurl down the shady vale of Tempe to the ground and show the groves to the Sun." Supply *est*: *his* is possessive dat. with *labor*, nom. subject of unexpressed *est*; both pres. act. infinitives are predicate nom.

88   **Nemeen** Greek acc. sing. f., with pf. pass. pple. *accisam*, lit. "Nemea cut down"; direct object of *praecipitare* in the next line

    Tempe Greek acc. n. pl., modified by adj. *umbrosa*; direct object of *praecipitare* in the next line

89   **solo** dat. of direction with *praecipitare*

    Phoebo by METONYMY for *soli*, "to the sun"; dat. of indirect object with *ostendere*

90   **sternitur** Statius signals his engagement with the model of (1) Ennius by reusing the *simplex* of an Ennian verb (*consternitur*, *Ann.* 177, in this volume) and (2) Vergil by opening the passage with a passive verb that echoes Vergil's introduction of his imitation of Ennius' passage (*itur*, *Aen.* 6.179, also in this

volume). The subject is *silua* in the next line. The adv. *extemplo*, much favored in the republican period, falls out of use in imperial Latin and its archaic flavor here pointedly underlines Statius' allusion to the Ennian passage, as does *ueteres*.

incaedua verbal adj., modifying *silua* in the next line, used elsewhere only by Ovid, when describing an uncut forest of great age and sanctity (*Am.* 3.1.1, *Fast.*1.243)

ferro instrumental abl. with the verbal idea implicit in verbal adj. *incaedua*, "unfelled," which modifies *silua* in the next line

90-91 **ueteres . . . | . . . comas** acc. of respect with *incaedua . . . silua*; lit. "a forest unfelled by iron [i.e., the axe] in respect to its ancient foliage"

91 **largae . . . umbrae** gen. of quality with *non opulentior*, "not more rich in abundant shade"

qua abl. of comparison, introducing a rel. clause whose antecedent is *silua*; for the construction, cf. below 117.

92 **Argolicos inter saltusque . . . Lycaeos** Statius' erudite geographical reference extends from the Argolid, whence four (Adrastus, Capaneus, Hippomedon, Amphiaraus) of the Seven came, to Mt. Lycaon in Arcadia, whence one (Parthenopaeus) hailed.

educta nom. sing. f., pf. pass. pple., modifying *opulentior* (for which supply *silua*); subject of *extulerat* in the next line

93 **caput** acc. sing. n., direct object of *extulerat*

stat cf. *stabat* at Ov. *Met.* 8.743 (in this volume), describing an old oak tree sacred to Ceres

sacra Supply *silua.*

senectae gen. of description with *numine*, causal abl., in the next line

94 **transgressa** pf. act. pple. of deponent verb *transgredior*, modifying *silua*

ueterno abl. of respect of a rare noun (*ueternus, -i*, m.) used by Statius here in the otherwise unparalleled sense of "old age"; see *OLD* s.v. 2.

95   **mutasse** by SYNCOPE for *mutauisse*

    superstes nom. sing. f. adj., modifying *silua*, "remaining alive after the death of another"; *OLD* s.v. 3

96   **luco** dat. with *aderat*; "a pitiable death was at hand for the grove"

97   **fugere** = *fugerunt*

    nidos tepentes acc. pl. m., direct object of *absiliunt* in the next line

98   **cadit** Like Ennius and Vergil, in his tree-felling episode Statius employs verbs that commonly appear in epic contexts of battlefield killing; see *OLD* s.v. 9, and cf. my note on Enn. *Ann.* 175.

    fagus Statius innovates in the tradition by adding the beech to the catalogue of trees felled for a funerary pyre; it is normally associated with pastoral poetry (Verg. *Buc.* 1.1) rather than epic.

99   **Chaonium . . . nemus** nom. sing. n., governed by *cadit* in the previous line. The adj. *Chaonius* refers to a district in northwestern Greece where Jupiter's famous oracle at Dodona gave responses emanating from the rustling leaves of his sacred oak-tree; translate "the oak-grove." The epithet may hint at the sanctity of the grove the Argives fell; cf. Erysichthon's impiety in felling Ceres' oak-tree (Ov. *Met.* 8.741–76, in this volume) and Caesar's in desecrating a grove sacred to the Druids (Luc. *BC* 3.399–452, in *Silver Latin Epic*).

    brumae dat. with *inlaesa*, which modifies *cupressus, -us,* f. The cypress-tree was a widespread symbol of death in the ancient Mediterranean, and at Rome Augustus had planted his Mausoleum with cypresses.

100   **procumbunt piceae** Statius quotes a hemistich from Vergil's tree-felling scene; see my note on *Aen.* 6.180. The list of trees that follows (Stat. *Theb.* 6.101–6: *orni, iliceae trabes, taxus, fraxinus, robur, abies, pinus, alnus, ulmus,* all nom.) encompasses all those mentioned by Statius' Latin epic predecessors

to offer the largest number of types, as the Flavian epicist challenges his earlier models for poetic primacy.

flammis . . . supremis dat. of indirect object with *alimenta*, which stands in apposition to *piceae*.

101   **iliceae . . . trabes** "holm-oak beams"; Statius varies Vergil's "ash beams" (*fraxineae . . . trabes*, *Aen.* 6.181, in this volume).

101-2   **metuenda . . . suco | taxus** "the yew-tree, to be feared because of its poisonous sap"; *suco* is causal abl. with gerundive *metuenda*, which modifies *taxus*.

102-3   **infandos belli potura cruores | fraxinus** "the ash-tree which will drink war's unholy gore"; fut. act. pple. *potura* modifies *fraxinus*, which like most tree-species is f. The ash-tree is conventionally associated with war as the wood from which the battle spear was made (cf. Homer's Priam "of the ash-spear").

103   **situ** causal abl., "due to rot," with *expugnabile*, an adj. that normally means "capable of being captured by assault" (*OLD* s.v.).

104   **odoro uulnere** descriptive abl., "with fragrant wound"

105   **scinditur** cf. Verg. *Aen.* 6.182 (in this volume), which also opens with this verb.

       terrae dat. of direction with *adclinant*; the subject of the verb is *intonsa cacumina* (nom. pl. n.).

106   **alnus . . . ulmus** both nom. sing. f., in apposition to *intonsa cacumina* in the previous line

       fretis . . . uitibus both dat. with adj. *amica* and *inhospita* respectively

107   **dat gemitum tellus** cf. Ov. *Met.* 8.757-73 (in this volume), where it is the sacred oak that first groans (8.758), then announces her own death and foretells Erysichthon's punishment (8.771-73); and Luc. *BC* 3.445-46 (in *Silver Latin Epic*), where the Gallic population groans at the sight of Caesar's impious assault on the Druids' grove (*gemuere uidentes | Gallorum populi*).

107-10 **non sic ... | ... cum** In a SIMILE, Statius compares the noise
of the trees falling to the ground with the roar of the winds
Boreas and Notus. His predecessors also emphasize the noise
of logging; cf. Enn. *Ann.* 178–79, Verg. *Aen.* 6.180, Ov. *Met.*
8.770 (all in this volume). Statius draws on the common Homeric SIMILE comparing the noise or frenzy of human battle to
that of the natural elements (e.g., *Il.* 14.394–99, where the roar
of battle is compared to the roar of Boreas and a forest fire).

108   **Ismara** n. pl. noun, with *euersa*, subject of *feruntur* in the previous line; Mt Ismarus is in southern Thrace.

       Boreas Greek nom. sing. m., subject of *extulit*; the north wind

       antro abl. of separation with *extulit*

109   **grassante Noto** abl. absolute; on the south wind *Notus*, see my
note on V. Fl. *Arg.* 2.505–8.

109-10 **nocturna ... | flamma** nom. sing. f., subject of *peregit* (109)

110-13 The Argive assault on the grove drives the gods of the local
countryside from their forest home: Pales, a tutelary deity of
flocks and herds (111); Silvanus, a Roman god of forests (111);
semidei, the demigods (112); and the tree Nymphs (113).

110   **flentes** nom. pl. m., with the roster of gods in the following
lines

110-11 **dilecta locorum | otia** "the beloved leisure of the place"; *di-
lecta otia* is direct object of *linquunt.*

111   **cana Pales** nom. sing. f., "silvery Pales"

       arbiter umbrae Silvanus is a connoisseur of the shady coun-
tryside; *umbrae* is objective gen. with *arbiter.*

112   **semideum** partitive gen. with *pecus*

       migrantibus ... illis dat. with *aggemit*; "the forest groans in
sympathy with them as they depart"

113   **nec** negates the main verb, *dimittunt*; the Nymphs cannot dis-
miss the trees from their embrace.

114   **ut cum** introducing another SIMILE that likens the logging of
the grove to the sack of a city

auidis uictoribus dat. of indirect object with *dedit* in the next line; "the general grants the eager victors [the opportunity] to plunder the citadel of which they have taken possession"

115   **raptare** complementary infinitive with *dedit*

       signa audita Supply *sunt.*

116   **inuenias** potential subjunctive in primary sequence, taking *dedit* (115) as a true perfect

117   **immodici** nom. pl. m., best translated adverbially: "excessively, without restraint"; Statius' moralizing comment aligns the Argive logging expedition with the impious tree-felling of Erysichthon in Ov. *Met.* 8.741–76 (in this volume) and Caesar in Luc. *BC* 3.399–452 (in *Silver Latin Epic*).

       quo abl. of comparison, introducing a relative clause whose antecedent is *fragor*

       bella gerebant Statius explicitly draws the comparison between war and logging that Ennius and Vergil leave implicit; see my notes on Enn. *Ann.* 175–79.

ᴏᴠ *Silius Italicus,* PUNICA *1.1–28*
Proem and foundation of Carthage

The final entry in the *Reader*, Silius Italicus' *Punica*, relentlessly reprises the subject matter of Ennian and Vergilian epic in a final flowering of Roman historical epic. In the proem to Silius' seventeen-book epic on Rome's second war with Carthage, the poet pays homage to the Vergilian substructure of the epic in his account of Dido's foundation of Carthage. The passage is dense with verbal echoes of the *Aeneid.*

1   **ordior arma** Silius begins his epic with a (deponent) verb meaning "begin/undertake," and his second word reprises the opening word of the *Aeneid* (1.1, in this volume); translate "I undertake to tell of arms . . ." Silius follows his tribute to Vergil in the opening line with a tribute to Lucretius in the next line, whose first word (*Aeneidum*) is the first word of *De Rerum Natura.*

quibus instrumental abl.

caelo dat. of direction

2   **Aeneadum** On the form, see my note on Lucr. 1.1; it depends on *gloria* in the preceding line.

    Oenotrius, -a, -um adj., "of or belonging to the Oenotri," a people inhabiting southern Italy in early times; Vergil sets the adj. into epic circulation in the *Aeneid*.

2–3   **ferox Oenotria iura | Carthago** an elegant CHIASMUS, with subject *ferox Carthago* (nom. f. sing.) enclosing direct object *Oenotria iura* (acc. pl. n.). It is paradoxical that "fierce Carthage" should "endure" (*patitur*) "the laws of the Oenotri."

3   **da, Musa, . . . memorare** Supply *mihi* and translate "allow me, Muse, to narrate . . . " Silius retains Vergil's syntax of imperative + vocative in the invocation of the Muse (cf. Verg. *Aen.* 1.8, with my note), but replaces *memora* with *da* in pres. act. imperative, and varies the syntax by constructing *da* with complementary infinitive *memorare*, thereby scrupulously preserving Vergil's diction. This veneration of Vergil's model, attested in Silius' personal life as well (Martial reports that he owned Vergil's tomb), is typical of the Flavian poet's compositional techniques in the *Punica*.

3–4   **decus . . . laborum | antiquae Hesperiae** "the glory of ancient Italy's exploits"; *decus* is acc. sing. n., direct object of *memorare*. With *antiquae*, Silius implicitly contrasts legendary republican morality and martial success with the decadence of his contemporary Rome. Both *labores* and *Hesperia* mark Silius' debt to Vergil in his conception of the epic. For Vergil's characterization of Aeneas as a Herculean hero who performs epic *labores*, cf. Verg. *Aen.* 1.10 (in this volume). Throughout the first half of the *Aeneid*, Vergil specifies Aeneas' destination as *Hesperia*, the "Westland" (e.g., at *Aen.* 1.530, 2.781).

4–5   **quantosque ad bella crearit | et quot Roma uiros** two indirect questions, also governed by *memorare*; translate "and how great and how many the men Rome bore for war."

4   **crearit** = *creauerit* by SYNCOPE; pf. act. subjunctive in indirect question in primary sequence (*da . . . memorare*)

5   **sacri . . . pacti** an unusual gen. of respect with *perfida*, which modifies nom. sing. f. subject *gens Cadmea* (i.e., the Carthaginians) in the next line. Roman authors conventionally characterize the Carthaginians as "treacherous" because of the history of conflict between the two empires in the three Punic Wars; see my note on Verg. *Aen.* 1.349.

     cum introduces a temporal clause.

6   **Cadmea** "of or belonging to Cadmus," son of Agenor the Phoenician (cf. 1.15 below). Silius employs the mythical genealogy to refer to the historical foundation of Carthage from the Phoenician city of Tyre.

     super prep. + abl., here in the sense "about"; Roman authors commonly characterize the Punic Wars as a contest between Rome and Carthage for hegemony over the whole of the Mediterranean.

7   **quaesitumque** Supply *est*; impers. pf. pass. indicative introducing indirect question in secondary sequence (*qua . . . poneret arce*). Translate "and for a long time it was unclear . . . "

     qua . . . arce local abl. of the interr. rel., introducing indirect question

     poneret 3rd sing. impf. act. subjunctive in indirect question in secondary sequence; the subject is *Fortuna* in the next line.

8   **Marte** by METONYMY for *bello*, instrumental abl.

9   **Ioui** dat. of indirect object with *iuratum*, which normally takes *per* + acc. The treaty was sworn "to Jupiter" rather than "by" the god.

     patrum = *Patrum*, i.e., the "Fathers," the members of the Roman Senate.

10   **Sidonii . . . duces** nom. pl. m., subject of *fregere* (= *fregerunt*), "the Sidonian generals"; Sidon was a town on the Phoenician coast.

impius Silius again refers to the Carthaginians' treachery in breaking peace-treaties with Rome; cf. *perfida* (5).

11   **placitam . . . pacem** "the peace that had won approval"

suasit Supply *eis*, of the Carthaginians; *suasit* governs complementary infinitive *rumpere* instead of introducing indirect command with *ut* + subjunctive: "the impious sword persuaded them to break the peace that had won approval."

temerando gerund in instrumental abl.; "by desecration"

12   **medio . . . bello** temporal abl. Silius specifies the subject of the poem as the second Punic War; lit. "in the middle war."

uicissim adv., "in a reciprocal manner, reciprocally"; *OLD* s.v. 3

13   **molitae** Supply *sunt*; the two "peoples" (*gentes*, nom. pl. f.) "labor to bring about" each other's "end" (*finem*) and "destruction" (*excidium*).

13–14   "and those to whom victory was granted came closer to destruction"

13   **fuere** = *fuerunt*; the subject has to be supplied from the relative clause in the following line.

periclo = *periculo*, dat. with *propius*

14   **quis** = *quibus*, dat. of indirect object with *datum*

superare pres. act. infinitive, subject of impers. verb *datum* (with which supply *est*)

14–15   **reserauit . . . arces | . . . Agenoreas, obsessa Palatia** an example of HYSTERON PROTERON, a rhetorical figure in which an item that naturally comes first is placed last. Here Silius has reversed the chronology of events in the Second Punic War: Hannibal besieged Rome (211 BCE) before Carthage sued for peace (201 BCE).

Dardanus . . . | ductor Scipio was "the Dardan general" to whom Carthage "opened her citadel" (*arces | . . . Agenoreas*). Silius employs Vergilian vocabulary in his characterization of the Romans as Trojans by ancestry; cf. *Dardanius . . . nepos Veneris*, of Ascanius, at Verg. *Aen.* 4.163 (in this volume).

arces | . . . Agenoreas The Phoenician king Agenor was the father of Cadmus, Europa, and Phoenix (the eponymous ancestor of the Phoenicians). Silius characterizes Carthage as Phoenician by applying an adj. derived from Agenor's name to the city fortress; in this he follows Vergil, who calls Carthage *Agenoris urbem* (*Aen.* 1.338, in this volume).

15 **obsessa** Supply *sunt* and construe with *Palatia* (poetic pl.); Silius names Rome's most famous hill by METONYMY for the city itself.

15–16 **uallo | . . . muris** both instrumental abl.

17–18 **causas . . . odium . . . | . . . arma** acc., all three direct objects of *aperire* (1.19)

17 **tantarum . . . irarum** objective gen. with *causas*; Silius returns directly to Vergil's proem (cf. Verg. *Aen.* 1.8, *Musa, mihi causas memora*; 1.11 *tantaene animis caelestibus irae*; both in this volume).

17–18 **perenni | . . . studio** instrumental abl.

18 **nepotibus** dat. of indirect object with *mandata*, pf. pass. pple. modifying *arma*; with *nepotibus*, Silius recalls Dido's final imprecation before she kills herself, cursing Carthage and Rome to battle in every generation (Verg. *Aen.* 4.629, *pugnent ipsique nepotesque*).

19 **fas** Supply *est* and translate "It is right to disclose the causes of such great anger, the hatred preserved by constant zeal, and the arms entrusted to her [i.e., Dido's] descendants."

superas . . . mentes = *superum mentes* (poetic pl.); "the purpose of the gods"

20 **repetam primordia** Silius announces his intention to return to the Vergilian origins of the enmity between Carthage and Rome, in Statian diction (cf. *gentis . . . canam primordia dirae*, *Theb.* 1.4). For the murder of Dido's husband Sychaeus by her brother Pygmalion, see Verg. *Aen.* 1.343–68 (in this volume).

21   **Pygmalioneis ... terris** abl. of separation; Dido (23) flees (*fugiens*, 22) "from Pygmalion's territory." The adj. *Pygmalioneus, -a, -um*, is a Silian coinage, derived from the name Vergil gives to Dido's brother, Pygmalion (cf. Verg. *Aen.* 1.347, 364; in this volume).

   per caerula "over the blue waters" of the sea

22   **fugiens** pres. act. pple., nom. sing. f., modifying Dido in the next line

   fraterno crimine instrumental abl.

23   **fatali ... orae** dat. of direction with *appellitur*; "Dido is driven to the destined shore of Libya."

   Libyes Greek gen. sing. f., dependent on *fatali ... orae*

24   **pretio** abl. of price

   mercata nom. sing. f., pf. act. pple. (with Dido); *locos* is acc. of direct object. For the construction, cf. Verg. *Aen.* 1.367, *mercati ... solum* (in this volume).

25   **qua** local abl., "where"

   secto ... tauro instrumental abl., "with the bull hide cut into pieces." Silius says *tauro* by METONYMY for *taurino tergo*, the phrase that Vergil employs in his version of the aetiological tale at *Aen.* 1.368 (in this volume).

   permissum Supply *est*.

26–27 **Argos ... | ... Agamemnoniam ... Mycenen** both Greek acc., objects of prep. *ante*; Silius refers to Vergil's collocation of the two cities at *Aen.* 6.838, *Argos Agamemnoniasque Mycenas* (not in this volume). Argos was an important city in the Peloponnese and a major cult center of Juno, while Agamemnon's Mycenae was important to the goddess as the city that led the Greek forces against Troy.

26   **(sic credidit alta uetustas)** Silius alludes to Vergil's report early in the *Aeneid* of Juno's preference for Carthage over her most famous center of worship in ancient Greece—Samos (*posthabita Samo, Aen.* 1.16, not in this volume). Silius'

parenthesis has the air of an Alexandrian footnote (for the term see my note on Cat. 64.76), and may allude specifically to Vergil's *fertur* there (*Aen.* 1.15).

27   **gratissima tecta** acc. pl. n., in apposition to *Agamemnoniam . . . Mycenen*, the whole line elegantly arranged in CHIASMUS abBA

28   **profugis** dat. of advantage; Silius uses the word of Dido's Phoenician exiles here, in IRONIC reminiscence of Vergil's characterization of Aeneas, in the proem to the *Aeneid*, as an unnamed exile from Troy (*profugus Aen.* 1.2, in this volume).

      condere gentem Silius directly recalls the final words of Vergil's proem to the *Aeneid* (*tantae molis erat Romanam condere gentem*, "so great an undertaking was it to found the Roman people," *Aen.* 1.33; not in this volume), but he reverses their application from Rome to Carthage, where Juno plans to establish an eternal city for the Phoenician exiles. The adj. *aeternam* seems particularly IRONIC here, since Latin authors refer to Rome as "the eternal city."

Appendix A

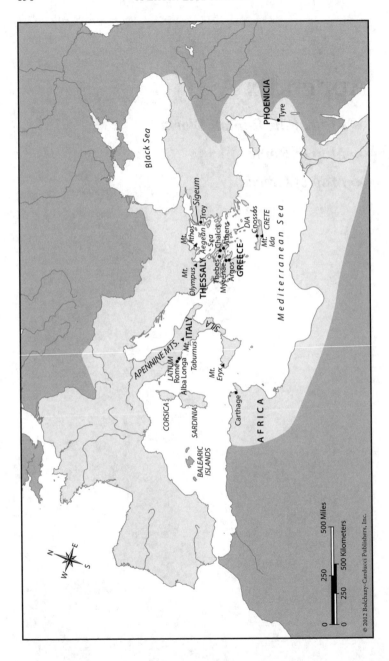

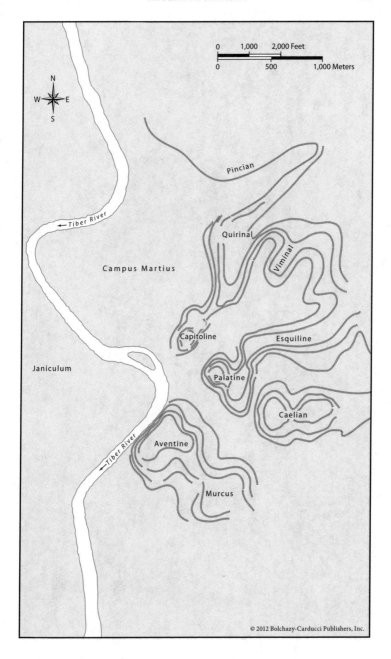

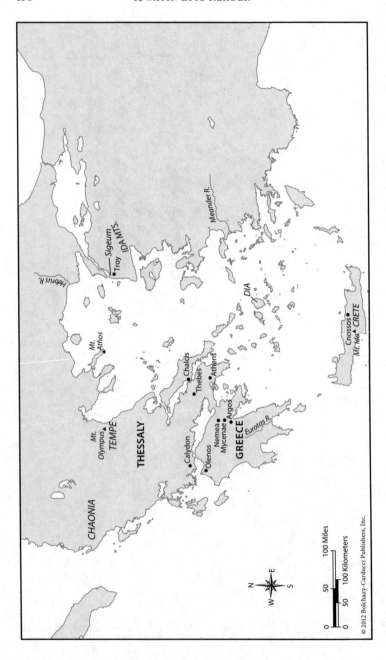

Appendix B

∾ *Glossary of Literary Terms*

ADNOMINATIO juxtaposition of two different forms of the same verbal root (e.g., Cat. 64.55 *uisit uisere*)

ALLITERATION repetition of consonants in close succession

ANAPHORA repetition of a word at the beginning of successive clauses (e.g., Cat. 64.63–5 *non*)

ANTITHESIS the contrast of opposites

APOSTROPHE a direct address to a person or thing, often in an appeal

ASSONANCE repetition of vowels in close succession

ASYNDETON the omission of a conjunction (e.g., Lucr. 1.14 *ferae pecudes*)

ATTRACTION when a word is drawn by the influence of its context to take an irregular construction

CAESURA "cutting," word break within a foot

CHIASMUS crossed arrangement of words in a phrase, corresponding to one another in the scheme ABBA

COLON, COLA (pl.) "member," "members"; clause(s) or other syntactical structure characterized by its own rhythm (e.g., the HEMISTICH)

DIAERESIS "dividing," word break between feet

ECPHRASIS set-piece description, commonly used for descriptions of works of art

EPANALEPSIS "resumption," "repetition" of a word from one line to the next

EPIGRAM see *SENTENTIA*

FIGURA ETYMOLOGICA juxtaposition of two or more words from the same root

HEMISTICH "half-verse"; in dactylic hexameter, the line is divided into two "half-verses" by the main CAESURA

HENDIADYS the use of two nouns joined by a conjunction in place of noun + adj. (e.g., Verg. *Aen.* 12.712 *clipeis atque aere sonoro*, "with shields of resonant bronze")

HYPALLAGE the interchange of cases, also referred to as transferred epithet (e.g., Cat. 64.50 *priscis figuris* for *hominum priscorum*)

HYPERBATON disruption of normal prose word order, for example, through wide separation of noun and modifier

HYPERBOLE exaggeration

HYSTERON-PROTERON "following preceding"; a rhetorical figure in which an item that naturally comes first is placed last

IAMBIC SHORTENING (= *breuis breuians*) shortening of a long syllable preceded by a short syllable may occur if the word accent falls on the syllable immediately following the long syllable (e.g., Lucr. 1.10 *patefactast*, where the e, though long by nature, is shortened after the initial *breue* and before the penultimate *longum* that receives the word accent)

IRONY the poet says one thing but means the contrary

METAPHOR employment of one expression for another that has some resemblance to it, often concrete for abstract (e.g., *ignis* for *amor*)

METONYMY use of a related word conveying the same idea for another (e.g., *Mars* for *bellum*)

OXYMORON juxtaposition of seeming contraries to one another

PARONOMASIA wordplay, often to underline an etymological relationship (in which case it can be called *figura etymologica*)

PERIPHRASIS description of something in a roundabout way, by various attending circumstances, rather than directly

PLEONASM over-fullness of expression (redundancy)

POLYPTOTON juxtaposition of different cases of the same substantive (e.g., Lucr. 1.26–27 *omni* | *omnibus*)

POLYSYNDETON redundancy of conjunctions

SENTENTIA "epigram," the use of a short maxim or witty paradox, often at the close of a verse paragraph

SIMILE the illustration of a statement by a comparison

SYNCOPE omission of a short unaccented vowel (e.g., Ov. *Met.* 1.96 *norant* for *nouerant*), literally "cutting out"

SYNIZESIS "settling together," the treatment of two adjoining vowels in the same word as a single vowel; a related phenomenon is the treatment of *i* and *u* preceding another vowel as consonantal

TRICOLON grammatical construction of three COLA that correspond syntactically

ZEUGMA two nouns share a verb that has a different meaning with each

Complete Vocabulary

ā, *exclamation*, ah!

ā, ab, *prep. + abl.*, from, out of, away from; by (*agent*)

abdō, -ere, -didī, -ditum, to place out of sight, hide, conceal; to conceal oneself, go and hide

abeō, -īre, -iī, -itum, to go away, depart

abhorreō, -ēre, -uī, -itum, shrink back from, shudder at

abiēs, -etis, *f.,* the silver-fir, a species of fir-tree

abigō, -ere, -ēgī, -actum, to drive away; to banish

abrumpō, -ere, -rūpī, -ruptum, to break (off); to sever, rupture

abscīdō, -ere, -cīdī, -cīsum, to cut off; to separate

absiliō, -īre, -ī(u)ī, —, to spring forth or away

absinthium, -(i)ī, *n.,* wormwood; an infusion or tincture of wormwood

abstineō, -ēre, -uī, -tentum, to keep away, restrain

absum, abesse, āfuī, —, to be physically absent; to be (at a specified distance) away

ac. *See* **atque**

accendō, -ere, -cendī, -censum, to kindle, set on fire; to inflame, excite

ācer, ācris, ācre, *adj.,* violent, intense

Actaeus, -a, -um, *adj.,* of or connected with Attica, Attic, Athenian

ad, *prep. + acc.,* to, up to, towards

adclīnō (1), to lean on; to incline to

addō, -ere, -idī, -itum, to add, attach, insert

addūcō, -ere, -duxī, -ductum, to bring; to draw or pull towards one

adeō, -īre, -(i)ī, -itum, to come or go near, approach; to meet, incur, undergo, submit to

adeō, *adv.,* to that point, so far

adferō, adferre, attulī, allatum, to bring, take, or carry

adglomerō (1), to wind in a ball; to add

adhūc, *adv.,* up to the present time, as yet, so far

adigō, -ere, -ēgī, -actum, to drive, to force

adiuuō, -āre, -iūuī, -iūtum, to help, assist, support

adloquor. *See* **alloquor**

adnō (1), to swim to, swim near

adsultō (1), to leap violently upon, attack

adsum, adesse, adfuī, —, to be present, be at, be near

aduentus, -ūs, *m.,* coming, approach, arrival

aduoluō, -ere, -uoluī, -uolūtum, to roll

adulterium, -(i)ī, *n.,* adultery

Aeacidēs, -ae, *m.,* son of Aeacus; Telemon or Peleus

aeger, -gra, -grum, *adj.,* sick, ill, diseased

Aegīdēs, -ae, *m.,* the son of Aegeus, i.e., Theseus

Aeneadēs, -ae, *m.,* person related to or associated with Aeneas, companion ofAeneas, Trojan; descendant of the companions of Aeneas, i.e., Roman

Aenēās, -ae, *m.,* the son of Venus and Anchises and reputed ancestor of the Romans

aequō (1), to make equal, equalize

aequor, -oris, *n.,* level surface; surface of the sea

aequus, -a, -um, *adj.,* even, level; equal, equitable

āēr, āeris, *m.,* air

āerius, -a, -um, *adj.,* airy, aerial, rising aloft

aerumna, -ae, *f.,* toil, hardship, distress

aes, aeris, *n.,* copper, bronze or brass; copper or bronze as a metal of currency, money

aetās, -ātis, *f.,* period of life, time of life; space of time, age

aeternus, -a, -um, *adj.,* eternal

aethēr, -eris, *m.,* heaven, the sky

aeuum, -ī, *n.,* an age

afferō. *See* **adferō**

Africus, -a, -um, *adj.,* African

Agamemnonius, -a, -um, *adj.,* belonging to Agamemnon

Agēnor, -oris, *m.,* a king of Tyre

Agēnoreus, -a, -um, *adj.,* relating to Agenor (a king of Phoenicia)

ager, agrī, *m.,* land, piece of land, field

aggemō, -ere, —, —, to groan at, weep at

agmen, -inis, *n.,* a mass in movement; a stream, band, or train, especially of persons; an army on the march

agnoscō, -ere, -nōuī, -notum, to recognize, acknowledge

agō, -ere, ēgī, actum, to do, act; to drive, urge, push; (*in imperative*) come, come now

āla, -ae, *f.,* wing; upper arm; flank

alacer, -cris, -cre, *adj.,* quick, lively, animated

Albānus, -a, -um, *adj.,* of, belonging to, or near Alba Longa; Alban

albus, -a, -um, *adj.,* white, light-colored; bright, shining, clear

Alcīdēs, -ae, *m.,* son of Alceus; Hercules

alga, -ae, *f.,* seaweed; water-plants; something worthless or uncountable

alimentum, -ī, *n.,* food, fuel

aliquis, aliquae, aliquid, *indef. pron.,* somebody, something

aliter, *adv.,* otherwise, else, in another way

alius, -a, -ud, *pron.,* different in identity, other; different in quality, of a different sort; **alius . . . alius,** this . . . that, the one . . . the other

alloquor, -ī, -locūtus sum, to address

allūdō, -ere, -lūsī, -lūsum, to frolic beside, play against, sport with

almus, -a, -um, *adj.,* nourishing, cherishing, bountiful

alnus, -ī, *f.,* the alder-tree

alō, -ere, -uī, altum *or* **alitum,** to nurse, nurture

altē, *adv.,* on high, highly; deeply

alter, -tera, -terum, *adj.,* one of two, the one, the other

alternus, -a, -um, *adj.,* one after the other, by turns, alternate

altiuolans, -ntis, *adj.,* high-flying

altus, -a, -um, *adj.* (from *alō*), grown great, high, lofty; deep

amābilis, -e, *adj.,* worthy of love, lovely

amārus, -a, -um, *adj.,* bitter

ambāgēs, -um, *f. pl.,* meanderings, wanderings, digression

ambiguus, -a, -um, *adj,* unsettled, undecided, doubtful; of uncertain direction, unsteady

ambō, -ae, -o, *adj.,* both, two together

amictus, -ūs, *m.,* upper garment, mantle cloak; clothing, dress

amīcus, -a, -um, *adj.,* friendly, favorable to

amnis, -is, *m.,* a stream of water, a river

amō (1), to like, love

amoenus, -a, -um, *adj.,* pleasant, delightful, charming

amor, -ōris, *m.,* sexual passion, love

Amphitrītē, -ēs, *f.,* the wife of Neptune; the sea

amplector, -ī, -plexus sum, to embrace

amplexus, -ūs, *m.,* an embrace

Androgeōnēus, -a, -um, *adj.,* of, or connected with, Androgeos

Androgeōs, -ō, *m.,* the son of Minos and Pasiphae, whose death Minos avenged on the Athenians

anguis, -is, *m., f.,* a snake, serpent

angustus, -a, -um, *adj.,* narrow, confined

animō (1), to fill with breath; to be animate, living

animus, -ī, *m.,* mind, soul

Anna, -ae, *f.,* the sister of Dido

annōsus, -a, -um, *adj.,* full of years, aged

annus, -ī, *m.,* a year

ante, *prep. + acc.,* before, in front of

antīquus, -a, -um, *adj.,* old, ancient, former

antrum, -ī, *n.,* a cave

anus, -ūs, *f.,* old woman

aper, aprī, *m.,* a wild boar

aperiō, -īre, -uī, apertum, to open, uncover

apertus, -a, -um, *adj.,* (from **aperiō**) open

appellō, -ere, -pulī, -pulsum, to drive to, bring to

Appennīnus, -a, -um, *adj.,* of the Apennine mountains

aqua, -ae, *f.,* water

āra, -ae, *f.,* altar

arbiter, -trī, *m.,* a witness, spectator; a judge; a ruler, master

arbor, -oris, *f.,* tree

arbustum, -ī, *n.,* wood, copse, plantation

arbuteus, -a, -um, *adj.,* of the arbutus or wild strawberry tree; made of arbutus-wood

Arctos, -ī, *f.,* the lands or peoples of the North

arcus, -ūs, *m.,* a bow

ardeō, -ēre, arsī, —, to burn, glow, be on fire

arduus, -a, -um, *adj.,* tall, lofty; steep, precipitous

argentum, -ī, *n.,* silver

Argolicus, -a, -um, *adj.,* Argolic, of Argos

Argos, *n. sing.,* Argos, the capital of Argolis in the Peloponnese

argūmentum, -ī, *n.,* a piece of evidence, proof, argument

arguō, -ere, -uī, -ūtum, to show, reveal

Ariadna, -ae (or **Ariadnē, -ēs**), *f.,* daughter of King Minos of Crete who assisted Theseus to escape from the Labyrinth and was abandoned by him at Naxos; she was subsequently loved by Bacchus, and her crown was made into a constellation

ariēs, -etis, *m.,* a male sheep, ram; battering ram

arma, -ōrum, *n. pl.,* armor, weapons of war; war

armentum, -ī, *n.,* herd

armipotens, -entis, *adj.,* strong in war, valiant

armus, -ī, *m.,* shoulder, flank

arrigō, -ere, -rexī, -rectum, to stand on end, raise, excite

ars, artis, *f.,* skill, art, craft, trick, stratagem

artus, -ūs, *m.,* the joints, the limbs

aruum, -ī, *n.,* a ploughed field, a field, arable land

arx, -cis, *f.,* a fortress, citadel, stronghold

Ascanius, -iī, *m.,* the son of Aeneas and founder of Alba Longa; also called Iulus

aspectus, -ūs, *m.,* sight, view, vision; a sight, vision

aspergō, -ginis, *f.,* moisture in the form of drops, spray

aspiciō, -ere, aspexī, aspectum, to notice with the eyes, catch sight of, observe

aspirō (1), to emit air or breath, breathe; to blow or breathe on; to give assistance (to), favor, aid

assiduus, -a, -um, *adj.,* constant, persistent, unremitting

astō, -āre, -itī, —, to stand by, at, on; to stand still, waiting

astrum, -ī, *n.,* a star, a constellation

at, *conj.,* but, however, on the other hand, while, whereas; at least, yet, at any rate

Athēnae, -ārum, *f. pl.,* city of Athens

Athos, *m. sing.,* a mountain on the peninsula of Acte in Chalcidice

atque, ac, *conj.,* and, and also

attingō, -ere, -tigī, -tactum, to reach, arrive at, enter

attollō, -ere, —, —, to lift up, raise up; to erect

auārus, -a, -um, *adj.,* greedy

audax, -ācis, *adj.,* bold; daring, courageous; audacious, rash

audeō, -ēre, ausus sum, to intend or dare (to do something); to be bold

audiō, -īre, -ī(u)ī, -ītum, to hear, listen to

Auentīnus, -a, -um, *adj.,* of the Aventine, one of the seven hills of Rome; (sc. *mons*) the Aventine hill

auersus, -a, -um, *adj.,* having the back turned, facing in the opposite direction

auferō, auferre, abstulī, ablātum, to carry away; to remove, take away

augur, -uris, *m.,* one who observes and interprets the behaviour of birds, an augur

augurium, -iī, *n.,* the observation and interpretation of omens, augury

auidus, -a, -um, *adj.,* desirous, eager, greedy

auis, -is, *f.,* bird

aura, -ae, *f.,* breeze

aureus, -a, -um, *adj.,* golden, made of gold

auris, -is, *f.,* ear

Aurōra, -ae, *f.,* the dawn; goddess of the dawn

aurum, -ī, *n.,* gold

auspicium, -iī, *n.,* divination by means of birds, auspices

aut, *conj.,* or, and; **aut . . . aut,** either . . . or

autem, *conj.,* but, however

auus, -ī, *m.*, grandfather, ancestor

auxilium, -iī, *n.*, help, aid

bacchāns, -antis, *f.*, bacchant, votary of Bacchus

Baleāricus, -a, -um, *adj.*, of or belonging to the Balearic islands, Balearic; *m. pl.*, the inhabitants of the Balearic islands, famous as slingers

bellum, -ī, *n.*, war

bellus, -a, -um, *adj.*, pretty, handsome, charming

belua, -ae, *f.*, a beast, wild animal

bene, *adv.*, well, fittingly, rightly

bibulus, -a, -um, *adj.*, fond of drinking; absorbent, porous, soaked

biformis, -is, -e, *adj.*, (of monsters) consisting of two parts of different kinds, two-formed

bipennis, -is, -e, *adj.*, having two wings; (of an axe) having two blades or edges

bipēs, -edis, *adj.*, having two feet

bis, *adv.*, twice, two times

blandus, -a, -um, *adj.*, flattering, fondling, caressing; enticing, alluring, tempting

Boreās, -ae, *m.*, the north wind

bra(c)chium, -(i)ī, *n.*, arm

breuis, -e, *adj.*, short, shallow, slight

brūma, -ae, *f.*, winter, wintry cold; the winter solstice

Byrsa, -ae, *f.*, the citadel of Carthage

cacūmen, -minis, *n.*, peak, top, tip

Cadmēus, -a, -um, *adj.*, Theban

cadō, -ere, cecidī, cāsum, to fall, to drop, sink; to be killed, die

caecus, -a, -um, *adj.*, blind

caedēs, -is, *f.*, killing, slaughter

caedō, -ere, cecīdī, caesum, to strike, smite, beat; to kill, slay, murder

caelestis, -is, -e, *adj.*, celestial, heavenly, divine

caelō (1), to adorn in relief, emboss, engrave

caelum, -ī, *n.*, the sky, the heavens

caerula, -ōrum, *n. pl.*, the blue expanse (of the sky); the blue waters (of the sea)

caerulus, -a, -um, *adj.*, blue, dark blue

calidus, -a, -um, *adj.*, hot, warm

Calydōn, -ōnis (*acc.* -a), *f.*, a very ancient city in Aetolia

campus, -ī, *m.*, plain, field

candidus, -a, -um, *adj.*, shining white; clear, bright

cāneō, -ēre, -uī, —, to be or become covered in white

canis, -is, *m.*, dog, hound

canō, -ere, cecinī, cantum, to sing, chant, celebrate

cānus, -a, -um, *adj.*, whitish-grey, grey; old

capessō, -ere , -īuī, -itum, to catch at eagerly, lay hold of

capiō, -ere, cēpī, captum, to take

captō (1), to snatch at eagerly or frequently, try for

caput, -itis, *n.,* head; life; person, individual

carcer, -eris, *m.,* prison; the starting-place of a racecourse

careō, -ēre, -uī, -itum, to be without; to be free from

carmen, -minis, *n.,* song, poem, incantation

carpō, -ere, -sī, -tum, to pluck, seize

Carthāgo, -inis, *f.,* Carthage

cārus, -a, -um, *adj.,* dear, beloved

Cassiopē, -ēs, *f.,* the wife of Cepheus and mother of Andromeda, afterwards changed into a constellation; the constellation

castus, -a, -um, *adj.,* pure, chaste, unstained

cāsus, -ūs, *m.,* (from **cado**) fall; event, accident, chance, fortune; disaster, misfortune, danger

catēna, -ae, *f.,* a chain, chains, fetters; a causal series of events

cauda, -ae, *f.,* tail

cauea, -ae, *f.,* a hollow place, cavity; a den for animals

caueō, -ēre, cāuī, cautum, to take precautions, be on one's guard; to guard against

causa, -ae, *f.,* cause, reason, origin, source

cautēs, -is, *f.,* a rough sharp rock

cauus, -a, -um, *adj.,* hollow, concave

Cēcropidēs, -ae, *m.,* a male descendant of Cecrops

Cecropius, -a, -um, *adj.,* of Cecrops or his descendants; Athenian

cēdō, -ere, cessī, cessum, to go, proceed; to go away, withdraw, depart; to come to an end; to give way, yield, submit, surrender

celeber, -bris, -bre, *adj.,* widely known, notorious, distinguished

celer, -ris, -re, *adj.,* swift, fast, speedy, agile, quick

celerō (1), to hurry, hasten

cēlō (1), to conceal, hide

celsus, -a, -um, *adj.,* upraised, high, lofty

Cēpheus, -ei, *m.,* a king of the Cephenes (usually located in Ethiopia) and father of Andromeda

Cereālis, -e, *adj.,* of, belonging to or associated with Ceres

Cerēs, -eris, *f.,* Ceres, the goddess of grain and fruits

cernō, -ere, crēuī, crētum, to distinguish, discern, see; to perceive; to look at, examine

certāmen, -inis, *n.,* a contest, struggle

certātim, *adv.,* with rivalry, in competition

certō (1), to contend, struggle

ceruix, -īcis, *f.,* neck

cēterus, -a, -um, *adj.,* the rest, the remaining part

cētus, -ī, *m.,* any large sea-creature

Chalcidicus, -a, -um, *adj.,* of or belonging to Chalcis

Chāonius, -a, -um, *adj.,* Chaonian, of or from Chaonia

chaos, -ī, *n.,* the formless state of primordial matter, chaos

chorēa, -ae, *f.,* a round dance; dancers

chorus, -ī, *m.,* a dance in a circle, a choral dance; the persons singing and dancing

cibus, -ī, *m.,* food, nutriment

cieō, -ēre, cīuī, citum, to cause to move; to move, stir

cingō, -ere, cinxī, cinctum, to surround, encircle; to gird, equip

circum, *prep.* + *acc.,* around, about; *adv.,* round about, on all sides

circumdō, -dare, -dedī, -datum, to put or place (round or near)

circumfundō, -ere, -fūdī, -fūsum, to pour around; to surround, encompass

circumsonō, -āre, -uī, -ātum, to resound all around; to surround (with noise)

circueō, -īre, -iī, -itum, to make the circuit of, go round, circle; to surround, encircle, envelope

circus, -ī, *m.,* circle, orbit; an oval course for races

citō (1), to excite, start up; to summon, call forward

citus, -a, -um, *adj.,* (from **cieō**) quick, speedy

clādēs, -is, *f.,* calamity, disaster

clam, *adv.,* secretly

clamō (1), to shout, utter a loud noise; to declare plainly, proclaim

clāmor, -ōris, *m.,* a shout, shouting; shout of protest, outcry; shout of approval, applause

clārus, -a, -um, *adj.,* clear; bright, shining; illustrious, distinguished

classis, -is, *f.,* class; fleet, naval force; band, group

claudō (clūdō), -ere, clausī, clausum, to close, shut; to shut up, confine

clipeus, -ī, *m.,* shield

Cnōsius, -a, -um, *adj.,* of or pertaining to Cnossos in Crete

coeō, -īre, -iī, -itum, to come together, meet, assemble

coepī, -isse, coeptum, (*only pf. stem normally used*) to begin; to undertake

coeptum, -ī, *n.,* something undertaken, undertaking, enterprise

coerceō, -ēre, -cuī, -citum, to restrain, confine; to control, check cognoscō, -ere, -gnōuī, -gnitum, to become acquainted with, get to know, learn

cōgō, -ere, coēgī, coāctum, to force, compel

collis, -is, *m.*, a hill, high ground

collum, -ī, *n.*, the neck

colō, -ere, -uī, cultum, to live in, inhabit; to till, cultivate; to worship, cherish

color, -ōris, *m.*, color, hue

coma, -ae, *f.*, the hair of the head; the leaves of trees

comes, -itis, *m./f.*, companion, follower, attendant

commisceō, -ēre, -miscuī, -mixtum, to mix together, to combine

commoueō, -ēre, -mōuī, -mōtum, to move, shake, agitate, disturb, upset

commūniō, -īre, -īuī, -ītum, to fortify on all sides; to strengthen

commūnis, -e, *adj.*, common, general, universal, public

cōmō, -ere, compsī, comptum, to put together, form; to arrange, adorn

compellō (1), to address, speak to

compleō, -ēre, -ēuī, -ētum, to fill, fill up

complexus, -ūs, *m.*, embrace

comptus, -a, -um, *adj.*, (from cōmō) adorned, neat

concelebrō (1), to visit a place often or in large companies; to pursue eagerly; to celebrate

concha, -ae, *f.*, mollusc, shell-fish; the shell of a mollusc, sea-shell

concidō, -ere, -cidī, —, to fall down, collapse; to fall dead, die or be killed

concieō, -ēre, -cīuī, -citum, to stir up or set in violent motion, rouse up

concipiō, -ere, -cēpī, -ceptum, to lay hold of, take in, receive; to conceive, become pregnant; (with *flammam*) to catch fire, be set alight

concitō (1), to move quickly or violently, to stir up, to excite

concurrō, -ere, -currī, -cursum, to hurry together, meet, accumulate; to charge; to run together, collide

concutiō, -ere, -cussī, -cussum, to shake together, agitate; to excite

condō, -ere, -didī, -dītum, to put together, build, found, establish; to store; to hide

confodiō, -ere, -fōdī, -fossum, to stab, pierce through

congeminō (1), to double, increase; to produce or employ in a repeated action

congerō, -ere, -gessī, -gestum, to bring together, amass

congestus, -a, -um, *adj.*, crowded together, piled up

cōniciō, -ere, -iēcī, -iectum, to throw together; to throw

coniugium, -(i)ī, *n.*, marriage, wedlock

coniunx, -iugis, *m./f.,* husband, wife, spouse

cōnor, -ārī, -ātus sum, to undertake, endeavor, attempt

conscius, -a, -um, *adj.,* sharing knowledge (especially secret knowledge), privy to; conscious of guilt, guilty

consistō, -ere, -stitī, -stitum, to stop moving, come to a halt

conspectus, -ūs, *m.,* view, sight

conspiciō, -ere, -spexī, -spectum, to catch sight of, notice, see; to stare at, watch

consternō (1), to stretch upon the ground; to overcome

constō, -stāre, -stitī, stātum, to stand together; to stand firm, be established; to be composed of

consul, -is, *m.,* consul

consūmō, -ere, -sumpsī, -sumptum, to consume, use up; to destroy

contegō, -ere, -texī, -tectum, to cover over, clothe; to conceal, hide

contendō, -ere, -tendī, -tentum, to draw tight, stretch; to exert, strain; to engage in a contest, compete

contentus, -a, -um, *adj.,* content, satisfied

contingō, -ere, -tigī, -tactum, to touch, reach; to take hold of, seize

contrā, *adv.,* opposite, over against, on the opposite side, facing (it/him/etc.); in return

contremescō, -ere, -muī, —, to tremble, shake violently; to tremble with fear, be greatly perturbed

conuallis, -is, *f.,* a valley shut in on all sides

cōnūbium, -(i)ī, *n.,* marriage, intermarriage

conueniō, -īre, -uēnī, -uentum, to assemble, meet, convene

conuentum, -ī, *n.,* an agreement, compact

conuertō, -ere, -uertī, -uersum, to cause to rotate, turn, direct; to invert, turn back, change, alter, shift

coorior, -īrī, -ortus sum, to originate, be born

cor, cordis, *n.,* the heart

cornū, -ūs, *n.,* horn

cornum, -ī, *n.,* the fruit of the cornelian cherry, cornel-berry

corona, -ae, *f.,* wreath, garland, crown

corpus, -oris, *n.,* body

corripiō, -ere, -ipuī, -eptum, to seize, grasp; to hasten, hurry, carry off

corruō, -ere, -uī, —, to fall down, collapse; to topple

cortex, -icis, m./f., bark, cork; rind, husk

coruscus, -a, -um, *adj.,* moving rapidly, trembling

costa, -ae, *f.,* rib

crēber, -bra, -brum, *adj.,* thick, close, numerous, abundant, dense

crēdō, -ere, -idī, -itum, to trust, believe, entrust

creō (1), to procreate, give birth to; to bring into being, create

crepitō (1), to rattle, creak, crackle

crescō, -ere, crēuī, crētum, to grow, increase

Crēta, -ae, *f.,* the island of Crete

crīmen, -inis, *n.,* an accusation, charge; crime, fault

crūdēlis, -e, *adj.,* cruel, merciless, savage

crūdescō, -ere, -duī, —, to become hard, violent

crūdus, -a, -um, *adj.,* bleeding, raw; fresh; unripe; rough, cruel

cruentus, -a, -um, *adj.,* bloody; bloodthirsty

cruor, -oris, *m.,* blood, the shedding of blood

culmen, -inis, *n.,* the top, summit; roof

culpa, -ae, *f.,* blame, reproach, guilt, offense

cum, *prep.* + *abl.,* with, together with, along with, by means of; *conj.,* when, since, although

cunctor, -ārī, -ātus sum, to delay, linger, hesitate

cunctus, -a, -um, *adj.,* all, the whole, total

cuneus, -ī, *m.,* wedge

cupidē, *adv.,* eagerly, zealously, with alacrity

cupīdō, -inis, *f.,* longing, desire

cupidus, -a, -um, *adj.,* longing, passionate, desirous

cupiō, -īre, -ī(u)ī, -ītum, to long for, desire, wish

cupressus, -ī, *f.,* the cypress

cūr, *adv.,* why

cūra, -ae, *f.,* anxiety, worry, care, distress; attention, concern

cūrō (1), to look after, give heed to, worry about

currus, -ūs, *m.,* chariot

cursus, -ūs, *m.,* a running, a rapid motion; course, march, journey

curuus, -a, -um, *adj.,* curved, bent; winding

daedalus, -a, -um, *adj.,* skillful

Daedalus, -ī, *m.,* Daedalus, a mythical Athenian hero, the builder of the labyrinth and the father of Icarus

daps, -pis, *f.,* sacrificial meal; feast, banquet

Dardanius, -a, -um, *adj.,* of or descended from Dardanus; Trojan

Dardanus, -a, -um, *adj.,* Trojan

Daunius, -a, -um, *adj.* Rutulian; son of Daunus

dē, *prep.* + *abl.,* from, about, concerning

dēcidō, -ere, -ī, —, to fall down, fall off

dēcipiō, -ere, -cēpī, -ceptum, to catch, ensnare; to deceive, cheat

dēclīnō (1), to turn away, turn aside

decus, -oris, *n.,* glory, splendor, ornament

dēdō, -ere, -didī, dēditum, to give away, give up; to surrender, yield

dēdūcō, -ere, -duxī, -ductum, to lead or bring out, extend; to draw out, compose

dēfendō, -ere, -fendī, -fensum, to repel, repulse, drive away; to defend, protect

dēferō, -ferre, -tulī, -lātum, to bring down, carry down; to bring away; to offer

defigō, -ere, -fixī, -fixum, to fasten down; to fix in

dēgener, -eris, *adj.,* of inferior stock, degenerate, ignoble, soft

dehiscō, -ere, -hiuī, —, to split open, yawn, gape

dēlābor, -ī, -lapsus sum, to fall, drop, slip down, sink, glide down

dēniquē, *adv.,* then; at last

dens, dentis, *m.,* a tooth

Dēōius, -a, -um, *adj.,* of or belonging to Deo (Demeter)

dēpōnō, -ere, -posuī, -positum, to put or lay down, drop; to take off

dēqueror, -ī, -questus sum, to complain of, bewail

dērigō (dīrigō), -ere, -rexī, -rectum, to arrange in a line; to form up (an army or similiar); to direct

descendō, -ere, -scendī, -scensum, to come or go down, descend

dēserō, -ere, -uī, -tum, to leave, depart; to desert, fail, abandon; to fall short, give up

dēsinō, -ere, -(i)ī, -itum, to leave off, desist, finish, stop

despondeō, -ēre, -spondī, -sponsum, to pledge, tpromise, betroth

destinō (1), to fix in position; to determine on, intend, purpose

destituō, -ere, -uī, -ūtum, to set up, fix; to leave in an isolated position by one's departure, abandon

dēsum, -esse, -fuī, —, to be wanting or lacking; to fail

dēterreō, -ere, -terruī, -territum, to deter, discourage; to frighten, terrify

detruncō (1), to lop off, behead, mutilate

dēueniō, -īre, -uēnī, -uentum, to arrive, reach

dēuincō, -ere, -uīcī, -uictum, to defeat decisively, subdue

deus, -ī, *m.,* god; **dea, -ae,** *f.,* goddess

Dīa, -ae, *f.,* an island in the Aegean Sea, more commonly known as Naxos

dīcō, -ere, dixī, dictum, to say, tell of, recite

Dīdō, -ōnis, *f.,* Dido, the queen and foundress of Carthage, widow of Sychaeus and lover of Aeneas

diēs, -ēī, *m.,* day

difficilis, -e, *adj.,* hard to deal with, troublesome, difficult

diffundō, -ere, -fūdī, -fūsum, to pour out; to spread, scatter, diffuse

dīlectus, -a, -um, *adj.,* beloved, dear

dīligō, -ere, -lexī, -lectum, to choose; to prize; to love

dimittō, -ere, -mīsī, -missum, to send forth; to send away, let go; to abandon

dīmoueō, -ēre, -mōuī, -mōtum, to part, disperse, remove

dīrus, -a, -um, *adj.,* awful, dire, dreadful

dīs, dītis, *adj. (compar.* **dītior,** *superl.* **dītissimus, -a, -um),** wealthy, rich

discessus, -ūs, *m.,* parting, splitting apart, departure

discors, -ordis, *adj.,* that is at variance or in conflict, discordant

discutiō, -ere, -cussī, -cussum, to dash to pieces, break up; to shake violently; to shake off

dissensus, -ūs, *m.,* disunion, disagreement

distinctus, -a, -um, *adj.,* distinct, varied

diū, *adv.,* by day; for a long time; a long time ago

dīuersus, -a, -um, *adj.,* differing, opposite, set apart, separate

dīuidō, -ere, -uīsī, -uīsum, to separate, divide

dīuus, -a, -um, *adj.,* divine

dīuus, -ī, *m.,* god; **dīua, -ae,** *f.,* goddess

dō, dare, dedī, datum, to give

doleō, -ēre, -uī, -itum, to suffer, grieve

dolor, -ōris, *m.,* pain, grief, distress

dolus, -ī, *m.,* trick, plot, malice

domus, -ūs, *f.,* house, home

dōs, dōtis, *f.,* dowry

dracō, -ōnis, *m.,* snake, (also of various mythical beasts)

dryas, -adis, *f.,* wood-nymph, dryad

dūcō, -ere, duxī, ductum, to lead, drive, bring, draw

ductor, -ōris, *m.,* a leader

dulcis, -e, *adj.,* sweet; pleasant, agreeable

dum, *conj., (with indicative)* while, during the time that; *(with subjunctive)* until

duo, -ae, -o, *adj.,* two

dūrus, -a, -um, *adj.,* hard, solid; robust, hardy; harsh, hard to bear

dux, ducis, *m./f.,* leader, guide, general

ē. *See* **ex**

ecce, *exclamation,* See! behold! look!

ecflō (eff-) (1), to blow out, to breathe out

ecfor, -ārī, -ātus sum, to utter, say; to announce, declare

edō, esse, ēdī, ēsum, to eat, to spend (money) on food; to consume

edō, -ere, -idī, -itum, to eject, emit; to bring forth; to utter, pronounce, declare

ēdūcō, -ere, ēduxī, ēductum, to bring out, draw forth

efferō, efferre, extulī, ēlātum, to carry out; to carry off; to lift up

efficiō, -ere, -fēcī, -fectum, to do, produce, effect

effigiēs, -ēī, *f.,* statue, portrait; model, example; copy, reproduction

effingō, -ere, -finxī, -finctum, to form, fashion; express, represent, portray

effor, -ārī, -ātus sum, to utter, say

effugiō, -ere, -fugī, —, to flee, slip away, escape

egens, -entis, *adj.,* (from **egeō**) poverty-stricken, needy, indigent

egeō, -ēre, eguī, to need, want, require; to find oneself in need of and without

ego, meī, *pron.,* I

ēgredior, -ī, -gressus sum, to go out, set out, leave

ēheu, *interjection.,* alas!

ēligō, -ere, ēlēgī, ēlectum, to select, choose, pick out

ēmicō, -āre, ēmicuī, ēmicātum, to spring out, leap forth; to shine forth

ēmineō, -ēre, -minuī, —, to project, stand out

ēminus, *adv.,* at a long range

emittō, -ere, -mīsī, -missum, to send forth, send out; to dispatch; to let go

ēnarrābilis, -e, *adj.,* that can be described or explained

enim, *conj.,* for

ēnō (1), to swim out, fly out

ensis, -is, *m.,* sword

eō, īre, iī *or* **īuī, itum,** to go

ephēbus, -ī, *m.,* a young man between eighteen and twenty

equidem, *adv.,* indeed, in truth

equus, -ī, *m.,* horse

Erebus, -ī, *m.,* the abode of the dead

ergō, *adv.,* therefore

ērigō, -ere, -rexī, -rectum, to set up, place upright, lift up, erect

errō (1), to wander, stray, rove; to err, be mistaken

error, -ōris, *m.,* a wandering, a maze; uncertainty, perplexity; mistake, (moral) lapse

Erycīna, -ae, *f.,* cult-title of Venus

Eryx, -rycis, *m.,* a mountain and city in Sicily

et, *conj.,* and

etiam, *conj.,* still, yet, even now, yet again; also, in addition, as well, too; even, actually; indeed, yes

ēuertō, -ere, -uertī, -uersum, to turn out, eject; to overturn; to overthrow, destroy

Eurōtās, -ae, *m.,* a river in Laconia, on which Sparta stands

Eurydica, -ae, *f.,* Eurydice, the mythological wife of Aeneas

ex, ē, *prep.* + *abl.,* out of, out from; from, from among; immediately after; with, by means; in accordance with; by the standard of

exardescō, -ere, -arsī, -arsum, to catch fire, burst into flame; to burn, be inflamed

excēdō, -ere, -cessī, -cessum, to withdraw (from), leave

excellō, -ere, -celuī, -celsum, to stand out, be distinguished

excidium, -iī, *n.,* destruction

excīdō, -ere, -cīdī, -cīsum, to cut out or off, hew or cut down

excitō (1), to cause to move, start, disturb; to rouse from sleep, wake up; to excite, stir

exclūdō, -ere, -clūsī, -clūsum, to shut out, exclude

exerceō, -ēre, -cuī, -citum, to train by practice, exercise; to put to use, employ

exertō (1), to thrust or put out; to lay bare, expose

exhauriō, -īre, -hausī, -haustum, to draw off, drink up, remove, exhaust, drain

exigō, -ere, -ēgī, -actum, to drive out or off; to thrust, hurl; to enforce, exact

exiguus, -a, -um, *adj.,* small, little, scanty

exim, *adv.,* (= *exinde*) from there, from here; after that, then, furthermore; hence, accordingly

exorior, -īrī, exortus sum, to rise out, come forth

expectō (1), to look out, wait for, expect

expōnō, -ere, -posuī, -positum, to put outside; to put on view, set forth, explain

expugnābilis, -e, *adj.,* that may be taken by storm

exsoluō, -ere, -uī, -ūtum, to pay for; perform, discharge

exspīrō (1), to breathe out, exhale

exstillō (1), to drop moisture, drip, trickle

exstinguō, -ere, -stinxī, -stinctum, to extinguish, quench, put out, kill, wipe out

exstō, -āre, -(s)titī, —, to project, stand out; to be conspicuous, catch attention; to exist

exsultō (1), to spring up, dance; to exult

extemplō, *adv.,* immediately

externō (1), to drive out of one's wits, provoke to panic

exterreō, -ēre, -uī, -itum, to frighten out of; to frighten badly, scare, terrify

extrēmum, -ī, *n.,* limit, edge, end

faber, -bra, -brum, *adj.,* of the craftsman or his work

faciēs, -ēī, *f.,* shape, form, figure

faciō, -ere, fēcī, factum, to make, build, create, prepare, produce; to achieve, do, accomplish, act

factum, -ī, *n.,* deed, action, fact, achievenment

fāgus, -ī, *f.,* the beech-tree

falcātus, -a-, -um, *adj.,* furnished with curved blades; curved like a scythe or pruning-hook, sickle-shaped

fallācia, -ae, *f.,* deceptive behavior, deceit, trick

fallax, -ācis, *adj.,* deceitful, treacherous; misleading, deceptive; false, fallacious; spurious

fallō, -ere, fefellī, falsum, to deceive, trick, mislead, cheat

fāma, -ae, *f.,* report, rumor, talk, story, reputation

famulus, -ī, *m.,* slave, servant, attendant

fās, *n. indecl.,* divine command, divine law; that which is lawful

fastīgium, -(i)ī, *n.,* sharp point, apex, slope, peak, height

fātālis, -e, *adj.,* relating to destiny or fate; deadly, fatal

fateor, -ērī, fassus sum, to assent, concede, acknowledge; to profess, declare

fātum, -ī, *n.,* prophecy, utterance; fate; doom, death

Faunī, -ōrum, *m. pl.,* Fauns, forest gods

Fauōnius, -(i)ī, *m.,* the west wind

faux, faucis, *for* **fauces, -ium,** *f. pl.,* the throat

fax, facis, *f.,* torch, light

fēmina, -ae, *f.,* woman

fera, -ae, *f.,* a wild animal, wild beast

ferō, ferre, tūlī, lātum, to bring, bear, carry; to tell

ferox, -ōcis, *adj.,* fierce, savage, defiant

ferrum, -ī, *n.,* iron, steel; sword

ferus, -a, -um, *adj.,* untamed, wild, savage

festus, -a, -um, *adj.,* appropriate to a holiday; festive, merry

fētus, -a, -um, *adj.,* having recently given birth, bearing young

fētus, -ūs, *m.,* offspring; fruit

fidēs, -ēī, *f.,* trust; promise; honesty, good faith

fīgō, -ere, fixī, fixum, to drive in, fix in, transfix, fasten

figūra, -ae, *f.,* shape, form, figure, appearance

fīlum, -ī, *n.,* thread, cord, filament

fingō, -ere, finxī, fictum, to form, fashion, create; to groom

fīnis, -is, *m./f.,* boundary, territory, limit, end

fiō, fierī, factus sum, (used as passive of **faciō**) to be made, become; to be done, happen

fissilis, -is, -e, *adj.,* easily split

flagrō (1), to burn, flame, blaze

flamma, -ae, *f.,* flame, fire

flātus, -ūs, *m.,* a blowing, blast, breathing

flāuus, -a, -um, *adj.,* yellow, golden; blond(e)

flectō, -ere, flexī, flexum, to bend, curve; to avert, turn aside; to alter; to prevail on, influence

fleō, -ēre, flēuī, flētum, to weep; to lament

flōreō, -ere, -uī, —, to blossom, bloom; to be bright or gay; to be prosperous, be at the height of one's powers, fame etc.

flōs, flōris, *m.,* flower

fluctuō (1), to rise in waves, surge, billow; to be in a state of agitation or turmoil, seethe

fluctus, -ūs, *m.,* wave, billow, waters of the sea

fluentisonus, -a, -um, *adj.,* resounding with the noise of waves

fluitō (1), to flow, run, stream; to float, drift

flūmen, -inis, *n.,* river, stream

fluō, -ere, fluxī, fluxum, to flow, run, stream; to originate, derive, proceed

fluuius, -(i)ī, *m.,* river

foedus, -deris, *n.,* treaty, compact, bond, tie

fons, fontis, *m.,* spring, source; origin, fount

forās, *adv.,* out of doors, out, forth

foris, -is, *f.,* door

forma, -ae, *f.,* form, appearance, figure, shape

fors, -tis, *f.,* chance, luck; destiny; accident

forsan, *adv.,* perhaps

fortē, *adv.,* by chance, as it happened

fortis, -e, *adj.,* strong, vigorous, brave

fortūna, -ae, *f.,* fortune, chance

fossa, -ae, *f.,* ditch, trench

frāga, -ōrum, *n. pl.,* wild strawberries

fragor, -ōris, *m.,* a breaking; a noise of breaking, crack, crash

frangō, -ere, frēgī, fractum, to break, break to pieces, shatter, shiver

frāternus, -a, -um, *adj.,* of a brother, brotherly, fraternal

fraxineus, -a, -um, *adj.,* made of ash-wood

fraxinus, -ī, *f.,* an ash-tree

fremitus, -ūs, *m.,* a roaring, murmuring, growling sound

fremō, -ere, -uī, -itum, to roar, rumble, growl, mutter; to clamor

fretum, -ī, *n.,* a channel, strait

frīgidus, -a, -um, *adj.,* cold, chilly

frondēns, -entis, *adj.,* leafy; full of trees or leafy plants

frondifer, -era, -erum, *adj.,* leaf-bearing, leafy

frondōsus, -a, -um, *adj.,* full of leaves, leafy

frons, -ntis, *f.,* forehead, brow

frūgifer, -era, -erum, *adj.,* fruit-bearing, fruitful, fertile

frux, -ūgis, *f., (especially pl.* **fruges)** produce, crops, harvest

fuga, -ae, *f.,* flight, fleeing

fugiō, -ere, fūgī, fūgitum, to run away, flee; to escape, elude; to vanish, pass away; to avoid, shun

fulgeō, -ēre, fulsī, —, to flash, gleam, shine

fulmen, -inis, *n.,* lightning, thunderbolt

fulmineus, -a, -um, *adj.,* of lightning, like lightning

funda, -ae, *f.,* sling

funditus, *adv.,* from the depths; utterly, completely

fundō, -ere, fūdī, fūsum, to pour, spread, scatter

fundus, -ī, *m.,* ground, foundation; soil, farm, estate

fūnis, -is, *m.,* rope, cable

fūnus, -eris, *n.,* funeral, burial; death; corpse

furia, -ae, *f.,* rage, madness, fury

furor, -ōris, *m.,* violent madness, frenzy; rage, fury, anger; passionate desire or longing

furtīuus, -a, -um, *adj.,* stolen; stealthy, secret

furtō, *adv.,* secretly

futūrus, -a, -um, *adj.,* future

galea, -ae, *f.,* helmet

gaudeō, -ēre, gauīsus sum, to be glad, be pleased, rejoice

gelidus, -a, -um, *adj.,* cold, icy, frosty

geminus, -a, -um, *adj.,* twin, twin-born; two-figured

gemitus, -ūs, *m.,* groan, moan

gemma, -ae, *f.,* eye, bud; jewel, gem

generātim, *adv.,* by or according to classes, kinds (with reference to the natural division of animals or plants into species)

genetrix, -īcis, *f.,* she who has borne or produced, mother

genitābilis, -e, *adj.,* productive, generative

genitor, -ōris, *m.,* father; creator, originator

gens, -ntis, *f.,* race, nation, people

genu, -ūs, *n.,* knee

genus, -eris, *n.,* race, kind, species, stock

germana, -ae, *f.,* sister

germānus, -a, -um, *adj.,* having the same parents

germanus, -ī, *m.,* full brother

gerō, -ere, gessī, gestum, to bear, carry; to wear, show; to perform, do; to spend time

gignō, -ere, genuī, genitum, to bring into being, create, give birth to

glaciēs, -ēī, *f.,* ice

glans, glandis, *f.,* acorn; beachnut; bullet thrown from a sling

glaucus, -a, -um, *adj.,* bluish-
or greenish-grey

glōria, -ae, *f.,* praise or honor
accorded to persons or
other recipients by general
consent, glory

gnārus, -a, -um, *adj.,* having
knowledge or experience of,
acquainted with

gnāta, -ae, *f.,* (= *nāta*)
daughter

gnātus, -ī, *m.,* (= *nātus*) child,
son

Gorgō, -gonis, *f.,* the Gorgon,
Medusa

Gorgoneus, -a, -um, *adj.,* of the
Gorgon

Gortȳnius, -a, -um, *adj.,* of
or coming from Gortynia;
Cretan

gradus, -ūs, *m.,* step, pace

grandō, -inis, *f.,* hail, hail-
storm

grassor, -ārī, -ātus sum, to
walk about; to proceed

grātus, -a, -um, *adj.,* grateful;
welcome, pleasant

grauidus, -a, -um, *adj.,* heavy,
weighed down, pregnant

grauis, -e, *adj.,* heavy, weighty;
difficult, oppressive

gremium, -iī, *n.,* lap, bosom

grex, gregis, *m.,* a herd, flock; a
troop, band

gubernō (1), to steer a ship,
to be at the helm; to steer,
direct, govern

gurges, -itis, *m.,* a whirlpool,
eddy, abyss

habēna, -ae, *f.,* reins, bridle

habeō, -ēre, -uī, -itum, to have,
hold, posess; to command;
to occupy, inhabit, keep

haereō, -ēre, haesī, haesum, to
stick, adhere, cling; to hold
on tightly; to stay put

hāmus, -ī, *m.,* hook, curved
object

harēna, -ae, *f.,* sand, seashore,
beach

hasta, -ae, *f.,* spear

haud, *adv.,* not

Hebrus, -ī, *m.,* a river in
Thrace

herba, -ae, *f.,* herb, grass

hērōs, hērōis, *m.,* hero;
demigod

Hesperia, -ae, *f.,* the western
land; Italy

heu, *interjection,* alas

hic, haec, hoc, *demonstrative
pron.,* this; (*pl.*) these

hiems, hiemis, *f.,* winter; storm

hinc, *adv.,* from here, hence

homō, hominis, *m.,* human
being, person, man

honor (-ōs), -ōris, *m.,* honor

horrendus, -a, -um, *adj.,*
terrible, fearful

horreō, -ēre, -uī, —, to bristle;
to be rough

horrificus, -a, -um, *adj.,*
causing terror, dreadful

horror, -ōris, *m.,* a bristling,
shuddering; dread, fright

hospes, -pitis, *m.,* a host; a
guest-friend, friend; a
stranger

hostis, -is, *m.,* an enemy; a stranger

humus, -ī, *f.,* the ground, earth

iaciō, -ere, iēcī, iactum, to lay; to throw, cast, hurl; to utter

iactō (1), to throw, toss

iaculor, -ārī, -ātus sum, to throw (a javelin); to shoot at; to aim at

iam, *adv.,* at this point in time, now, yet

iamdudum, *adv.,* some while ago now

iānua, -ae, *f.,* door, entrance

Īcarus, -ī, *m.,* the son of Daedalus, who fell into the Icarian sea while escaping from Crete with wings made by his father

iciō *or* **icō, -ere, īcī, ictum,** to strike

ictus, -ūs, *m.,* stroke, thrust, blow

Īdaeus, -a, -um, *adj.,* of Mount Ida

idcircō, *adv.,* for that reason, on those grounds

Īdē, -ēs, *f.,* a mountain range in Phrygia

īdem, eadem, idem, *demonstrative pron.,* same, the same one

ignārus, -a, -um, *adj.,* unaware, ignorant, unknown

ignipotens, -entis, *adj.,* having power over fire; god of fire, Vulcan

ignis, -is, *m.,* fire

ignōbilis, -e, *adj.,* unknown, obscure, of low birth, base

ignōtus, -a, -um, *adj.,* unknown, unfamiliar, obscure, ignorant

īle, -is, *n.,* intestines, guts

īlex, -icis, *f.,* the holm-oak, a species of oak-tree

īliceus, -a, -um, *adj.,* of holm-oak

ille, illa, illud, *demonstrative pron.,* that; (*pl.*) those

illīc, *adv.,* at that place, over there, there

imāgō, -inis, *f.,* image, ghost, representation shape, form

imber, -bris, *m.,* a rain shower or storm

immānis, -e, *adj.,* (*compar.* **-ior**), savage, brutal; vast, huge

immemor, -ris, *adj.,* not remembering, forgetful; heedless (of obligations or consequences)

immittō, -ere, -mīsī, -missum, to cause to go, send in; throw, let fly

immōtus, -a, -um, *adj.,* not moved, motionless; undisturbed, unshaken; emotionally unmoved, unrelenting, inflexible

immūnis, -e, *adj.,* exempt, immune, free (from)

impauidus, -a, -um, *adj.,* fearless

impellō, -ere, -pulī, -pulsum, to push, drive, or strike against; to beat, compel, push imperitō (1), to exercise authority, control

imperium, -(i)ī, n., power, command; dominion, empire

impius, -a, -um, adj., impious, showing no regard for duty

impleō, -ēre, -ēuī, -ētum, to fill (in, up, over, out)

imprōuidus, -a, -um, adj., without forethought, improvident

impulsus, -ūs, m., shock, impact; incitement, impulse

īmus, -a, -um, adj., deepest, innermost; in the depths of

in, prep. + abl., in, on, within, among; (with acc.) into, onto

Inachidēs, -ae, m., a descendant of Inachus

inānis, -e, adj., empty; false, illusory

inarātus, -a, -um, adj., unploughed, untilled

inarō (1), to plough in, cultivate

incaeduus, -a, -um, adj., not cut, unfelled

incautus, -a, -um, adj., unwary, unguarded

incēdō, -ere, -cessī, -cessum, to move forwards, advance, march

incertus, -a, -um, adj., uncertain; not yet decided; not clearly ascertained

incipiō, -ere, -cēpī, -ceptum, to start, begin

inclūdō, -ere, -clūsī, -clūsum, to shut up, confine, imprison

inclutus, -a, -um, adj., celebrated, famous, renowned

incumbō, -ere, -cubuī, -cubītum, to lie upon, lean upon

incurrō, -ere, -currī (-cucurrī), -cursum, to run into; to attack; to meet

incutiō, -ere, -cussī, -cussum, to strike, dash, beat against; to strike into, inspire

inde, adv., from there, then; then, thereupon

indicō (1), to point out, reveal, show, declare, disclose, reveal

indīgestus, -a, -um, adj., not properly arranged, disorderly, confused

indō, -ere, -didī, -ditum, to put in, put on; to give as a name

indomitus, -a, -um, adj., untamed; untamable, fierce, wild; unconquerable; violent, unrestrained

indūcō, -ere, -duxī, -ductum, to draw or spread over; to lead or bring in

induperātor, -ōris, m. (= imperātor), one who gives orders, a commanding officer, general

iners, -tis, adj., without skill; inactive, not moving

inextrīcābilis, -e, adj., impossible to disentangle, pathless

infandus, -a, -um, adj., unutterable, unnatural, abominable

infēlix, -īcis, *adj.,* unhappy,
  miserable; unfruitful,
  barren
inferō, -ferre, -tulī, illātum, to
  carry in, import
inferus, -a, -um, *adj.,* below,
  beneath, lower
infīgō, -ere, -fixī, -fixum, to
  drive in, attach, plant
inflectō, -ere, -flexī, -flexum,
  to bend, curve, turn
informis, -e, *adj.,* formless,
  featureless; ugly, unsightly
infrā, *adv.,* below; (*prep. + acc.*)
  below, under
infundō, -ere, -fūdī, -fūsum, to
  pour in or on
ingeminō (1), to redouble
ingenium, -(i)ī, *n.,* natural
  disposition, temperament,
  talent
ingens, -gentis, *adj.,* huge,
  great, remarkable
inhibeō, -ēre, -buī, -bitum, to
  restrain, hold back, check
inhiō (1), to stand open, gape;
  to open the mouth wide,
  gape at
inhospitus, -a, -um, *adj.,*
  inhospitable
inhumātus, -a, -um, *adj.,*
  unburied
inimīcus, -a, -um, *adj.,*
  unfriendly, hostile, harmful
inīquus, -a, -um, *adj.,* uneven;
  unequal, unfair; inimical,
  hostile
initus, -ūs, *m.,* entrance,
  approach, arrival

iniūria, -ae, *f.,* injustice, a
  wrong, an insult, injury
iniustus, -a, -um, *adj.,* unjust,
  unfair
inlaesus, -a, -um, *adj.,* unhurt,
  uninjured
inlīdō, -ere, -līsī, -līsum, to
  strike, beat, dash against
inmensus, -a, -um, *adj.,*
  immeasurable, vast,
  boundless
inmodicus, -a, -um, *adj.,*
  immoderate, excessive;
  unrestrained
inmōtus. *See* **immotus**
innābilis, -is, -e, *adj.,* in which
  swimming is impossible
innītor, -ī, -nixus *or* **-nisus
  sum,** to lean or rest upon
innumerus, -a, -um, *adj.,*
  that cannot be numbered,
  innumerable, countless
innuptus, -a, -um, *adj.,*
  unmarried
inpellō. *See* **impello**
insānia, -ae, *f.,* madness,
  frenzy
inscius, -a, -um, *adj.,* unaware,
  ignorant
insequor, -ī, -secūtus sum, to
  pursue, chase, follow
insignis, -e, *adj.,* distinguished,
  conspicuous, remarkable
insiliō, -īre, -siluī, —, to leap,
  spring, jump in or on
insomnia, -ae, *f.,* sleeplessness
instabilis, -e, *adj.,* unsteady,
  unstable; that cannot be
  stood upon

instar, *n.,* (*indecl.*) equivalent in measure, effect, condition, worth, etc.; counterpart, equal; **ad instar,** according to the standard or pattern (of)

instō, -āre, -itī, —, to press on with; to assail, press; to loom, threaten, be upon one

insuētus, -a, -um, *adj.,* accustomed

insum, inesse, infuī, —, to be in or on; to be present

intactus, -a, -um, *adj.,* untouched, undamaged, unharmed

integer, -gra, -grum, *adj.,* whole, complete, entire, intact

inter, *prep.* + *acc.,* among, between

intereā, *adv.,* meanwhile

intimus, -a, -um, *adj.,* innermost, inmost; deepest; most secret, intimate

intonō, -āre, -uī (-auī), —, to thunder

intonsus, -a, -um, *adj.,* unshorn; with long hair or beard; rude, rough; wooded

intractābilis, -is, -e, *adj.,* unmanageable, intractable

intremō, -ere, -uī, —, to tremble, quake

intrō (1), to go into, enter

intumescō, -ere, -tumuī, —, to swell, swell up

inuādō, -ere, -uāsī, -uāsum, to attack, inuade, set on, plunge into

inuehō, -ere, -uexī, -uectum, to carry in, import; (*pass.*) to ride, drive, sail in

inueniō, -īre, -uēnī, -uentum, to encounter, come upon, find; to devise, invent

inuītus, -a, -um, *adj.,* unwilling, reluctant

ipse, -a, -um, *pron. and adj.,* himself, herself, itself, oneself; the very

īra, -ae, *f.,* anger, rage, indignation

irritus, -a, -um, *adj.,* not ratified, invalid, null, void; empty, unrealized, unfulfilled

is, ea, id, *pron.,* he, she, it, they

Ismara, -ōrum, *n. pl.,* a mountain in Thrace

ita, *adv.,* thus, so; therefore

Ītalia, -ae, *f.,* Italy

Italus, -a, -um, *adj.,* Italian, of or belonging to Italy or its people

iter, itineris, *n.,* journey, march, route

iterō (1), to do again, repeat; to traverse again, revisit

iterum, *adv.,* again

iubeō, -ēre, iussī, iussum, to order, command, decree

iūdex, -icis, *m.,* judge; juror

iugālis, -e, *adj.,* of the yoke; of or belonging to marriage, matrimonial, nuptial

iugō (1), to fasten, bind, join; to marry

iugum, -ī, *n.,* yoke; bondage; team of animals

iungō, -ere, iunxī, iunctum, to yoke, harness, join, fasten, attach

Iūnō, -ōnis, *f.,* the goddess Juno, wife and sister of Jupiter

Iūppiter, Iouis, *m.,* Jupiter

iūrō (1), to take an oath, swear, vow

iūs, iūris, *n.,* law, code, rule, right

iuuenca, -ae, *f.,* a young cow, heifer

iuuenis, -is, *m.,* youth, young man

iuuentūs, -ūtis, *f.,* the youth

iuuō, -āre, iūuī, iūtum, to help, assist, benefit

Karthāgō, -inis, *f.,* Carthage, the capital of the Phoenician empire in North Africa

labefaciō, -ere, -fēcī, -factum, to make unsteady, loosen; to subvert, weaken the resolve of

lābor, -ārī, lapsus sum, to glide, slide, flow

labor, ōris, *m.,* effort, work, toil; distress, hardship

lābrum, -ī, *n.,* lip

lac, lactis, *n.,* milk

lacertus, -ī, *m.,* upper arm, arm, shoulder; (*pl.*) strength, muscles, vigor, force

lacessō, -ere, -ī(u)ī, -ītum, to provoke, stimulate, excite, irritate

lacrima, -ae, *f.,* tear, weeping

lacrimō *or* **lacrumō** (1), to shed tears, weep

lactens, -ntis, *adj.,* milk-white

laedō, -ere, laesī, laesum, to injure, damage, harm, hurt, injure, wrong

laetitia, -ae, *f.,* joy, gladness, pleasure

laetor, -ārī, -ātus sum, to rejoice, be joyful, be glad

laetus, -a, -um, *adj.,* joyful, cheerful, glad

laeuus, -a, -um, *adj.,* left, on the left side; awkward, stupid; of ill omen

lambō, -ere, -ī, -itum, to lick, lap

lampas, adis, *f.,* torch, light (of the sun)

lapsus, -ūs, *m.,* gliding, sliding; slipping and falling

largus, -a, -um, *adj.,* abundant, plentiful, profuse

latex, -icis, *m.,* a liquid, fluid

Latīnus, -a, -um, *adj.,* of or belonging to Latium, Latin

Latīnus, -ī, *m.,* a mythical king of Latium

Latium, -(i)ī, *n.,* an area of central Italy

latus, -eris, *n.,* side; flank

Lāuīnia, -ae, *f.,* the daughter of Latinus, who was married to Aeneas

lauō (1), to wash, bathe; wet, moisten, bedew

laus, laudis, *f.,* praise, fame, glory

laxus, -a, -um, *adj.,* wide, loose, spacious, open

lectulus, -ī, *m.,* couch, bed

legō, -ere, lēgī, lectum, to gather, pick; read

lēnis, -e, *adj.,* gentle, kind, light; smooth, mild, easy, calm

lepōs *or* **lepor, -ōris,** *m.,* pleasantness, agreeableness, charm

lētum, -ī, *n.,* death, ruin, annihilation

leuis, -e, *adj.,* light, small, slender, slight; gentle

lex, lēgis, *f.,* motion, bill, law, statute; principle; condition

Līber, -erī, *m.,* Italian god of vegetation, god of wine, Bacchus

lībrō (1), to balance, swing; to hurl

Libycus, -a, -um, *adj.,* of or belonging to North Africa, African

Libyē, -ēs, *f.,* Libya

licet, -ēre, licuit, licitum esse, *impers. verb,* (*with dat. and subjunctive*) it is allowed; (*with subjunctive*) although

lignum, -ī, *n.,* wood, timber

ligō (1), to tie, bind fast

līmen, -inis, *n.,* threshold, entrance, door

līmēs, -itis, *m.,* cross-path, boundary

lingua, -ae, *f.,* tongue, speech, language

linquō, -ere, līquī, —, to go away, leave, quit; forsake, abandon, desert

līquens, -entis, *adj.,* liquid, flowing

liquidus, -a, -um, *adj.,* clear, limpid, pure, unmixed; liquid; flowing, without interruption; smooth

liquor, ōris, *m.,* fluidity; fluid, liquid

lītus, -oris, *n.,* seashore, coast, beach, riverbank

līuens, -entis, *adj.,* dull or greyish bue, livid, discolored; jealous, envious, spiteful

locus, -ī, *m.,* place, spot; rank, position

longē, *adv.,* a long way off, far off, at a distance

longus, -a, -um, *adj.,* long

loquella, -ae, *f.,* speech, utterance

lōrum, -ī, *n.,* strap; (*pl.*) horse's reins

luctus, -ūs, *m.,* grief, mourning, sorrow

lūcus, -ī, *m.,* grove; sacred grove

lūdificor, -ārī, -ātus sum, to make game of, mock; to delude, cheat

lūdō, -ere, -sī, -sum, to play, sport; to delude, deceive

lūmen, -inis, *n.,* light; eye

lupa, -ae, *f.,* she-wolf

lustrō (1), to purify, encircle, shine light over, irradiate

lustrum, ī, *n., usually pl.,* haunts of wild beasts; rough or wooded country, wilds

lustrum, -ī, *n.,* an expiatory sacrifice offered every five years; a period of five years

lux, lūcis, *f.,* light, daylight

Lycaeus, -a, -um, *adj.,* Lycaean

madeō, -ēre, -uī, —, to be wet

Maeandros, -ī, *m.,* a river of Phrygia, famous for its winding course

maestus, -a, -um, *adj.,* unhappy, sad, mournful; gloomy, grim, distressing

magis, *adv.,* more

magister, -trī, *m.,* leader, chief

magnanimus, -a, -um, *adj.,* noble in spirit, brave, generous

magnus, -a, -um, *adj.,* great, large; lofty, noble

maior, maius, *adj., compar. of* **magnus**

malum, -ī, *n.,* trouble, distress; misfortune, evil

malus, -a, -um, *adj.,* bad, evil, harmful

mandō (1), to commit to one's charge, entrust

maneō, -ēre, mansī, mansum, to stay, wait, remain

manifestus, -a, -um, *adj.,* clear, plain, manifest

manus, -ūs, *f.,* hand; a band or body of men

mare, -is, *n.,* sea, the sea

margo, -ginis, *m./f.,* edge, brink, margin

marīta, -ae, *f.,* a wife

marītus, -ī, *m.,* a husband

marmor, -oris, *m.,* marble

Mars, -tis, *m.,* the god of war; warfare, fighting, battle

māter, -tris, *f.,* mother

māteria, -ae, *f.,* stuff, matter, material

Māuors, -ortis, *m., see* **Mars**

medeor, -ērī, -itus sum, to heal, cure

meditor, -ārī, -ātus sum, to ponder, reflect, intend, plan

medium, -iī, *n.,* middle part, center; midst; mean

medius, -a, -um, *adj.,* central, middle, moderate

medulla, -ae, *f.,* marrow

mel, mellis, *n.,* honey

membrum, -ī, *n.,* limb

Memmiadēs, -ae, *m.,* a descendant of the Memmii

Memmius, -a, -um, *adj.,* the name of a Roman *gens*; especially C. Memmius, a contemporary of Cicero and friend of Lucretius

memor, -oris, *adj.,* mindful of (*with gen.*), remembering

memorō (1), to mention, call to mind, recount

mens, -tis, *f.,* mind; sanity

meō (1), to go, pass

mercor, -ārī, -ātus sum, to buy, purchase, trade

mereō, -ēre, -uī, -itum, to earn, win, gain, deserve

mergō, -ere, mersī, mersum, to dip, immerse

metuō, -ere, -uī, -ūtum, to fear, be afraid

metus, -ūs, *m.,* fear, dread

meus, -a, -um, *poss. adj.,* my

migrō (1), to remove from one place to another, migrate; to depart

mīles, -itis, *m.,* soldier, foot soldier

mīlitia, -ae, *f.,* performance of the duties of a soldier, military service

mille, *indecl. adj. and substantive,* a thousand; (*pl.*) **mīlia, -ium**

minae, -ārum, *f. pl.,* threats, menaces

ministrō (1), to attend, serve, provide

Mīnōius, -a, -um, *adj.,* of or belonging to **Minos;** Cretan

minor, -us, *adj.,* less, smaller, inferior

Mīnos, -ōis *or* **-ōnis,** *m.,* king and lawgiver of Crete, husband of Pasiphaë, father of Ariadne, Phaedra, etc.; after his death, one of the judges in the Underworld

Mīnōtaurus, -ī, *m.,* the monster (half-man, half-bull) resulting from Pasiphaë's union with a bull; housed in the Labyrinth, it was killed by Theseus

mīrus, -a, -um, *adj.,* extraordinary, remarkable, astonishing, wonderful

misceō, -ēre, -uī, mixtum, to mix, blend, combine, unite

miser, -era, -erum, *adj.,* poor, wretched, unfortunate; distressing, grievous; wretched, miserable

miserābilis, -e, *adj.,* miserable, wretched, unhappy

miseror, -ārī, -ātus sum, to feel sorry for

mitra, -ae, *f.,* oriental headdress fastened with ribbons under the chin

mittō, -ere, mīsī, missum, to send

modo, *adv.,* only, merely, but

modus, -ī, *m.,* mode, way

moenia, -ium, *n. pl.,* defensive walls

moenus *or* **mūnus, -eris,** *n.,* a function, task

mōlēs, -is, *f.,* shapeless, heavy mass

mōlior, -īrī, -ītus sum, to set in motion; to contrive; to labor at

mollis, -e, *adj.,* soft, mild, gentle

monimentum (*also* **monu-**), **-ī,** *n.,* statue, monument, memorial

mons, -tis, *m.,* mountain

monstrifer, -era, -erum, *adj.,* productive of monsters or portents

monstrum, -ī, *n.,* portent; monster, monstrosity

montānus, -a, -um, *adj.,* of or
belonging to a mountain,
mountainous

mora, -ae, *f.,* delay

**mordeō, -ēre, momordī,
morsum,** to bite

morior, -ī, mortuus sum, to die

moror, -ārī, -ātus sum, to
delay, wait, remain

mors, -tis, *f.,* death

morsus, -ūs, *m.,* bite; jaws, teeth

mortālis, -e, *adj.,* mortal

mōrum, -ī, *n.,* mulberry,
blackberry

mōs, mōris, *m.,* manner

mōtus, -ūs, *m.,* a motion,
movement

moueō, -ēre, mōuī, mōtum, to
move, shake, change, disturb

mox, *adv.,* soon

mūgiō, -īre, -īuī *or* **-iī, -ītum,**
to bellow as an ox; to moo

mulceō, -ēre, mulsī, mulsum,
to stroke, caress

multiplex, -icis, *adj.,* having
many folds or windings

multus, -a, -um, *adj.,* much,
many

mundus, -ī, *m.,* world

Murcus, -ī, *m.,* Murcus (an old
name for the Aventine Hill)

murmur, -uris, *n.,* rumble,
roar, mutter, murmur

mūrus, -ī, *m.,* wall, city-wall

Mūsa, -ae, *f.,* a muse; goddess of
music, literature, and the arts

mūsaeus, -a, -um, *adj.,* of,
belonging to, or inspired by
the Muses

mussō (1), to mutter, whisper

mūtō (1), to move, shift; to
change, alter

mūtus, -a, -um, *adj.,* dumb,
silent, speechless

Mycēnē, -ēs, *f.,* Mycenae, a city
in Argolis

myrtus, -ī, *f.,* myrtle-tree

nam, *conj.,* for, because

namque, *conj., (affirmative)*
certainly, yes; *(explanatory)*
for; *(causal)* for, because, for
instance; *(expository)* now,
well then

nascor, -ī, nātus sum, to be
born

nātūra, -ae, *f.,* nature

nātus. *See* **gnātus**

nāuiger, -era, -erum, *adj.,* ship-
bearing, navigable

nāuigō (1), to sail, set sail

nāuis, -is, *f.,* ship

nē, *conj.,* that not, lest, so that
not

-ne *or* **-n,** *interr. particle*
(introducing a question,
direct or indirect; also
introducing an alternative in
a question, direct or indirect)

nec. *See* **neque**

necdum, *adv.,* not yet; *(conj.)*
and (but) not yet

nectar, -aris, *n.,* nectar, the
drink of the gods

nectō, -ere, nex(u)ī, nexum, to
tie, bind

nefandus, -a, -um, *adj.,* wicked,
impious, heinous

nefās, *n. indecl.,* an offense
against divine law, an
impious act, sacrilege, crime

Nemea, -ae, *f.,* a valley in
Argolis, where Hercules
killed the Nemean lion and
where the Nemean games
were held every other year

nemus, -oris, *n.,* wood, forest,
grove

nepōs, -ōtis, *m.,* grandson,
descendant

Neptūnus, -ī, *m.,* Neptune, god
of the sea

neque *or* **nec,** *conj. and adv.,*
not, and . . . not; not . . .
either, not even; **neque . . .
neque,** neither . . . nor

neu, *conj.,* or not, and not

nīdus, -ī, *m.,* a nest; nestlings

nihil (nīl), *n.,* nothing

nimbus, -ī, *m.,* rain-cloud,
cloud, rain

nisi, *conj.,* if not; except, unless

niteō, -ēre, -uī, -itum, to shine,
glisten

nitidus, -a, -um, *adj.,* shining,
bright

nītor, -ī, nixus sum, to rest
one's weight on, lean

niuālis, -e, *adj.,* snowy

Nixus, -ī, *m.,* the kneeling
constellation, i.e., Hercules

nō (1), to swim, float

nocturnus, -a, -um, *adj.,* by
night, nightly, nocturnal

nōdōsus, -a, -um, *adj.,* full of
knots, knotty

nōmen, -inis, *n.,* name

nōn, *adv.,* not

nondum, *adv.,* not yet

nōs, nostrum, *pers. pron.,* we

noscō, -ere, nōuī, nōtum, to
come to know; to know

noster, -tra, -trum, *poss. adj.,* our

nōtus, -a, -um, *adj.,* (*from*
noscō) known

Notus, -ī, *m.,* the south wind

nouēnī, -ae, -a, *pl. adj.,* nine each,
nine apiece; **annīs nouēnīs,** at
nine-yearly intervals

nouitās, -ātis, *f.,* newness;
rareness, strangeness

nouus, -a, -um, *adj.,* new

nox, noctis, *f.,* night

nubēs, -is, *f.,* cloud; dark cloud

nūbifer, -fera, -ferum, *adj.,*
cloud-bearing, cloud-bringing

nūbilum, -ī, *n.,* a cloudy sky; (*in
pl.*) the clouds

nūbō, -ere, nupsī, nuptum, to
veil oneself; to marry; to be
married

nūdō (1), to strip bare, uncover,
expose

nūdus, -a, -um, *adj.,* naked,
unclothed

nullus, -a, -um, *adj.,* no, none,
not any

nūmen, -inis, *n.,* a nod of the
head; consent; the divine
will; divinity; a deity

nunc, *adv.,* now

nuntius, -(i)ī, *m.,* messenger,
message

Nympha, -ae, *f.,* a semi-divine
female spirit of nature,
nymph

ō, *interjection,* oh! (*exclamation*)

ob, *prep.* + *acc.,* before, because of

oblīquus, -a, -um, *adj.,* slanting; oblique

oblīuiscor, -ī, oblītus sum, to forget

obnītor, -ī, -nixus sum, to press against; to strive against, oppose

oborior, -īrī, -ortus sum, to spring up, rise up, occur

obruō, -ere, -ruī, -rutum, to cover over; to bury; to fall, collapse

obsideō, -ēre, -sēdī, -sessum, to sit down near; to beseige

obsitus, -a, -um, *adj.,* covered (with), overgrown (with), smothered (in); enveloped (in)

obstipescō, -ere, -uī, —, to be struck dumb, be stunned, dazed, or astounded by any powerful emotion

obstō, -āre, -stitī, -stātum, to stand in the way, hinder

occupō (1), to seize, capture; take up, occupy

occurrō, -ere, -currī, -cursum, to run to meet

ocellus, -ī, *m.,* (little) eye; darling, term of endearment

oculus, -ī, *m.,* eye

odium, -(i)ī, *n.,* hatred, dislike

odor, -ōris, *m.,* scent, fragrance, aroma

odōrus, -a, -um, *adj.,* sweet-smelling; strong-smelling

Oenōtria, -ae, *f.,* old name of the southeast part of Italy

Ōlenius, -a, -um, *adj.,* of or belonging to Olenos in Aetolia

ōlim, *adv.,* once, formerly

ōmen, -inis, *n.,* omen, augury

omnipotens, -ntis, *adj.,* almighty, omnipotent

omnis, -e, *adj.,* all, every, whole

onerō (1), to load, heap, encumber

onus, -eris, *n.,* a load, burden

opera, -ae, *f.,* trouble, pains, service, exertion

operiō, -īre, -uī, opertum, to cover (over)

oppidum, -ī, *n.,* town

opprobrium, -(i)ī, *n.,* reproach incurred, shame, scandal, opprobrium; source of reproach, shame

ops, opis, *f.,* power, means, resources, wealth

optō (1), to wish; choose, decide on

opulentus, -a, -um, *adj.,* rich, wealthy, opulent

opus, -eris, *n.,* work

ōra, -ae, *f.,* edge, border, coast

orbis, -is, *m.,* disc, sphere, globe

ordior, -īrī, orsus sum, to begin

ordō, -inis, *m.,* row, rank, order

orīgo, -inis, *f.,* origin, source

Orīōn, -onis, *m.,* a mighty hunter transformed into the constellation Orion

ornō (1), to equip, furnish; to decorate, embellish

ornus, -ī, *f.,* the mountain-ash
ōrō (1), to speak as an orator; to beg, pray, entreat
ōs, ōris, *n.,* mouth; face, countenance
ōtium, -(i)ī, *n.,* leisure, ease; rest, quiet
ouō (1), to rejoice, exult

pābulor, -ārī, -ātus sum, to forage, eat fodder, graze
pābulum, -ī, *n.,* food, nourishment; fodder
paciscor, -ī, pactus sum, to bargain, contract, agree; to betroth
pactum, -ī, *n.,* pact, convention, manner
Palātium, -(i)ī, *n.,* the Palatine Hill in Rome
Palēs, -is, *f.,* the tutelary goddess of herds and shepherds
palleō, -ēre, -uī, —, to be or become pale; to pale
pallescō, -ere, palluī, —, to grow pale, turn pale, lose color
pallidus, -a, -um, *adj.,* pale, pallid
pallor, -ōris, *m.,* paleness, wanness, pallor
pangō, -ere, pepigī, pactum, to insert firmly, fix by driving in; to fix, set; to compose poetry
papilla, -ae, *f.,* nipple, teat
parātus, -ūs, *m.,* preparation, provision, equipment

parens, -entis, *m.,* parent, father, mother
pariter, *adv.,* equally; together
parō (1), to provide, supply, prepare
pars, -tis, *f.,* part, some (of)
pascō, -ere, pāuī, pastum, to feed, lead to pasture
Pāsiphaē, -ēs, *f.,* a daughter of Helios, the wife of Minos and mother of Phaedra, Ariadne, and the Minotaur
passim, *adv.,* here and there; dispersedly, at random
patefaciō, -ere, -fēcī, -factum, to lay open, disclose, bring to light
pateō, -ēre, -uī, —, to be open
pater, -tris, *m.,* father
patior, -ī, passus sum, to experience, undergo, suffer, bear, endure
patria, -ae, *f.,* one's native land, city, etc.
patrius, -a, -um, *adj.,* of or relating to a father, fatherly, paternal
patulus, -a, -um, *adj.,* standing open; wide-spreading
pauidus, -a, -um, *adj.,* terror-struck, frightened
paulus, -a, -um, *adj.,* little, small; *(acc. as adv.)* a little
pax, pācis, *f.,* peace
pectus, -oris, *n.,* breast, chest; heart
pecus, -udis, *f.,* a head of cattle, an animal, one of a herd
pelagus, -ī, *n.,* the sea

pellō, -ere, pepulī, pulsum, to
beat, push, strike; to drive,
impel; to stir, rouse; to expel,
banish

Penātēs, -ium, *m.,* the tutelary
gods of the Roman larder,
regarded as controlling
the destiny of the Roman
household

pendeō, -ēre, pependī, —, to
hang upon, rely upon

pendō, -ere, pependī, pensum,
to pay; to weigh, consider;
to value

penitus, *adv.,* internally,
inwardly; deeply

penna, -ae, *f.,* wing, feather

per, *prep.* + *acc.,* through, by

peragō, -ere, -ēgī, -actum, to
carry through, complete; to
live out (a period of time)

percellō, -ere, -culī, -culsum,
to beat down, upset; to urge
on, excite

perdō, -ere, -didī, -ditum, to
lose; to ruin, destroy

peregrīnus, -a, -um, *adj.,*
foreign, strange

perennis, -e, *adj.,* perennial,
everlasting

perfidus, -a, -um, *adj.,*
faithless, treacherous

perfundō, -ere, -fūdī, -fūsum,
to pour over, wet; to sprinkle

**pergō, -ere, perrexī,
perrectum,** to continue,
proceed

perhibeō, -ēre, -uī, -itum, to
tell, regard, hold

perīculum (perīclum), -ī, *n.,*
test, trial, proof; danger

permittō, -ere, -mīsī, -missum,
to let go through; to let go,
hurl; to yield; to permit

perpetuus, -a, -um, *adj.,*
continuous, constant,
perpetual

perpōtō (1), to drink heavily,
drink the whole of, drink up

persequor, -ī, -secūtus sum, to
follow perseveringly, pursue;
to follow out

Perseus, -eī, *m.,* Perseus, the
son of Zeus and Danaë,
who killed the Gorgon and
rescued Andromeda

**perspiciō, -ere, -spexī,
-spectum,** to see through; to
look at attentively

persultō (1), to leap, gambol,
skip about

**pertaedeō, -ēre, —, -taesum
est,** (*impers.*) to fill with
weariness or disgust

**peruertō (peruortō), -ere,
-uertī, -uersum,** to turn
upside down, overturn,
overthrow

peruolō (1), to fly through,
about, to

pēs, pedis, *m.,* foot

pestis, -is, *f.,* plague, pestilence

petō, -ere, -īuī *or* **-iī, -ītum,** to
fall upon, attack; to demand,
seek, require

pharetra, -ae, *f.,* a quiver

Phoebē, -ēs, *f.,* goddess of the
moon, Diana

Phoebēus, -a, -um, *adj.,* of or
associated with **Phoebus**

Phoebus, -ī, *m.,* god of the sun,
Apollo

Phoenix, -īcis, *m.,* a Phoenician

Phorcus, -ī, *m.,* Phorcus, son of
Neptune, father of Medusa
and the other Gorgons

Phrygius, -a, -um, *adj.,*
Phrygian, Trojan

piāculum, -ī, *n.,* a victim
offered by way of atonement,
expiatory offering

picea, -ae, *f.,* a spruce

piceus, -a, -um, *adj.,* of pitch;
pitch-black

pictus, -a, -um, *adj.,* painted,
colored

Pīerius, -a, -um, *adj.,* of or
belonging to the Muses

pietās, -ātis, *f.,* an attitude of
dutiful respect towards
those to whom one is bound
by ties of religion; piety

pīnus, -ūs, *f.,* a species of pine-
tree

Pīraeus, -ī, *m.,* port of Athens

Pīsaeus, -a, -um, *adj.,* Pisaean

piscis, -is, *m.,* fish

pistris, -is, *f.,* a sea-monster; a
whale; a shark

pius, -a, -um, *adj.,* pious,
dutiful

placeō, -ēre, -uī, -itum, to
please, to be agreeable to

placidus, -a, -um, *adj.,* gentle,
quiet, still

plācō (1), to quiet, calm,
appease

plausus, -ūs, *m.,* clapping,
applause

plēnus, -a, -um, *adj.,* full, filled

plērumque, *adv.,* for the most
part, commonly, generally

plumbum, -ī, *n.,* lead

pōculum, -ī, *n.,* cup, goblet

poena, -ae, *f.,* penalty,
punishment

Poenī, -ōrum, *m. pl.,* the
Carthaginians

polluō, -ere, -uī, -ūtum, to
befoul, defile, pollute

polus, -ī, *m.,* pole; the sky, heaven

pondus, -eris, *n.,* weight

pōnō, -ere, posuī, positum, to
place, set, put, set up, erect,
establish

pontus, -ī, *m.,* the sea; (*as
substantive*) **Pontus,** the Sea
(a deity)

populor, -ārī, -ātus sum, to lay
waste, ravage, devastate

populus, -ī, *m.,* people, nation

porrigō, -ere, -exī, -ectum, to
stretch out, extend

portō (1), to carry, convey

possideō, -ēre, -sēdī, -sessum,
to possess, have, hold

possum, posse, potuī, —, to be
able, have power; can

post, *adv.,* behind, backwards,
afterwards; *prep.,* after

posterus, -a, -um, *adj.,* future,
later, next

postillā, *adv.,* after that,
afterwards

postquam, *conj.,* after, when,
ever since

potius, *adv.*, rather

pōtō (1), to drink

praebeō, -ere, -buī, -bitum, to offer, furnish, supply

praeceps, -cipitis, *adj.*, headlong; swift, rushing; steep

praecingō, -ere, -cinxī, -cinctum, to surround, encircle, gird

praecipitō (1), to hurl or throw down; to fall headlong

praeda, -ae, *f.*, booty, plunder, spoil taken in war

praefīgō, -ere, -fixī, -fixum, to attach in front

praemium, -(i)ī, *n.*, profit, reward

praepes, -etis, *adj.*, swiftly flying, winged

praescius, -a, -um, *adj.*, having foreknowledge, prescient

praeter, *adv.*, beyond; except

praetexō, -ere, -uī, -tum, to screen, clothe (with); to put forward as a pretext, pretend

precor, -ārī, -ātus sum, to beg, entreat, pray

premō, -ere, pressī, pressum, to press, press hard upon

pretium, -(i)ī, *n.*, price, worth, pay

prīmordium, -(i)ī, *n.*, the first beginning, origin

prīmum, *adv.*, first; in the first place; at first

prīmus, -a, -um, *adj.*, first, the first

prior, prius, *adj.*, former, first

priscus, -a, -um, *adj.*, ancient, old, former

prius, *adv.*, before

prō, *prep.* + *abl.*, for, on behalf of, for the sake of

procella, -ae, *f.*, violent wind, storm, gale; violent emotion, passion

prōcērus, -a, -um, *adj.*, high, tall, long

procul, *adv.*, at a distance, away, apart; far away, far

prōcumbō, -ere, -cubuī, -cubitum, to fall forwards; to be beaten down

prōcursus, -ūs, *m.*, the act of running forward (especially in battle), onrush

proelium, -(i)ī, *n.*, battle

proficiscor, -ī, -fectus sum, to set out, depart, proceed

profugus, -a, -um, *adj.*, fleeing, fugitive, exile

profundō, -ere, -fūdī, -fūsum, to pour, pour out, shed copiously

profundus, -a, -um, *adj.*, deep, bottomless, boundless

prōgnātus, -a, -um, *adj.*, born, descended, sprung

prōiciō, -ere, -iēcī, -iectum, to give up, abandon, renounce

prōlēs, -is, *f.*, offspring, progeny

prōmissum, -ī, *n.*, promise, assurance

prōmoueō, -ēre, -mōuī, -mōtum, to move forwards, push onwards

prōnuba, -ae, *f.,* a married woman who conducted the bride to the bridal chamber

prōnus, -a, -um, *adj.,* inclined forwards, stooping forward; steep

propāgō, -inis, *f.,* offspring, children, stock

propior, -us, *adj.,* nearer

proprītim, *adv.,* particularly, specifically

prōsequor, -ī, -secutus sum, to follow or accompany forth; to attack, pursue

prospectō (1), to gaze out at, look out on, look for, watch, face towards

prospiciō, -ere, -spexī, -spectum, to see before, see in front; to look ahead, watch, survey

prosternō, -ere, -strāuī, -stratum, to knock over, throw to the ground; to overcome

prōtinus, *adv.,* straight on; immediately

proximus, -a, -um, *adj.,* nearest

pudor, -ōris, *m.,* shame, sense of shame; modesty

puella, -ae, *f.,* girl, maiden

puer, -erī, *m.,* child, boy; slave

pugna, -ae, *f.,* hand to hand combat, a fight, a battle

pugnō (1), to fight

pulcher, -chra, -chrum, *adj.,* (*also* **pulcer**) beautiful, handsome

pulsō (1), to strike repeatedly, beat, knock on, hammer at, batter, assail

puluis, -eris, *m.,* dust, powder

puniceus, -a, -um, *adj.,* scarlet, crimson

Pūnicus, -a, -um, *adj.,* of or associated with Carthage or its people; Carthaginian, Punic

Pygmaliōn, -ōnis, *m.,* a king of Tyre, brother to Dido

Pygmaliōnēus, -a, -um, *adj.,* of, belonging to, or descending from Pygmalion, king of Tyre

pyra, -ae, *f.,* a funeral pile, pyre

quā, *adv.,* by which way, on which side, where; how, in what manner

quaerō, -ere, -sīuī, -situm, to seek, look for

quālis, -e, *adj.,* such as, like

quam, *adv.,* than

quamquam, *conj.,* although

quamuīs, *adv.,* as much as you like, however much; very much, exceedingly

quantulus, -a, -um, *adj.,* how little, how small

quantum, *interr. adv.,* how much? how greatly?; (*rel. adv.*) to what extent, to the extent to which

quantus, -a, -um, *interr. adj.,* of what size? how great?l (*rel. adj.*) of what size, degree, amount; as much as

quasi, *adv.,* as if, just as
quassō (1), to shake or toss violently
quater, *adv.,* on four occasions, four times
quatiō, -ere, —, quassum, to shake, brandish
quattuor, *indecl. adj.,* four
-que, *conj.,* and; **-que . . . -que,** both ... and
queō, -īre, -īuī *or* **-iī, -itum,** to be able to
quercus, -ūs, *f.,* an oak-tree
queror, -ī, questus sum, to express discontent, regret, or similar; to complain, grumble, protest
quī, quae, quod, *pron. and adj.,* who, what, which
quia, *conj.,* because
quīcumque, quaecumque, quodcumque, *pron.,* whoever, whatever
quiēs, -ētis, *f.,* sleep, rest, repose
quiescō, -ere, -ēuī, -ētum, to rest, repose, sleep
quīn, *conj.,* so that not, without; that not; but that; that; **quin etiam,** moreover
quinque, *adj.,* five
quis, quae, quid, *interr. pron.,* who, which, what; (*indef. pron.*), any; *after* **sī, nisi, num, nē,** = **aliquis**
quisquam, quicquam (quidquam), *indef. pron.,* anyone, anything

quō, *adv. and conj.,* to which place, to which purpose; at which time, when
quom. *See* **cum,** *conj.*
quondam, *adv.,* formerly, once
quoniam, *adv.,* since, because
quoque, *adv.,* likewise, as well, also, too
quot, *indecl. adj.,* how many; **quot . . . tot . . . ,** as many ... so many
quotannīs, *adv.,* every year, annually

rabiēs, -es (-ēī), *f.,* madness, rage
radius, -(i)ī, *m.,* staff, rod; beam, ray
rāmus, -ī, *m.,* branch, bough
rapax, -ācis, *adj.,* grasping, greedy of plunder
rapidus, -a, -um, *adj.,* tearing away, seizing; tearing or hurrying along, swift, quick
rapiō, -ere, -uī, -tum, to seize and carry off; to violate, ravish
raptō (1), to seize and carry off, snatch, drag
rastrum, -ī, *n.,* a drag-hoe
ratiō, -ōnis, *f.,* reckoning, calculation; reason, account
ratis, -is, *f.,* a boat, a raft
recēdō, -ere, -cessī, -cessum, to go back, fall back, withdraw, recede
recipiō, -ere, -cēpī, -ceptum, to admit, accept; to take back; to receive

reclūdō, -ere, -sī, -sum, to open, uncover

recreō (1), to make or create anew, remake

rector, -ōris, *m.,* guide, director, ruler

rectus, -a, -um, *adj.,* straight; right, proper; (*n. sing. as substantive*) that which is morally right

recubō (1), to recline

recursō, -āre, —, —, to keep running back, to keep recurring to the mind

reddō, -ere, -idī, -itum, to give back, restore, reply, hand over

redeō, -īre, -iī, -itum, to go back, come back, return

referō, -ferre, -(t)tulī, -lātum, to bring, bear or carry back

reflectō, -ere, -flexī, -flexum, to bend back, turn round or back

rēgīna, -ae, *f.,* queen

regius, -a, -um, *adj.,* royal, regal; of royal blood

regnō (1), to rule as king, reign

regnum, -ī, *n.,* kingdom, royal power

regō, -ere, rexī, rectum, to guide, conduct, direct

rēiciō, -ere, -iēcī, -iectum, to throw back, cast back, reject

relegō, -ere, -lēgī, -lectum, to pick up again; to go back over, retrace

relinquō, -ere, -līquī, -lictum, to leave behind

remaneō, -ere, -mansī, -mansum, to stay or remain behind

remeō (1), to go or come back; to turn back; to return

remētior, -īrī, -mensus sum, to measure again, measure back; (*pf. pple. in passive meaning*) has been traversed

rēmigium, -(i)ī, *n.,* oarage

Remora, -ae, *f.,* the name proposed by Remus for Rome

remoueō, -ēre, -mōuī, -mōtum, to move back or away; to remove, banish

remūgiō, -īre, —, —, to moo in reply, to resound (with mooing)

rēmus, -ī, *m.,* oar

Remus, -ī, *m.,* Remus, brother of Romulus

renouō (1), to renew, restore

reparō (1), to recover, retrieve; to restore, repair

repellō, -ere, reppulī, repulsum, to drive or thrust back

repentē, *adv.,* suddenly, at once

repetō, -ere, -īuī *or* **-iī, -ītum,** to return to; to attack again

repōnō, -ere, -posuī, -positum *or* **-postum,** to put back, replace; to lay back

rēs, reī, *f.,* thing, matter, circumstance

reserō (1), to unlock, unclose, unbar

resistō, -ere, -stitī, —, to stand again; to resist, oppose

resoluō, -ere, -uī, -ūtum, to loosen, undo, unravel, relax; to undo, nullify

respiciō, -ere, -spexī, -spectum, to look behind, look back

respondeō, -ēre, -spondī, -sponsum, to respond, reply, answer; to correspond to

resupīnus, -a, -um, *adj.,* bent back, lying on one's back, supine

resurgō, -ere, -surrexī, -surrectum, to rise up again, appear again

retegō, -ere, -texī, -tectum, to uncover, strip, expose, reveal

retineō, -ēre, -tinuī, -tentum, to hold back, restrain, detain

retorqueō, -ere, -torsī, -tortum, to twist or bend back

retrō, *adv.,* backwards, behind

reuertor, -ī, -versus sum, to turn back; to come back, return

reuolō (1), to fly back

rex, rēgis, *m.,* king

Rhīpaeus, -a, -um, *adj.,* of or belonging to the Rhipaean mountains in Scythia

rīdeō, -ēre, -rīsī, -rīsum, to smile, laugh

rīpa, -ae, *f.,* bank, margin, shore

rōbur *or* **rōbor, -oris,** *n.,* a very hard kind of oak-wood; strength, hardness

Rōma, -ae, *f.,* Rome

Rōmānus, -a, -um, *adj.,* Roman

Rōmulus, -ī, *m.,* Romulus, founder of Rome, brother of Remus

rōstrum, -ī, *n.,* bill, beak; prow (of a ship)

rubēta, -ōrum, *n. pl.,* a thicket of brambles

rudis, -e, *adj.,* undeveloped, rough, wild; coarse

ruīna, -ae., *f.,* headlong rush or fall, downward plunge; collapse, ruin; *pl.* collapsed remains, ruins

rumpō, -ere, rūpī, ruptum, to burst, rupture, break

ruō, -ere, ruī, rutum, to rush, hasten

rūpes, -is, *f.,* cliff, rock

rursus, *adv.,* backward, back; again, once more

Rutulus, -a, -um, *adj.,* of or belonging to the Rutuli, a people of Latium; Rutulian

sacer, -cra, -crum, *adj.,* sacred, holy

sacrō (1), to consecrate, exalt, sanctify

saec(u)lum, -(u)lī, *n.,* generation; breed, race; age

saepe, *adv.,* often

saeuiō, -īre, -iī, -ītum, to rage

saeuus, -a, -um, *adj.,* savage, ferocious

sāl, salis, *m.,* salt; brine, salt water, sea

salictum, -ī, *n.,* a collection of willows, a willow-grove, osier-bed

saltus, -ūs, *m.,* a forest or mountain pasture; a dale, ravine, glade salūs, -ūtis, *f.,* health, safety, salvation

salutō (1), to greet, hail

sanciō, -īre, sanxī, sanctum, to make sacred

sanctus, -a, -um, *adj.,* sacred, holy

sanguineus, -a, -um, *adj.,* of blood, bloody

sanguis, -inis, *m.,* blood

sānus, -a, -um, *adj.,* healthy, sane

satis (sat), *indecl. adj.,* enough; (*adv.*), enough, sufficiently

sauciō (1), to wound, hurt

saucius, -a, -um, *adj.,* wounded

saxeus, -a, -um, *adj.,* of stone or rock; rocky; stony, unfeeling

saxum, -ī, *n.,* rock, boulder

scamnum, -ī, *n.,* support; bench, stool, step; throne

scelerātus, -a, -um, *adj.,* criminal, wicked

scelus, -eris, *n.,* crime

scindō, -ere, scidī, scissum, to cut, tear; to split, cleave

scopulōsus, -a, -um, *adj.,* rocky, full of cliffs

scopulus, -a, -um, *adj.,* cliff, crag, rock

scrībō, -ere, scripsī, scriptum, to write, draw

scrūtor, -ārī, -ātus sum, to examine, investigate

sē, suī, *reflex. pron.,* himself, herself, itself, themselves

secō, -āre, secuī, sectum, to cut; to wound, hurt

secundus, -a, -um, *adj.,* second; favorable

secūris, -is, *f.,* axe, hatchet

sēcūrus, -a, -um, *adj.,* untroubled, undisturbed, safe; negligent, indifferent

secus, *adv.,* otherwise

sed, *conj.,* but, yet, however

sedeō, -ēre, sēdī, sessum, to sit

sēdēs, -is, *f.,* seat; home, dwelling

sēditiō, -ōnis, *f.,* discord, turmoil, rebellion

sēdō (1), to allay, settle, still; sēdātus, calm

sēmen, -inis, *n.,* that which is sown, seed

sēmideus, -a, -um, *adj.,* half-divine

sēmita, -ae, *f.,* a side-path or track, an alley, lane, course

semper, *adv.,* always

senecta, -ae, *f.,* old age

sensus, -ūs, *m.,* sense, sensation, perception, consciousness, feeling, emotion

sentus, -a, -um, *adj.,* rough, rugged

septēnī, -ae, -a, *adj.,* seven, seven each, sevenfold

sepulchrum, -ī, *n.,* tomb, grave

sequor, -ī, secūtus sum, to follow, come after

sermo, -ōnis, *m.,* talk, conversation

serō, -ere, sēuī, satum, to sow, plant

sertum, -ī, *n.,* wreath, garland

seruātor, -ōris, *m.,* a savior, preserver

seruō (1), to save, preserve; to watch, observe

sēsē, *reflex. pron.*, (*emphatic form of* **sē, suī**), himself, herself, itself, themselves

sī, *conj.*, if

sīc, *adv.*, thus, so, in this way

siccus, -a, -um, *adj.*, dry

Sīdōnius, -a, -um, *adj.*, Phoenician, Sidonian

sīdus, -eris, *n.*, star, constellation

Sīgēus, -a, -um, *adj.*, Sigean, relating to Sigeus, a promontory in Troas

significō (1), to show by signs, indicate, signify

signum, -ī, *n.*, mark, sign, indication; a sign in the heavens, a constellation

Sīla, -ae, *f.*, a mountainous region of forest in the country of the Bruttii

sileō, -ēre, -uī, —, to be silent, be quiet

silua, -ae, *f.*, wood, forest

Siluānus, -ī, *m.*, a Latin god of woods and forests

similis, -e, *adj.*, like, resembling, similar

simul, *adv.*, at the same time, together; **simul ac**, as soon as

simulō (1), to put out, pretend, simulate

sine, *prep. + abl.*, without

sinister, -tra, -trum, *adj.*, left, on the left hand; wrong; unfavorable

sinō, -ere, sīuī, situm, to permit, allow

sinus, -ūs, *m.*, a bending, curve, fold; a bay, gulf

sistō, -ere, stetī, statum, to cause to stand, erect; to plant, place, or set firmly; to halt, stop

situs, -ūs, *m.*, neglect, disuse, deterioration, rottenness, mould

sīue, *conj.*, whether; or

sociō (1), to associate, to share, attach as a partner or associate

socius, -a, -um, *adj.*, associated, allied

sōl, -is, *m.*, the sun

sōlācium, -(i)ī, *n.*, soothing, comfort, consolation

soleō, -ēre, -uī, -itus, to be accustomed

sollicitus, -a, -um, *adj.*, worried, anxious, troubled

sōlor, -ārī, -ātus sum, to comfort, console

solum, -ī, *n.*, soil, earth, ground

soluō, -ere, soluī, solūtum, to loosen, untie, release

sōlus, -a, -um, *adj.*, alone, on one's own; lonely, forsaken; unaided, single-handed; only one, single

somnus, -ī, *m.*, sleep; sleepiness, lethargy

sonō, -āre, -uī, -itum, to sound, resound, make a noise

sonōrus, -a, -um, *adj.*, loud, sonorous

sonus, -ī, *m.*, noise, sound

sōpiō, -īre, -īuī, -ītum, to put or lull to sleep

sopōrus, -a, -um, *adj.,* sleep-bringing

soror, -ōris, *f.,* sister

sors, -tis, *f.,* lot, chance, fortune, destiny

spargō, -ere, sparsī, sparsum, to scatter, shower, spread out

spatiōsus, -a, -um, *adj.,* ample, wide, spacious, large

speciēs, -ēī, *f.,* a seeing, appearance

spectō (1), to look at

spēlunca, -ae, *f.,* cave

sperō (1), to hope

spēs, -eī, *f.,* hope

spīnōsus, -a, -um, *adj.,* thorny, spiny, spiky

spīritus, -ūs, *m.,* breath, breathing; spirit, life

sponte, *adv.,* freely, spontaneously

squāmiger, -era, -erum, *adj.,* equipped with scales, scaly

stabiliō, -īre, -īuī, -ītum, to make firm or stable; to fix, establish

stabulum, -ī, *n.,* abode, habitation; stable, stall; lair, haunt

stellans, -antis, *adj.,* starry, set with stars

sternō, -ere, strāuī, strātum, to stretch out, spread out; to strew, spread

stillō (1), to fall in drops, drip

stirps, -pis, *f.,* stem, plant; family stock

stō, stāre, stetī, statum, to stand; stand still; stand firm

strophium, -iī, *n.,* twisted breast-band; headband

studeō, -ēre, -uī, —, to be eager; to apply oneself

studium, -(i)ī, *n.,* zeal, eagerness, enthusiasm

stupeō, -ēre, -uī, —, to be paralyzed, stunned, dazed, speechless, dumbfounded

suādeō, -ēre, suāsī, suāsum, to recommend urge, advise, suggest

suāuiloquens, -entis, *adj.,* speaking pleasantly or agreeably

suāuis, -e, *adj.,* sweet, agreeable

sub, *prep. + abl. or acc.,* under, below, beneath

subdō, -ere, -didī, -ditum, to put under

subitō, *adv.,* suddenly

subitus, -a, -um, *adj.,* sudden

sublīmis, -e, *adj.,* high, lofty

subsīdō, -ere, -sēdī, -sessum, to sit down, to settle down

subter, *prep. + acc. or abl.,* below, beneath, underneath

subtīlis, -e, *adj.,* fine, delicate; precise, detailed

subtrahō, -ere, -traxī, tractum, to draw or drag from under, remove, withdraw, steal

subuolō (1), to fly up or upwards

succēdō, -ere, -cessī -cessum, to move below, move up, advance, succeed

succīdō, -ere, -dī, -sum, to cut from below or at the base

succumbō, -ere, -cubuī, -cubitum, to sink, collapse, give in, submit

sūcus, -ī, *m.,* juice, sap

sudō (1), to sweat, perspire

sūdor, -ōris, *m.,* sweat

sulcō (1), to drive a furrow across, plough, cleave, furrow

sum, esse, fuī, —, to be

summittō, -ere, -mīsī, -missum, to place under; to put forth from below

summus, -a, -um, *adj.,* highest, topmost, final, greatest, supreme, foremost

sūmō, -ere, sumpsī, sumptum, to take, take up

super, *prep. + acc. or abl.,* above

superbus, -a, -um, adj., proud; lofty

superō (1), to surpass, excel, outdo; to prevail over, overcome, defeat

superstes, -stitis, *adj.,* standing over or near; present, witnessing; surviving

superus, -a, -um, *adj.,* upper, heavenly; (*as substantive*) the deities

supplex, -icis, *m./f.,* suppliant

suppōnō, -ere, -posuī, -positum, to place under or beneath,

suprēmus, -a, -um, *adj., superl. of* **superus**; highest, uppermost

surgō, -ere, surrexī, surrectum, to rise, arise, spring up

suspendō, -ere, -pendī, -pensum, to hang, suspend

suspiciō, -ere, -spexī, -spectum, to look at from below, look up to; to mistrust, suspect

suspīrō (1), to draw a deep breath, sigh; to exhale

suus, -a, -um, *poss. adj.,* his, her, its, one's, theirs

Sychaeus *or* **Sȳchaeus, -ī,** *m.,* the husband of Dido

tabella, -ae, *f.,* tablet

Taburnus, -ī, *m.,* a mountain in Samnium

taceō, -ēre, -uī, -itum, to be silent, say nothing

tacitus, -a, -um, *adj.,* making no utterance, not speaking, silent, quiet

taeda, -ae, *f.,* pine-wood; torch

taeter, -tra, -trum, *adj.,* offensive, foul; shameful, disgraceful

tālāria, -ium, *n. pl.,* ankles, heels

tālis, -e, *adj.,* of such a kind

tamen, *adv.,* yet, nevertheless, still

tandem, *adv.,* at last

tangō, -ere, tetigī, tactum, to touch

tantum, *adv.,* so much, so far; hardly, only

tantus, -a, -um, *rel. adj.,* so great; (*correlative of* **quantus**) of such a size, as great, large, etc. (as)

tardus, -a, -um, *adj.*, slow in movement, moving slowly; making slow progress

taurīnus, -a, -um, *adj.*, of or derived from a bull

taurus, -ī, *m.*, bull

taxus, -ī, *f.*, a yew-tree

tectum, -ī, *n.*, roof, house

tegmen, -inis, *n.*, a cover, covering

tegō, -ere, texī, tectum, to cover, cover over; to protect

tellūs, -ūris, *f.*, the earth, the globe

tēlum, -ī, *n.*, dart, spear; weapon

temerō (1), to violate, defile, dishonor

Tempē, *n. pl.*, (*only in nom., vocative, acc.*) the valley of the Peneus, between Ossa and Olympus in Thessaly, noted for its beauty

tempestās, -ātis, *f.*, time, season, occasion

templum, -ī, *n.*, temple, sacred building

tempus, -oris, *n.*, time, period, circumstance

tendō, -ere, tetendī, tensum, to stretch, stretch out

teneō, -ēre, -uī, tentum, to have, hold

tener, -era, -erum, *adj.*, tender, delicate, soft

tenuis, -e, *adj.*, thin, fine

tenus, *prep.* + *abl. or gen.*, as far as, up to

tepeō, -ēre, —, —, to be warm or lukewarm

ter, *adv.*, three times, thrice

teres, -etis, *adj.*, smooth

tergum, -ī, *n.*, back, rear, hide of an animal

terō, -ere, trīuī, trītum, to rub, wear away

terra, -ae, *f.*, earth, the earth; land, ground, soil

terreō, -ēre, -uī, -itum, to terrorize, terrify

terribilis, -e, *adj.*, frightful, dreadful, terrible

tertius, -a, -um, *adj.*, third

texō, -ere, -uī, -tum, to weave, construct

textum, -ī, *n.*, a woven fabric, cloth

thalamus, -ī, *m.*, bedroom; (*metonymy*) marriage

thēsaurus, -ī, *m.*, treasure-chamber, treasure

Thēseus, -eī *or* -eos, *m.*, a hero of Attic legend, slayer of the Minotaur, husband of Phaedra, etc.

Thessalus, -a, -um, *adj.*, of or native to Thessaly, Thessalian

timeō, -ēre, timuī, —, to fear

timor, -ōris, *m.*, fear

tingō, -ere, tinxī, tinctum, to wet, moisten; to dye

Tītān, -nos, *m.*, one of the Titans, a race of gods descended from Heaven and Earth, who preceded the Olympians

tollō, -ere, sustulī, sublātum, to take up, lift up, raise

Tonans, -tis, *m.,* the Thunderer; Jupiter

torqueō, -ēre, torsī, tortum, to twist, turn

torquēs *or* **torquis, -is,** *m.,* a collar of twisted metal; a collar-like marking (applied to the windings of a sea-serpent)

torus, -ī, *m.,* a swelling; a muscle; a bed; a mound

tot, *indecl. adj.,* this, that many, so many

tōtus, -a, -um, *adj.,* the whole of, all, entire

trabs, trabis, *f.,* beam, timber; tree

tractō (1), to touch, handle; to treat, use

trāiciō, -ere, -iēcī, -iectum, to throw across, move, shift, travel across, cross; to pierce

trānō (1), to swim across

tranquillus, -a, -um, *adj.,* calm, tranquil

transgredior, -ī, -gressus sum, to go across, pass over

transmittō, -ere, -misī, -missum, to send across, transmit

tremō, -ere, -uī, —, to tremble, quake

tremulus, -a, -um, *adj.,* trembling, agitated

trepidus, -a, -um, *adj.,* agitated, anxious, restless, disturbed

Triopēius, -(i)ī, *m.,* the son of Triopas, king of Thessaly, Erysichthon

tristis, -e, *adj.,* sad, sorrowful; melancholy, harsh, severe

trisulcus, -a, -um, *adj.,* three-furrowed, three-pronged

triumphus, -ī, *m.,* a triumph, the procession of a victorious general

Trōia, -ae, *f.,* the city and territory of Troy, situated on the Asiatic side of the entrance to the Hellespont

Trōiānus, -a, -um, *adj.,* of or belonging to Troy, Trojan

Trōs, -ōis, *m.,* a Trojan

truncus, -ī, *m.,* trunk

tū, tuī, *pers. pron.,* you (*sing.*)

tuba, -ae, *f.,* trumpet

tueor, -ērī, tuitus sum, to look at, observe; to watch over, protect, guard; to preserve, look after, maintain

tum, *adv.,* then, on that occasion in the past; at that moment in the future; on such an occasion; at that, thereupon; in addition, besides, moreover

tumultus, -ūs, *m.,* commotion, confusion

tunc, *adv.,* then, at that time

tundō, -ere, tutudī, tunsum, to beat, thump

turba, -ae, *f.,* commotion, uproar; crowd

turbō (1), to disturb, agitate

Turnus, -ī, *m.,* a king of the Rutuli, rival to Aeneas for the hand of Lavinia, and defeated and killed by him

turris, -is, *f.,* a tower

tūtus, -a, -um, *adj.*, safe

tuus, -a, -um, *adj.*, your (*sing.*)

Tydeus (*dissyllabic*), -eī *and*
-eos, *m.*, son of Oeneus,
father of Diomedes

tyrannus, -ī, *m.*, monarch,
sovreign, tyrant

Tyrius, -a, -um, *adj.*, of or
belonging to the city of Tyre

Tyrus, -ī, *f.*, Tyre, a city on the
Phoenician coast, famous
for its crimson dye

uacuus, -a, -um, *adj.*, empty,
devoid of, free from

uādō, -ere, —, —, to go, walk;
to rush

uadum, -ī, *n.*, waters of the sea
or a river; shallow body of
water, sea or river bed

uagor, -ārī, -ātus sum, to
wander, roam

ualescō, -ere, —, —, to become
sound in health, to grow
strong

ualles, -is, *f.*, a valley

uallum, -ī, *n.*, a palisade; a
fortification

uānus, -a, -um, *adj.*, hollow,
insubstantial, empty, false,
vain

uariātus, -a, -um, *adj.*, of
varied colors, variegated

uarius, -a, -um, *adj.*, having
two or more contrasting
colors, particolored,
variegated; composed of
many different elements,
varied, multifarious, motley

uastus, -a, -um, *adj.*,
monstrous, immense, huge;
empty, unoccupied

uātēs, -is, *m./f.*, prophet, seer;
poet

uāticinor, -ārī, -ātus sum, to
foretell, prophesy

ūber, -ris, *n.*, a woman's breast
or teat; udder, teats, etc.

ubī, *interr., rel., and indef. adv.*,
where

-ue, *enclitic conj.*, or

uel, *conj. and adv.*, or, or rather,
or even,

uēlō (1), to cover, clothe;
conceal, veil

uēlox, -ōcis, *adj.*, swift, quick,
fleet

uēlum, -ī, *n.*, sail

uelut(ī), *adv.*, like, as if

uēna, -ae, *f.*, vein, blood-vessel

ueniō, -īre, uēnī, uentum, to
come

uentōsus, -a, -um, *adj.*, windy;
like the wind, changeable,
fickle, inconstant; puffed up,
vain

uentus, -ī, *m.*, wind

uēr, uēris, *n.*, spring;
springtime of life, youth

uerberō (1), to beat

uerbum, -ī, *n.*, word

uernus, -a, -um, *adj.*, of or
belonging to spring

uērō, *adv.*, in truth, really,
indeed

uersō (1), to whirl, twist

uersus, -ūs, *m.*, furrow; line,
verse

uertex, -icis, *m.,* crown of the head, top, highest point

uertō, -ere, uertī, uersum, to turn, turn round or about

uērus, -a, -um, *adj.,* real, genuine, true, actual

uestīgium, -(i)ī, *n.,* footprint, track, step

uestīgō (1), to follow the trail of, track down, search for

uestis, -is, *f.,* cloth, drapery; clothing, garment

ueternus, -ī, *m.,* age

uetus, -eris, *adj.,* old, veteran, long-established

uetustās, -ātis, *f.,* age; antiquity; long duration

uetustus, -a, -um, *adj.,* ancient, old

uexō (1), to trouble, harass, distress

uia, -ae, *f.,* road, way, path, course

uīcīnus, -a, -um, *adj.,* near, neighboring

uicis (*gen.*), *f.,* situation, plight; process of change, succession

uicissim, *adv.,* in turn; in a reciprocal manner, reciprocally

uictima, -ae, *f.,* an animal offered in sacrifice, victim

uictor, -ōris, *m.,* a conqueror, victor

uictōria, -ae, *f.,* victory

uideō, -ēre, uīdī, uīsum, to see; (*in pass.*) seem

uigeō, -ēre, -uī, -itum, to be vigorous, thrive, flourish

uinciō, -īre, uinxī, uinctum, to fasten, bind, wrap

uinclum *or* **uinculum, -ī,** *n.,* bond, chain, fetter, shackle

uindex, -icis, *m.,* defender, protector; avenger

uiolō (1), to violate, pollute, defile

uir, uirī, *m.,* man, husband

uirens, -entis, *adj.,* verdant

uirgineus, -a, -um, *adj.,* maidenly, of a maiden

uirgō, -inis, *f.,* maiden, virgin, young woman

uiridis, -e, *adj.,* green

uirtūs, -ūtis, *f.,* manliness, virtue, excellence, goodness, merit

uīs, uis, *f.,* strength, energy, vigor

uīsō, -ere, uīsī, uīsum, to view, behold, survey

uīsus, -ūs, *m.,* sight

uīta, -ae, *f.,* life

uītis, -is, *f.,* a grape-vine

uitta, -ae, *f.,* band, ribbon; fillet

uix, *adv.,* barely, with difficulty

ullus, -a, -um, *adj.,* any

ulmus, -ī, *f.,* the elm

ulna, -ae, *f.,* the forearm; *poetic, as a measure of length,* approximate to the span of the outstretched arms

ultrā, *adv.,* beyond, further

ululō (1), to utter drawn-out cries, howl, yell

umbra, -ae, *f.,* shadow, shade, ghost

ūmeō, -ēre, —, —, to be moist or wet

umerus, -ī, *m.,* the upper arm or shoulder

ūnanimus, -a, -um, *adj.,* sharing a single attitude or purpose, acting in accord

uncus, -a, -um, *adj.,* bent like a hook, hooked, curved

unda, -ae, *f.,* wave; sea

unde, *interr. and rel. adv.,* from what place, from where, whence; from whom, from what

undique, *adv.,* from all sides, on all sides, everywhere

unguis, -is, *m.,* nail, claw, talon

ūnus, -a, -um, *adj.,* one, a single, alone

uocō (1), to call

uolō (1), to fly

uolō, uelle, uoluī, —, to be willing, to wish

uolucris, -is, *f.,* bird

uolūmen, -inis, *n.,* anything rolled; a roll, whirl, fold

uoluō, -ere, uoluī, uolūtum, to roll, cause to roll

uoluptās, -tātis, *f.,* pleasure

uōmer, -eris, *m.,* ploughshare

uomō, -ere, uomuī, uomitum, to vomit, to spew

uōs, uestrum, *pron.,* you (*pl.*)

uōtum, -ī, *n.,* vow; votive offering

uox, uōcis, *f.,* voice, sound

urbs, urbis, *f.,* city

urgueō, -ēre, ursī, —, to press, squeeze; to threaten; to urge

urna, -ae, *f.,* urn, pitcher

ūsus, -ūs, *m.,* use

ut, *adv.,* just as, like; as if

uter, -tra, -trum, *interrog. adj.,* which of two

uterque, utraque, utrumque, *adj.,* each of two, both

ūtilis, -e, *adj.,* useful, fit, serviceable, profitable, beneficial

utpote, *adv.,* as one might expect, as is natural

uulgus, -ī, *n.,* crowd, mob, common people

uulnus, -eris, *n.,* wound

uultus, -ūs, *m.,* expression, look, countenance, face

Venus, -eris, *f.,* Venus, goddess of love

Zephyrus, -ī, *m.,* a west wind

B͞C LATIN Readers

Series Editor: RONNIE ANCONA, HUNTER COLLEGE
AND CUNY GRADUATE CENTER

Other Readers Also Now Available

An Apuleius Reader
Selections from the
METAMORPHOSES
ELLEN D. FINKELPEARL
(2012) ISBN 978-0-86516-714-8

A Caesar Reader
Selections from BELLUM
GALLICUM *and* BELLUM
CIVILE, *and from Caesar's
Letters, Speeches, and Poetry*
W. JEFFREY TATUM
(2012) ISBN 978-0-86515-696-7

A Cicero Reader
*Selections from Five Essays
and Four Speeches,
with Five Letters*
JAMES M. MAY
(2010) ISBN 978-0-86515-713-1

A Livy Reader
Selections from
AB URBE CONDITA
MARY JAEGER
(2010) ISBN 978-0-86515-680-6

A Lucan Reader
Selections from
CIVIL WAR
SUSANNA BRAUND
(2009) ISBN 978-0-86516-661-5

A Martial Reader
Selections from Epigrams
CRAIG WILLIAMS
(2009) ISBN 978-0-86516-704-9

A Plautus Reader
*Selections from
Eleven Plays*
JOHN HENDERSON.
(2009) ISBN 978-0-86516-694-3

A Roman Verse Satire Reader
*Selections from Lucilius,
Horace, Persius,
and Juvenal*
CATHERINE C. KEANE
(2010) ISBN 978-0-86515-685-1

A Sallust Reader
Selections from
BELLUM CATILINAE,
BELLUM IUGURTHINUM,
and HISTORIAE
VICTORIA E. PAGÁN
(2009) ISBN 978-0-86515-687-5

A Seneca Reader
*Selections from
Prose and Tragedy*
JAMES KER
(2011) ISBN 978-0-86515-758-2

A Suetonius Reader
Selections from the
LIVES OF THE CAESARS
and the LIFE OF HORACE
JOSIAH OSGOOD
(2010) ISBN 978-0-86515-716-2

A Terence Reader
Selections from Six Plays
WILLIAM S. ANDERSON
(2009) ISBN 978-0-86515-678-3

Forthcoming in 2012 and Beyond

An Ovid Reader
CAROLE E. NEWLANDS
ISBN 978-0-86515-722-3

A Propertius Reader
P. LOWELL BOWDITCH
ISBN 978-0-86515-723-0

A Roman Army Reader
DEXTER HOYOS
ISBN 978-0-86515-715-5

A Roman Women Reader
SHEILA K. DICKISON and JUDITH P. HALLETT
ISBN 978-0-86515-662-2

A Tacitus Reader
STEVEN H. RUTLEDGE
ISBN 978-0-86515-697-4

A Tibullus Reader
PAUL ALLEN MILLER
ISBN 978-0-86515-724-7

VISIT THE SERIES WEBSITE FOR UPDATES
ON AVAILABLE VOLUMES:
www.bolchazy.com/readers